THE DONOGHUE STRATEGIES

BY WILLIAM E. DONOGHUE *with Thomas Tilling*
William E. Donoghue's Complete Money Market Guide
William E. Donoghue's No-Load Mutual Fund Guide

BY WILLIAM E. DONOGHUE
Donoghue's Mutual Fund Almanac
William E. Donoghue's Guide to Finding Money to Invest
Donoghue's Investment Tips for Retirement Savings

BY WILLIAM E. DONOGHUE *with Dana Shilling*
William E. Donoghue's Lifetime Financial Planner

BY WILLIAM E. DONOGHUE *with Robert Chapman Wood*
The Donoghue Strategies

THE DONOGHUE STRATEGIES

Ten Minutes a Week to
INVESTMENT SUCCESS

BY **WILLIAM E. DONOGHUE**

WITH *Robert Chapman Wood*

BANTAM BOOKS
NEW YORK · TORONTO · LONDON · SYDNEY · AUCKLAND

THE DONOGHUE STRATEGIES
A Bantam Book / March 1989

Grateful acknowledgment is made to the following:
Chart on page 70 from Ibbotson, Roger G., and Rex A. Sinquefield, *Stocks, Bonds, Bills, and Inflation*
(SBBI), 1982, updated in *SBBI 1988 Yearbook*, Ibbotson Associates, Inc., Chicago.
Glossary from *Guide to Finding Money to Invest* by William E. Donoghue. Copyright © 1985 by William E.
Donoghue. Reprinted by permission of Harper & Row Publishers, Inc.

Library of Congress-Cataloging-in-Publication Data
Donoghue, William E.
    The Donoghue strategies.

    Includes index.
    1. Investments.   2. Finance, Personal.
I. Wood, Robert Chapman   II. Title.
HG4521.D644   1989   332.6'78   88-33349
ISBN 0-553-05343-4

Published simultaneously in the United States and Canada

Bantam Books are published by Bantam Books, a division of Bantam Doubleday Dell Publishing Group, Inc.
Its trademark, consisting of the words "Bantam Books" and the portrayal of a rooster, is Registered in U.S.
Patent and Trademark Office and in other countries. Marca Registrada, Bantam Books, 666 Fifth Avenue,
New York, New York 10103

Printed in the United States of America

DH 0 9 8 7 6 5 4 3 2 1

To Retta Kelly,
my love and inspiration

CONTENTS

ACKNOWLEDGMENTS

Reg Greene, former public relations director for the Investment Company Institute, said in print, "Bill Donoghue revolutionized the way America saves." Thanks, Reg, but lots more people than Bill Donoghue have done this. I have named many of them in my previous books, but a few deserve particular mention here.

Some very special people made this book possible. Robert Chapman Wood, "Woody," my collaborator, has contributed unparalleled energy, insight, and attention to detail, as well as the willingness to work the long hours the project required.

Providing invaluable research assistance have been Paul Pacun, our quantitative analyst, whose computer wizardry unearthed many investment secrets; Greg Yost and Tina Baughman, single premium life insurance experts par excellence; Jay Schabacker, Dick Fabian, and Paul Merriman, three fellow mutual fund experts who have provided impressive philosophical insights into this business; Chuck Chakrapani, who contributed the germ of the CounterBalance portfolio strategy; Bill Crawford, mutual fund database builder extraordinaire; Cyndi Andrade, CFA, whose research skills are essential to all our books; Conrad Grundlehner, who has been my investment guru for nearly twenty years; and Walter Frank, our economist.

Special mention should be given to three people who made this book and the past year a very special professional experience: Ann Harris, our editor at Bantam Books, who "got the point" of the book quickly and sharpened that point tactfully and well; Peter Ginsberg, my literary agent, for his confidence and wisdom; and Michelle Atkinson, my dear friend, astute advisor, and professional assistant, who helped me sort out my professional and business life and gave me the space to write this book.

THE
DONOGHUE
STRATEGIES

1
INVEST TEN MINUTES A WEEK AND PROSPER FOR A LIFETIME

"Easy money" is the great American dream. What appears to be "easy money," however, has traditionally resulted only from long hours of hard work. You had to discover the keys to investment success yourself. You had to earn your "easy money" the hard way by disciplining yourself to implement your investment strategy with attention and finesse. You had to develop the guts to invest when others were fearful, to buy while there was "blood in the streets." Easy money comes harder than we would like.

Now you are in luck. The hardest work has already been done for you. If you are willing to invest a few hours to read this book and ten minutes a week to implement its strategies, I believe investment success can be yours.

I have studied the investment techniques of the wisest and most successful investors in America and translated them into terms which the average person can understand and follow. The strategies in this book are built on a few basic

1

cause-and-effect relationships acknowledged by all savvy investment experts.

I believe I can now teach you how to invest in well-diversified investment pools managed by the highest-paid and most effective investment managers in the country and, over the long term, achieve returns at least 50 to 100 percent greater than the average client.

"EASY MONEY" CAN BE EASY FOR THE WISE

As you read through the pages of this book, a path to confident investment success will unfold slowly before you. We will take time to explain each step in the strategies patiently and honestly and to describe carefully each investment tool that you should use. We will tell you how to manage your own money to stay on the path of investment success.

This book is called *The Donoghue Strategies*, plural, because there are **several** paths to investment success. All use investments with which you and millions of Americans are already familiar (or which you will soon come to know well). Your choice of strategy will take into account your investment goals, how comfortable you feel with risk, how actively involved you are willing to be, and how complex a tax-sheltering strategy you want to manage.

Then, it only takes ten minutes a week to achieve investment success.

Over the next five to ten years, if historic relationships continue, you are likely to average returns of 15 to 20 percent or more — safely, confidently, and proudly.

WHY THIS BOOK IS SPECIAL

The great management philosopher Peter Drucker once said, "Efficiency is doing things right, *effectiveness is doing the right things*." Read on and we will tell you how to make the investment decisions that are right and therefore effective for you.

Pride is a key issue. Pride keeps many an investor from

investment success. The only dumb question in life is the one to which you don't know the answer and which you're embarrassed to ask. If you read on patiently (don't be afraid to read and reread — I wrote and rewrote), we will answer all of your questions.

My entire investment career has been preparation for writing *The Donoghue Strategies*. For twenty years I have been carefully evaluating thousands of investment tools and techniques designed for the independent investor. For over a decade I have been teaching investors to manage their money better. The result is the investment system detailed in this book.

When we tested this system over the eight-year period ending December 31, 1987, it improved the yield on 46 of the best no-load (no sales charge) U.S. stock market mutual funds by an average factor of 124.41 percent!

Let's take a specific example. Suppose you had bought $10,000 worth of Value Line Special Situations Fund on January 1, 1980, and held it until December 31, 1987 (after the crash of 1987). You would have wound up with $19,330.

On the other hand, if you had followed the stock market investment system outlined in this book, switching your money to a money market mutual fund when the Donoghue Interest Rate Signal said, "Sell," and buying back in when the Donoghue Signal said, "Buy," you would have had an account valued at $53,910! That is an improvement of $34,580, or 370.63 percent. You could even have improved the performance of the venerated Fidelity Magellan Fund, the best-performing of all funds in this period, by 46.94 percent. If you had been prescient enough to use this system to invest in Magellan, you could have turned $10,000 into an amazing $104,460 in eight years!

Equally important, the system in this book substantially reduces risk. To achieve these returns you would have shifted your money into virtually riskless money market mutual funds at least 40 percent of the time in order to stay out of the stock market during periods when interest rates were rising — exactly the periods when most investment experts agree that risk is greatest. You would have accomplished this by shifting your money between a stock fund and a money fund an average of twice a year.

THIS BOOK IS DESIGNED FOR YOU

My mother told me, a few years ago, "Your father never trained me to be a widow." The real truth is that few of us were trained to manage our own finances.

This book has been written for the investor who wants to earn the highest and safest returns with the least management effort. It is written for investors who know that they **must** make the most of their investments — that success or failure can determine the quality of the rest of their lives. It is written for ordinary people who have little, if any, training in investments and finance but who must make responsible decisions about their money.

It will teach you how savvy, confident investors can invest for big returns not only in the stock market but in the risk-free money market and in the often quirky bond market as well. It will also advise you on the safest ways to execute the generally risky "buy, hold, and pray" strategy, in case you aren't ambitious or confident enough to implement the slightly more demanding strategies I advocate.

So even if you aren't ready to go for the truly big returns you can achieve through disciplined switching between stock market and money market funds, you can still come out way ahead on whatever investments you choose.

The investment tools are ones you are already familiar with: money funds, mutual funds, bank deposits, Treasury bills, individual retirement accounts (IRAs), etc. To these are added a few that are generally available but require the advice of a professional to buy — for example, single premium life insurance policies.

"WHAT MAKES YOU THINK I CAN REALLY EARN UP TO 20 PERCENT A YEAR?"

I have been studying the relationship between interest rates and investment returns for nearly twenty years. I've learned that the most important key to investment success today is to understand interest rate trends. If you follow interest rate trends when you invest, you can expect superior returns.

The investment geniuses of history have all recognized that the stock market tends to rise when interest rates fall and fall when interest rates rise. Since interest rates today are higher and more volatile than in the past, moreover, the opportunities to profit from interest rate changes are greater than ever before. At the Donoghue Organization, we've demonstrated that investors can dramatically increase their investment returns by paying attention to interest rate changes.

Back in 1978 I realized that higher levels of interest rates would dominate the investment markets for decades. Rising-interest-rate periods would offer excellent returns for people who kept their cash in short-term money market investments such as money market mutual funds. Declining-interest-rate periods, on the other hand, would produce dramatic opportunities for profit in the stock market.

In the late 1970s, interest rates were rising, so I developed two newsletters that made me a key leader of the financial services revolution: *Donoghue's Money Fund Report* (a newsletter analyzing the money market mutual fund industry for money fund professionals) and *Donoghue's Moneyletter* (which helped consumers obtain maximum returns). My *Complete Money Market Guide* was a national best-seller, and taught millions of investors to take charge of their financial lives.

Then interest rates started to decline in the early 1980s. I was ready to show investors how to capitalize on that phase of the interest rate cycle, too. In 1982, I wrote my *No-Load Mutual Fund Guide*, also a best-seller, which introduced the SLYC (Safety, Liquidity, Yield, and Convenience — Crash-proofing, too) investment system. We told investors to shift their money gradually from stock mutual funds to money funds (in nice, patient 25 percent segments), using an easy-to-follow interest-rate-based investment guideline.

The results? Excellent. If you had followed this system over the period 1982–86, and invested in the top five stock market funds featured in *Donoghue's Moneyletter*, you would have made seven switches in five years and averaged 26.61 percent average annual returns.

My books and newsletters led consumers in the big move from dependence on the crummy yields paid by banks and the dubious advice usually offered by stockbrokers to the free, higher returns anyone could achieve by seizing control of his or her own financial destiny.

WHAT ABOUT THE CRASH OF 1987?

The crash of October 1987 was a humbling experience for everyone involved, investors and investment advisors alike. Most of us (myself included, to some extent) did not have the discipline or guts to avoid being sucked into the heady atmosphere of a soaring market. We overstayed our welcome. Many of us paid the price. But *Moneyletter*'s hot line telephone service issued warnings a week and a half before the crash. Moreover, our advice for the year as a whole was good enough so that our readers made money, though it was not as much as it would have been had we at the Donoghue Organization assiduously followed our own indicators.

The losses that followed what was euphemistically called that "market break" sent us back to the drawing board. In the process of scrutinizing the assumptions on which we had based our investment strategies, we utilized the power of the computer to test literally hundreds of different alternatives.

It was like being single again. It was time to start romancing a fresh strategy. We looked anew at many alternatives, analyzed the best choices, and ended up reaffirming that we had been using the correct assumptions, but needed to season them with the wisdom and experience the crash had provided. Mature choices are the best choices.

This reassessment provided us with more sophisticated

approaches to our basic investment system. It increased the probability of safer as well as higher returns. It is these findings that are embodied in *The Donoghue Strategies*. The system of investments presented here is unlikely to become obsolete and will work extremely well in the money, bond, and stock markets. If followed over the period of 1980–87, a tricky period for all investors, it would have improved the returns of the no-load and low-load stock market funds we tested in our postcrash analysis by an astounding 124.41 percent, and improved the returns on nineteen bond funds we tested by 31 percent!

WHAT CAN THIS BOOK DO FOR YOU?

As you read through these chapters, you will discover some gems of investment strategies. Here are a few of them:

▶ **The knowledge of how and where to invest.** I can show you how to save thousands of dollars in wasted commissions, in bad investments, and in unnecessary taxes. Knowing how to invest in no-load mutual funds alone can save you significant money.

▶ **A reliable way of beating Wall Street.** You will learn the secrets of successful stock market fund investing, including a strategy for identifying the best funds and strategies for managing a portfolio of the top mutual funds.

▶ **A plan for battling the bond bombshells.** You will learn the secrets of successful bond fund investing; how to understand when bond funds are a serious threat to your financial security and when they are safe; how to avoid the biggest pitfalls in bond fund investing; and a much safer way to get a check a month from your mutual funds than taking on the enormous risks of relying on interest from bonds.

▶ **Ways to earn higher and safer money market profits.** You will learn the secrets to earning higher, safer returns from your money market investments; how to find the highest-yielding bank certificates of deposit (CDs); how to make extra profits from your federally insured CDs; and how to know when to invest in a money fund (and ride the interest rate curve upward) and when to buy a bank CD.

▶ **Several legal ways of beating the tax man.** You will learn the smartest ways to invest tax-free in money market, bond market, and stock market mutual funds.

ROMANCING YOUR FIRST INVESTMENT

If you think investing in today's highly volatile and confusing markets is scary and full of pitfalls, you should think back about your first date. I will never forget mine.

When I was a teenager, girls were a revelation to me. They were all different and each had her special allure. Retta had that lovely, moody blonde hair, Susie's red hair implied hidden passions, Debbie was a sultry brunette with dark fathomless eyes, and I will never forget Judy's smile. Each seemed so perfect and so unattainable.

Making my choice was so difficult! If I asked Retta out, Judy would know I liked Retta better. What if whoever I asked said "No"? Then I would be ruined forever. What if I wore the wrong clothes, said the wrong thing, took her to the wrong movie, ordered the wrong food — my mind boggled with the possibilities.

Somehow, I got through my first date and many others, and although I never quite figured out what made girls tick, I discovered that I rather liked discovering something new each time.

Investing is just as anxiety producing for many of us. As with dating, there seems to be no time in our education to learn the ropes. But somehow each of us learns despite this. And the rewards can be very satisfying.

THE "GO" SIGNAL TO INVESTMENT SUCCESS

Almost as exciting as learning how to read "go" signals from the opposite sex is learning to read "go" signals from the investment markets. If you are ready to enter the world of successful investing, the Donoghue Signals are ready to show you the way.

2
THE DONOGHUE SIGNALS

When the financial history of the last few decades of the twentieth century is written, it will be a story of unprecedented interest rate volatility propelling a seesaw stock market. If you can understand interest rates and their trends nowadays, you can read stock market trends almost like a book.

The go-go stock market years of the late 1960s were ended by a prime rate rise — to a then-record rate of 9 percent. The disaster of the stock market in the mid-1970s followed new interest rate increases; rates peaked in 1974 with the prime at 12 percent. Then, as rates eased off, the stock market soared, only to be driven into the cellar again and again by the prime rate, which eventually hit 20.5 percent in 1981 — three times!

Then, when the twin devils of high interest rates and high inflation were exorcised in 1982, declining rates set off one of the great bull markets in history — until rising interest rates triggered the crash of 1987.

VOLATILITY IS OPPORTUNITY

This interest rate roller coaster has produced both extraordinary opportunities and extraordinary challenges for investors (figure 2.1). Those who clung to the old "buy, hold, and pray/invest for the long term" philosophy saw their wealth

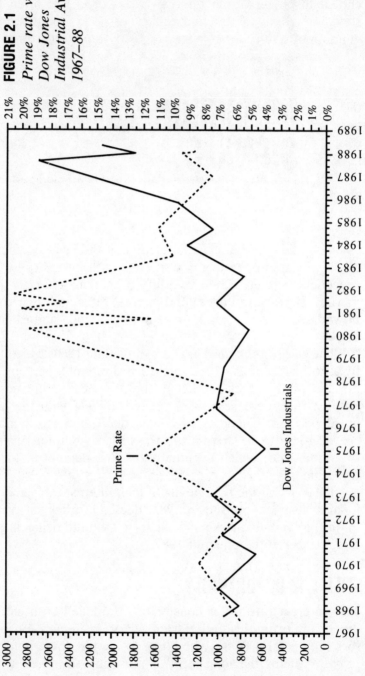

FIGURE 2.1
Prime rate vs.
Dow Jones
Industrial Average,
1967–88

ebb almost every time interest rates rose. Too often they stayed too long at the fair and then were frightened into jumping off the roller coaster at exactly the wrong times.

Witness the general paranoia after the 1987 crash. People who bailed out of the market right after the crash missed the 20 to 40 percent returns achieved by many mutual funds in the six months that followed. Many people have the feeling that "Every time I invest I lose money. Just as I gain confidence, the guy on the evening news reports that interest rates have risen and the stock market has fallen."

But we believe people can be smarter than that. Almost all big stock market declines, especially in the last twenty-five years, have been preceded by interest rate increases that started before the stock market turned dramatically down.

Thus the stock market investing problem today reminds me of an old joke:

"Doctor, it hurts when I raise my arm," says the patient.

"Don't raise your arm," replies the doctor.

An easy cure.

There is an answer to today's stock market volatility. **Do not invest in the stock or bond markets when interest rates are rising.** It is just that simple.

THE RATING GAME

The name of the game is to follow interest rates.

> **When interest rates are rising, stay on the sidelines, with your money invested in money market mutual funds. Money market funds are risk-free and they earn higher and higher yields as interest rates rise.**

> **When interest rates are falling, jump into the stock market (or, if you're more comfortable with fixed-income investing, the bond market) and you will prosper.**

WHY DO INTEREST RATES DRIVE STOCK PRICES?

There's no magic in the price declines that hit common stocks when interest rates rise. Basically, they have two causes:

► First, when fixed-income investments offer high interest rates, investors say, "Why should I take the risk of owning stocks when I can get such great returns from a federally insured CD?" They sell stocks and buy fixed-income securities, and the price of stocks falls.
► Second, business becomes more expensive when people must pay more to borrow, so business will slow and become less profitable. The threat of this slowing also reduces stock prices.

THE RELATIONSHIP IS ESPECIALLY POWERFUL TODAY

Let's look more closely at the first of these causes. The process of comparing investment yields is at the heart of Wall Street decision making. Sophisticated investors (definition: people who have lost money investing and learned from the experience) become skeptical about new investments. They ask each new investment, "What will you pay me for my money?" Then they look at the answers:

A **stock says,** "I will pay you dividends based on my company's earnings." And the investor asks, "What is the probability that you will earn money to pay dividends that increase over time?" Getting an answer, the investor retires to make his decision.

A **bond says,** "I will pay interest and return your money when I mature, and if I default, the assets pledged as collateral will be sold to repay you." The investor asks, "But what if I want to sell you before maturity? Will I get all my money back?" The bond replies, "I can't tell you that. If interest rates rise, my value will decline. You must decide whether you want to take that risk." Getting this answer, the investor tries to decide.

The investor will compare each risky alternative (i.e., each stock or long-term bond investment) to the rate of return he could receive without risk — perhaps a bank's CD interest rate. The most sophisticated investors "discount" the future benefits they expect from each investment alternative by the interest rates they could earn without risk.

Perhaps interest rate changes may have had relatively little impact on investment decisions in the 1960s, when rates remained between 3 and 6 percent and changed slowly. When, however, as in the past decade, interest rates fluctuate between 6 and 20 percent, the discount rate becomes very significant.

Wall Street computer models show, for example, that a $10 dividend ten years from now is worth $5.58 today at a 6 percent discount rate. But it's worth only $1.62 today at a 20 percent discount rate.

Thus a simple change in interest rates can reduce enormously the real value of the future stream of dividends from a stock. The effect may not show up immediately in the market value of the stock, but it will certainly show up eventually in price declines.

In August of 1981, for instance, you could have bought a thirty-month certificate of deposit that yielded over 19 percent. Let me tell you: When a riskless investment was yielding 19 percent, very few other investments were worthwhile. So stock and bond prices were down sharply.

DONOGHUE IS MY NAME, INTEREST RATES ARE MY GAME

If the name of the game is to follow interest rate trends, then I can help you. To follow these trends, the first place to look — the place where interest rate trends typically become established first — is the money market.

The money market is exactly what the name implies — a market for money. Specifically, the money market is where people make *short-term* loans at market-determined interest rates on which repayment is guaranteed by *highly reliable borrowers*. Billions of dollars' worth of short-term obligations of borrowers such as the U.S. Treasury and the largest banks and corporations are bought and sold every day.

To understand money market interest rate trends, study not what economists are saying but what they are doing with the short-term money they are paid to manage professionally. Their actions speak louder than their words to the press. "Put your money where your mouth is, and I'll believe you," I tell them.

MONEY MARKET TRUTH IS NO SECRET IF YOU KNOW WHERE TO FIND IT

The money market is an unusual market. An enormous share of the cash in the money market (10 to 15 percent) is invested in money market mutual funds. Since money market mutual funds are offered to the public, they must publicly disclose much of what they do.

Each week, at the appointed hour, over 500 money market mutual funds with over $330,000,000,000.00 (that's $330 billion, in case you were wondering what it looked like) under management report their vital statistics to the Donoghue Organization. Each tells its net assets (how much it has in shareholders' accounts), its 7-day yield and 30-day yield; the average maturity of its portfolio (the number of days from now until the average investment will mature or be repaid to the fund); and how much of this portfolio is invested in such categories of security as Treasury bills, government agency borrowings, repurchase agreements, certificates of deposit, etc.

Since the fund companies' management fees are also public information, their competitors can get a clear idea of their gross profits each week from the net assets statistics printed in the *Money Fund Report*. (See figure 2.2.)

Thus, highly competitive financial institutions in the money fund industry may know more about one another than the participants in any other industry in the world.

Clearly, we know a lot about what the money funds are doing. In fact, *the Federal Reserve Board has used Dono-*

Donoghue's
Money Fund Report ®
OF HOLLISTON, MA 01746
ISSN 0197 7091

Net Assets ($ mil)	TAXABLE FUNDS	Annualized Yields For Period Ended 7/19/88			Ave. Mat. (days)	Portfolio Holdings (%)								
		7-Day	30-Day	Compound 7-Day		U.S. Treas	U.S. Other	Repos	CDs	Bankers Accept	Comm'l Paper	Euros CDs, TDs	Yankees CDs, BAs	Non-Prime
	DOMESTIC PRIME & EUROS & YANKEES													
6.3	Alger Money Market Portfolio k	7.44	7.34	7.72	45	3	23	-	-	-	53	-	21	-
1,096.7	Cash Management Trust	7.19	7.05	7.45	18	-	10	3	10	1	74	-	2	-
327.5	Compass Cap. Cash Reserve Fund	7.03	6.90	7.28	32	-	-	-	8	1	60	28	3	-
209.2	Counsellors Cash Reserve k	7.08	6.97	7.33	30	-	-	11	5	-	12	69	3	-
849.3	ED Jones Daily Passport	6.60	6.49	6.82	43	-	-	2	11	-	55	16	16	-
34.4	EGT Money Market Trust	6.09	5.96	6.28	16	-	-	10	3	-	70	-	17	-
1,126.4	IDS Cash Management	6.87	6.77	7.11	23	-	-	-	1	-	74a	3	3	19
428.1	Integrated M.M. Securities	6.74	6.61	6.97	28	-	-	5	-	9	65a	17	4	-
261.8	Landmark Funds Cash Reserves	6.62	6.47	6.84	35	2	2	5	9	10	32	12	35	-
299.9	Lehman Management Cash Res.	6.79	6.64	7.02	41	-	5	-	16	-	2	72	17	-
227.4	Liquid Green Trust	6.59	6.49	6.81	36	-	-	3	-	-	80	-	17	-
100.0	Morgan Keegan Daily Cash	6.45	6.35	6.66	37	-	-	9	11	-	54	12	14	-
1,546.2	PaineWebber RMA MF/MM Port.	6.99	6.85	7.24	34	-	-	-	-	-	81	1	18	-
102.3	Phoenix M.M. Series	6.74	6.63	6.97	36	-	-	3	5	-	47	7	36	5
373.4	Piper Jaffray Inv. Tr., M.M.F. k	6.61	6.45	6.83	30	3	2	6	12	2	49	3	5	18
1,616.4	Prudential-Bache Command M.F.	6.93	6.81	7.17	46	-	6	-	7	-	60	18	9	-
5,246.1	Prudential-Bache MoneyMart Assets	6.85	6.71	7.09	40	-	-	3	5	8	77	9	1	-
651.5	Putnam Daily Dividend Trust	6.50	6.50	6.71	31	-	-	3	4	-	69	-	12	12
96.6	RNC Liquid Assets Fund, Inc. k	6.75	6.59	6.98	36	2	-	-	3	-	72	2	21	-
254.1	Renaissance Assets Trust/M.M.F.	6.92	6.81	7.16	27	-	-	-	5	-	59a	24	12	-
67.2	Sentinel Cash Management	6.64	6.59	6.86	36	-	-	-	10	23	43	-	24	-
362.5	Standby Reserve Fund, Inc.	6.88	6.74	7.12	41	3	-	4	18	17	45	6	-	-
297.0	Woodward M.M.F.	7.18	7.05	7.44	34	-	-	-	3	-	65a	24	8	-
$ 15,580.3	SUBTOTAL													
	AVERAGE YIELD & MATURITY	6.80	6.69	7.04	36									

FIGURE 2.2 *Sample table from* Money Fund Report

ghue's money fund data regularly for over a decade to learn what the critical indicators we have developed are saying.

HOW CAN YOU DETECT THE TRENDS?

In addition to the newsletters, we also distribute Donoghue's Money Market Funds table, which appears in over sixty major newspapers around the country and in *Barron's*, the financial weekly, which is available nationwide. (Appendix 8 lists some of the newspapers in which this table appears.) The data in the table can show you trends that indicate what strategic decisions you should make. The key information also appears in many newspapers that do not carry the complete table, such as *USA Today* and the *Wall Street Journal*, but not in a form that's as easy to work with.

The Money Market Funds table (figure 2.3) lists selected statistics on about 181 ordinary, taxable money market mutual funds, and on 76 money market funds that invest exclusively in tax-exempt securities and thus provide tax-free income. At the bottom of the taxable group of funds and the tax-free group of funds are given the overall average maturity and average yields for each group.

To invest wisely in the stock, bond, and money markets, we want to know: What is the underlying trend of interest rates? This trend can be deduced easily from our money market statistics.

THE DONOGHUE AVERAGE MATURITY SIGNAL

We have found the *average maturity* of taxable money funds to be an extremely useful **warning signal of higher rates ahead**. When money fund managers think that interest rates are going to rise, they "go short," or shorten the average maturity of the fund; that is, they reduce the number of days until the average investment in the portfolio matures.

In English, that means that when one of the fund's certificates of deposit matures or when the fund has additional assets to invest, the manager opts to invest the fund's money in a very short-term security — perhaps one that will mature in as little as a day or a week. That way, as interest rates rise, the manager will be able to reinvest the money sooner at the new, higher rates.

I call this the *Donoghue Average Maturity Signal*. It works for investors in two ways.

Risk-averse investors

If you keep your money primarily in bank certificates of deposit and similar investments, you will regularly be faced with a decision whether to "roll over" your certificate of deposit or to put your money in a highly liquid investment such as a money market mutual fund or money market deposit account. Certificates of deposit usually offer higher yields, but if interest rates rise, you're stuck with the current rate until your certificate matures. Thus, you're better off in a money market deposit account so you can ride the yields up as interest rates increase.

When you have money to invest, check the average maturity of taxable money funds in the Money Market Funds table, preferably for three or four weeks in a row. Generally, the average maturity ranges from 30 to 50 days. If the average maturity is **46 days or higher** and there is no sign of a declining trend — that is, the average maturity has not declined during the past three weeks — Wall Street's "smart money" definitely believes that interest rates are stable or falling. Consider buying a one-year CD (or an even longer CD, if the rate is good enough).

If the average maturity of taxable money funds is holding stable at **between 40 and 45 days**, that means that the smart money on Wall Street thinks that interest rates will *probably* remain stable or fall, but they are not sure. You are safe buying a six-month CD. You should also consider a six-month CD if the average maturity is over 45 days but shows a declining trend.

If the average maturity of all taxable money funds is **39 days or less**, however, that's a danger signal. Do not invest in a certificate of deposit until you have definite evidence that the interest rate rise that prompted fund managers to "go short" is over and interest rates are on the way down again.

TAX-FREE MONEY FUNDS

Tax-free money funds with assets of $100 million or more that are available to individual investors. For period ended June 6, 1988.

Fund	Assets ($ millio)	Average maturity (days)	7-day average yield (%)	7-day compound yield (%)
Alliance Tax-Exempt Reserves	673.4	59	4.4	4.5
Benham CA Tax-Free Trust	310.8	5	4.2	4.3
Boston Co. Mass. Tax Free M.F.	150.4	45	4.3	4.4
CMA Tax-Exempt	8,152.0	48	4.4	4.5
Calvert Tax-Free Reserves M.M.	727.0	44	4.9	5.0
Carnegie Tax-Free Income Trust	329.2	44	4.5	4.6
Centennial Tax-Exempt Trust	532.5	67	4.5	4.6
Compass Capital T-E Fund	159.0	45	4.7	4.8
DBL Tax Free Cash Fund Inc.	571.3	54	4.6	4.7
Dean Witter/Active Assets Tax Free	1,071.0	21	4.5	4.6
Dean Witter/Sears Tax Free Daily	943.8	20	4.4	4.5
Dreyfus CA Tax-Exempt M.M.F.	338.9	43	4.3	4.4
Dreyfus New York T-E M.M.F.	388.6	61	4.3	4.4
Dreyfus Tax-Exempt M.M.F.	2,632.6	40	4.3	4.4
FFB Tax-Free M.M.F.	142.9	51	4.4	4.5
Federated/Tax Free Instruments Tr.	1,426.6	47	4.4	4.5
Fidelity California Tax Free/MMP	566.3	45	4.4	4.5
Fidelity Mass. Tax Free/MMP	620.0	56	4.3	4.4
Fidelity NY Tax Free/M.M.P.	643.0	45	4.2	4.3
Fidelity Tax-Exempt M.M. Trust	3,634.1	39	4.5	4.6
First Lakeshore T-E M.M.F.	134.2	33	4.5	4.6
Flag Investors Tax Free/Cash Reserve	240.5	42	4.5	4.6
Franklin CA Tax-Exempt M.F.	674.4	24	4.7	4.8
Franklin Tax-Exempt M.M.F.	102.9	82	4.8	5.0
General CA Tax-Exempt M.M.F.	106.9	33	4.4	4.4
General Tax-Exempt M.M.F.	438.5	40	4.3	4.4
HighMark CA Tax Free Fund	108.4	28	4.4	4.5
Home Fed. Tax Free Res.	107.9	43	4.4	4.5
IDS Tax-Free M.F. Inc.	117.2	65	4.2	4.3
Kemper M.M.F. T-E Port.	174.7	21	4.6	4.7
Kidder Peabody CA T-E M.F.	149.5	59	4.3	4.4
Kidder Peabody T-E M.F.	796.5	57	4.4	4.5
Landmark Funds Tax Free Res.	148.5	26	4.2	4.3
Landmark NY Tax Free Res.	335.8	46	3.9	4.0
Lazard Freres Instit. Tax Free	214.3	53	4.8	4.9
Lazard Tax-Free M.M.F.	306.5	56	4.6	4.7
Lehman Mngmnt Tax Free Res.	103.8	63	4.3	4.4
Mariner NY Tax-Free M.M.F.	127.0	45	4.4	4.4
MarketMaster Tr. T-E Fund	122.8	40	4.6	4.7
McDonald Tax-Exempt M.M.F.	108.4	77	4.2	4.3
Merrill Lynch Instit. T-E	494.7	38	4.3	4.3
Metro Portfolio N.Y. Tax Free M.M.F.	111.6	42	4.0	4.1
Midwest Group Tax Free Tr. M.M.	121.1	76	4.5	4.6
Money Mngmnt Plus/T.F.	128.1	45	4.5	4.6
Municipal Cash Reserve Mgt	1,480.3	82	4.5	4.6
Neuberger & Berman Municipal M.F.	252.8	46	4.5	4.6
Nuveen CA Tax Free M.F.	207.4	20	4.5	4.6
Nuveen Tax-Free Reserves	424.9	37	4.4	4.5
PaineWeb. RMA Tax Free Fund	976.2	43	4.4	4.5
Pru-Bache NY M.M. Series	168.8	107	4.2	4.3
Prudential-Bache Command Tax Free	688.8	71	4.4	4.5
Prudential-Bache Tax Free M.F.	731.8	76	4.4	4.5
Reich & Tang/CT Daily Tax Free	254.3	47	4.0	4.1
Reich & Tang/Daily Tax Free	889.2	24	4.6	4.7
Reich & Tang/Empire Tax Free	219.4	92	4.2	4.3
Reserve Connecticut	246.8	41	4.0	4.1
Reserve Interstate	372.6	45	4.3	4.4
Scudder Daily Tax-Free Money Fund	394.5	67	4.6	4.7
Shearson Daily Tax-Free Div.	777.2	47	4.5	4.7
Shearson FMA Muni. Fund	1,098.5	40	4.5	4.6
Shearson-Lehman CA Daily Tax Free	191.9	24	4.4	4.5
Shearson-Lehman NY Daily Tax Free	220.5	52	4.2	4.3
Shearson/Provident: Muni Fund	1,808.6	44	4.7	4.8
Shearson/Provident: Muni. CA	935.7	37	4.6	4.7
Shearson/Provident: Muni. NY	400.1	44	4.5	4.7
SteinRoe Tax-Exempt M.F.	306.9	26	4.2	4.3
T. Rowe Price T-E M.F.	1,246.6	28	4.3	4.4
Tax-Exempt M.M.F.	1,749.8	15	4.5	4.6
Tecumseh PaPoose Tax-Free Port.	120.0	26	4.2	4.3
The Tax Free Money Fund Inc.	1,074.2	43	4.4	4.5
Thomson McKinnon Nat'l T-E	278.4	53	4.2	4.3
Tucker Anthony Tax-Exempt M.F.	250.9	34	4.4	4.5
USAA Tax-Exempt M.M.F.	619.9	49	4.7	4.8
UST Master Short-Term Tax-Exempt	536.2	41	4.7	4.8
Vanguard CA Tax Free M.M.F.	165.4	54	4.6	4.7
Vanguard Muni. Bond/M.M.	2,208.8	67	4.7	4.9
Vista NY Tax Free M.M.F.	250.4	51	3.9	4.0
Vista Tax Free M.M.F.	140.3	65	4.3	4.3
Woodward T-E M.M.F.	152.5	43	4.5	4.6
Donoghue's Tax Free Money Fund Avgs. *Averages for all 152 tax-free funds		44	4.36	4.45

30-day average yield 4.38

Yield columns represent annualized total return to shareholders for past seven days and 7-day compounded (effective) rates of return. Past returns are not necessarily indicative of future yields. Investment quality and maturity may vary among funds.

(r) - restricted availability.

Reprinted with permission from Donoghue's Money Fund Report, Holliston, 01746

18

MONEY MARKET FUNDS

Funds with assets of $100 million or more that are available to individual investors. For period ended June 7, 1988.

Fund	Assets ($ million)	Average maturity (days)	7-day average yield (%)	7-day compound yield (%)
Alex. Brown Gov't Series	281.1		6.6	6.9
Alex. Brown Prime	873.3	31	6.6	6.8
Alliance Capital Reserves	1,371.4	62	6.3	6.5
Alliance Gov't Reserves	330.8	67	6.3	6.5
American Capital Reserve	483.6	28	6.7	7.0
Arch Money Market Class A	337.2	24	6.7	6.9
Axe-Houghton M.M.F.	101.4	17	6.4	6.6
Bayshore Cash Reserve	306.5	48	6.8	7.0
Boston Company Cash Mgt	297.3	47	6.2	6.3
Bull & Bear Dollar Reserves	102.7	72	6.7	7.0
Capital Preservation Fund	2,095.4	40	5.9	6.0
Capital Preservation Fund II	468.2	1	6.2	6.4
Cardinal Gov't Securities	415.5	32	6.5	6.7
Carnegie Gov't Securities Trust	147.1	22	6.3	6.5
Cash Assets Trust	196.7	29	6.6	6.9
Cash Equivalent Fund M.M. Port.	5,814.1	21	6.4	6.6
Cash Equivalent Gov't Sec.	1,335.9	10	6.6	6.8
Cash Mngmt Trust	1,108.3	20	6.7	6.9
Centennial Money Mkt Trust	227.8	25	6.3	6.5
Churchill Cash Reserve Tr.	225.5	26	6.7	6.9
Colonial Gov't Money Market Tr.	103.8	52	6.0	6.2
Columbia Daily Income	474.9	30	6.4	6.6
Compass Cap. Cash Reserve Fund	288.0	33	6.7	6.9
Comp~ ~ U.S. Treas. Fund	~ 0.	39	6.5	6.?
C~ ~nt Co.		3?		
Merrill Lynch CBA M.F.	302.2	41	6.5	6.7
Merrill Lynch CMA Gov't	2,236.4	36	6.7	6.9
Merrill Lynch CMA M.F.	19,706.4	35	6.6	6.9
Merrill Lynch Gov't	1,508.5	36	6.1	6.3
Merrill Lynch Institutional	1,586.2	37	6.7	7.0
Merrill Lynch Ready	9,624?7	35	6.6	6.8
Merrill Lynch Ret. Res. M.F. (r)	3,324.6	33	6.3	6.5
Midwest Income ST Gov't	276.9	36	6.5	6.7
Money Market Mngmnt	188.1	47	6.3	6.5
Money Trust	151.5	13	6.7	6.9
Monitor Money Market Fund	260.8	32	6.8	7.0
Morgan Keegan Daily Cash	103.1	44	6.0	6.2
Mutual of Omaha M.M.A.	176.8	41	6.2	6.4
N.E. Cash Mgt Tr./M.M. Series	827.1	42	6.5	6.8
NLR Cash Portfolio	1,392.7	34	6.5	6.7
NLR Government Portfolio	115.6	48	6.3	6.5
Nationwide M.M.F.	404.2	31	6.4	6.6
Neuberger & Berman Gov't M.F.	237.4	55	5.6	5.7
Oppenheimer M.M.F. Inc.	722.2	25	6.5	6.7
Pacific American M.M.F. (r)	628.2	26	6.6	6.9
Pacific Horizon Funds/Gov't	879.9	59	6.5	6.7
Pacific Horizon Funds/M.M.P.	1~11.0	30	6.~	6.9
PaineWeb~ CASHFUND		30		~8
Donoghue's Money Fund Averages *				
* Averages for all 330 taxable funds		37	6.42	6.62
~We~ ...F./M.M. Port.				
~U.S. Co.				
~~0-d~ ~average yield 6.33				

Yield columns represent annualized total return to shareholders for past seven days and 7-day compounded (effective) rates of return. Past returns are not necessarily indicative of future yields. Investment quality and maturity may vary among funds.

(r) - restricted availability.

Reprinted with permission from Donoghue's Money Fund Report. Holliston, 01746

FIGURE 2.3 Donoghue's Money Market Funds table (which includes the Tax-Free Money Funds table) as it appears in the financial section of a typical newspaper. The key numbers are the average maturity and the 7-day average yield (circled, lower right).

19

What evidence are you looking for? Either a rising trend in the average maturity or a falling trend in the Donoghue Interest Rate Signal, described below.

Until you see that evidence, park your money in a money fund or bank money market account and wait for a chance to buy a long-term investment at a higher interest rate in the future. When more than 500 of the nation's best money market portfolio managers, with over $330 billion under management, put their money where their mouths are and reduce their average maturity, they are serious and should be heeded. They are expecting interest rates to rise.

Stock and bond market investors

As we already know, rising interest rates are a signal that the stock market is going to take a downturn. We will use another indicator for our "sell" and "buy" signals for stocks and long-term bonds, but the average maturity serves as an excellent "caution" signal.

When the average maturity falls to the 39- to 35-day range, trouble is brewing and you had better be on your guard.

The average maturity had shortened to 38 days for the two weeks before the October 19, 1987, crash that saw the market fall over 600 points in just two days. After the crash, the maturity lengthened as portfolio managers jumped into longer-term Treasury investments to take advantage of the "flight to quality" that followed and drove interest rates down.

By early January 1988, the average maturity had again shortened, this time to 35 days, before the 145-point decline of the Dow Jones Industrials on January 6.

When the market has been moving a bit too fast for comfort, the average maturity is a good caution signal to warn you not to stay in stock or bond market mutual funds. **It is to be heeded.**

THE DONOGHUE INTEREST RATE SIGNAL — WHERE THE BIG MONEY IS MADE

The money market is, first and foremost, a parking lot for the timid and the cautious. It is for people satisfied with returns usually in the 5 to 10 percent range. Five to 10 percent sure isn't enough for me if I am a long-term investor, however. If you want to earn higher returns, you have two choices:

▶ **For safe returns in the 8 to 13 percent range, you can buy and manage a portfolio that includes long-term bonds or bond mutual funds.** (However, you *must* learn when to *sell* bonds if you want to make money safely in the bond market, as we will demonstrate in chapters 8 and 9.)
▶ **If you want to earn returns of 20 percent or more, with risk only slightly greater than you would face in the bond market, you must learn to invest in the stock market.** You need to select the right stock market mutual funds to buy and also learn the right time to sell.

In either of these markets, you'll find the Donoghue Interest Rate Signal is your key to higher returns at lower risk.

Many investors believe that finding a rule that will tell them when to buy and when to sell is like finding the holy grail — highly desirable but hardly likely. But — don't tell 'em — we found it.

We set out to test the premise that interest rates and the stock market move in opposite directions most of the time and that if we could accurately interpret the interest rate trend, we could develop a powerful long-term strategy.

Several approaches we tried didn't perform as well as we'd hoped. Then we tried a technique that we had originally rejected: taking a "moving average" — an average of the values of an indicator for the current and a number of past periods.

Technical analysts use moving averages to smooth out short-term fluctuations and show a clear picture of a trend by eliminating "noise" (random, very short-term variations) in the statistics.

For instance, some analysts use the 39-week moving averages of the prices of individual mutual funds to forecast mutual fund trends. Each week, they add up the values for the current week and the previous 38 weeks of the dividend-adjusted price per share of a mutual fund they are following, then divide by 39. (Alternately, you can calculate a moving average with "exponential smoothing," which is easier each week and may actually be a better indicator. More on that below.)

Forecasting systems based on the 39-week moving average of the price per share have performed reasonably well over the past decade, but unfortunately no one knows why. When the price of a mutual fund rises above its 39-week moving average, this is said to indicate that an upward trend has been established and you should buy. Then you hold on, hopefully riding an uptrend for a while, until the price falls below its 39-week moving average. When that happens, you conclude that the uptrend is probably over and a downtrend is probably established, so you sell.

There is no discernable cause-and-effect relationship between the 39-week moving average and future prices, however. Thus it's hard to tell whether this system will continue to work in the future.

Some practical problems are even more serious:

▶ The price per share of the mutual fund must be adjusted for dividends, capital gains distributions, etc. This can be arduous.

▶ Events that have nothing to do with real trends can trigger a signal. For instance, the Boesky scandal scared the market into a tumble in the fall of 1986. Since the scandal had nothing to do with economics, the market soon rebounded. Moving-average market timers got out at the bottom and back in at the top.

▶ The moving average always gives its signals *after* the trend you are trying to catch has already begun. Therefore, you can lose all benefit of the signal if you neglect to check the average for one week and a big move passes you by. One newsletter delivered a "sell" signal based on the 39-week moving average after the close of trading on Thursday, October 15, 1987. If you got the signal and acted the next day, that was great. But if you didn't, you were fully invested when the market fell more than 500 points the following Monday.

There is a better, more rational way. Interest rates dominate the stock market. Money fund yields represent a sensitive indicator of interest rate trends. Rising interest rates tend to drive the stock market lower and falling interest rates bring stock price increases.

So we carefully analyzed how we could quantify this important cause-and-effect relationship. We wanted a way of using interest rate trends to forecast stock market trends.

We decided to use Donoghue's Money Fund Averages as the basis for our indicator. (Other money market rates could also be used, but no other standardized money market rate is available as widely as Donoghue's Money Fund Averages.)

We chose the Donoghue's 7-day average (uncompounded) yield of taxable money market funds, because this gives a picture of the latest interest rate trends. You'll find the 7-day average yield of taxable money market funds at the bottom of the list of taxable money market funds in Donoghue's Money Market Funds table every week. (See figure 2.3 above.) *And we hit pay dirt!*

THE ANSWER TO MARKET TIMING

A 25-week exponential moving average of Donoghue's Money Fund Average 7-day uncompounded yields did a superb job. I call this average the Donoghue Interest Rate Signal.

We tested it over the period from January 1, 1980, through December 31, 1987. The 1980–87 period contained two stock market crashes (1981 and 1987), two bond market crashes in 1987 alone and one in 1980–81, a period of high inflation that tested us all, and a great bull market. The results:

1 The Donoghue Interest Rate Signal generated only sixteen switch signals in eight years, so it would not be difficult for the average person to trade on.

2 Only four of those signals were false signals, and the loss on each was trivial.

3 If you had slavishly followed the "buy" and "sell" signals with each of the 46 stock market funds in the Donoghue fund universe that had an eight-year record, you would have improved your return in *every single fund*.

4 The average improvement was **124.41 percent** — dramatic indeed.

5 While the average fund returned about 14.52 percent a year using a buy-and-hold strategy (and some returned as little as 8.35 percent), **every single stock market fund averaged at least 18 percent a year if you switched in and out following the Donoghue Signal. The average performance was 23.69 percent!**

Moreover, by keeping your money in money market mutual funds during the dangerous periods when interest rates were rising, the Donoghue Signal sharply reduced the risks you would have faced.

To confirm that the signal works consistently, we carried out a separate test of the period from 1984–87, so as to eliminate both the high money market yields of the early 1980s and the enormous returns produced by the start of the bull market. For the 1984–87 period, the signal improved the return of the average fund by 116.10 percent (from an average return of 9.08 percent per year to an average return of 17.84 percent per year). **Another superb performance.**

These are, of course, "backcasted" results. I can't guarantee they predict the future. But they provide dramatic evidence of the value of the Donoghue Interest Rate Signal.

A GUIDE TO CALCULATING AND USING THE DONOGHUE INTEREST RATE SIGNAL

As we have noted, each week Donoghue's Money Market Funds table which contains the Donoghue's Money Fund

Averages, are published throughout the United States. (See appendix 8.) To calculate the Donoghue Interest Rate Signal **you need only two pieces of information:**

1 The current Donoghue's 7-day average (uncompounded) yield of taxable money market funds, and
2 The previous week's 25-week moving average.

Of course, you could learn the previous week's 25-week moving average by going to the library, looking up the Donoghue's Money Fund Averages for the last 25 weeks, adding them all up, and dividing by 25. That still wouldn't give you the "exponential" moving average that we use, but it would be close enough.

But you don't have to do all that. Instead, you can **just call 1-800-445-5900 (or in Massachusetts, 508-429-5930), and ask for the workbook. We will send you the previous week's Donoghue Signal Number and a free workbook you can use to keep track of the Signal Number each week.**

Moreover, because we are using that neat little variant on the 25-week moving average called "exponential smoothing," you don't have to add up 25 numbers every week. To calculate this week's Donoghue Signal Number, you just **multiply last week's Donoghue's Signal Number by .925 and this week's 7-day average (uncompounded) yield for taxable money market funds by .075. Then add up the two numbers you get.** That gives you this week's exponentially smoothed moving average, the Donoghue Signal Number.

In other words, the formula is:

$$\left(\begin{array}{c}\text{Last week's}\\\text{Donoghue}\\\text{Signal Number}\end{array}\right) \times .925 + \left(\begin{array}{c}\text{This week's}\\\text{taxable money fund}\\\text{7-day average yield}\end{array}\right) \times .075 = \begin{array}{c}\text{This week's}\\\text{Donoghue}\\\text{Signal Number}\end{array}$$

Figure 2.4 shows what a Donoghue Interest Rate Signal graph can look like. If the current 7-day average yield is **higher** than the 25-week average, the slope of the 25-week average will be rising. A rising interest rate trend is in ef-

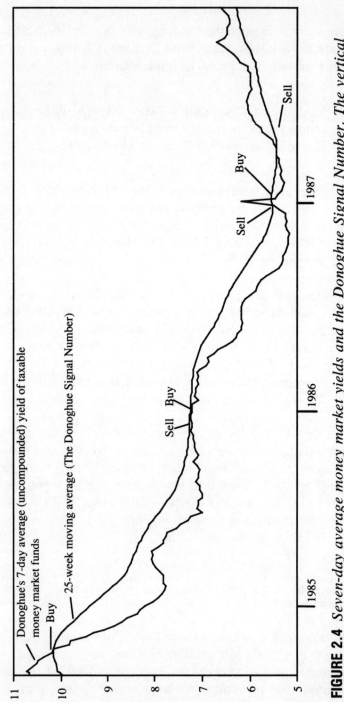

FIGURE 2.4 *Seven-day average money market yields and the Donoghue Signal Number. The vertical axis represents money market rates.*

fect — you have a **SELL** signal for stock or bond mutual funds. Your money should be in a money fund.

If the current 7-day average yield is **lower** than the 25-week average, that indicates a falling interest rate trend, a **BUY** signal. You should be invested in a stock market mutual fund (or a bond market mutual fund) from our list.

How to deal with trend reversals

If the current week's average 7-day yield of taxable money market funds crosses the 25-week moving average line (in other words, if the 7-day average yield was below the 25-week moving average last week and is above it this week, or vice versa), **that is your signal to move**. Do not wait for more confirmation. This system generates very few false signals and you take a significant risk of missed profits (or large losses) if you wait.

For example, if the current 7-day yield has just fallen below the 25-week moving average, go for it! You have a "buy" signal and you should jump back into the stock or long-term bond market.

Just one pitfall

Okay. You have obtained the previous week's Donoghue Signal Number from my office (or calculated a 25-week average yourself in a public library if you are the stubborn type). Now, keeping up to date should be easy, especially if a newspaper in your area carries the Donoghue Money Market Funds table or if you can sneak a peek at *Barron's* every weekend.

In newspapers, the Donoghue Money Market Funds table may appear on Thursday, Friday, Saturday, or Sunday. (Some papers publish it twice a week, but since we collect the data only once a week, the newspapers can only change the data once a week. They are just repeating the same table twice.)

The only danger is that you won't consistently use the same statistic. The Money Market Funds table includes several Donoghue's Money Fund Averages each week: the 7-day average yield, 7-day compound yield, and 30-day average yield for taxable money funds, and also the 7-day average yield, 7-day compound yield, and 30-day average yield for tax-free money funds. Note that all "average yields" are *un*-compounded.

When looking up the Money Fund Average every week, first find the listings for *taxable* mutual funds. (We use rates for taxable rather than tax-free funds because the rates for tax-free funds can be affected by other factors such as legislative moves in Congress.) The Donoghue's Money Fund Averages for taxable funds appear at the bottom of the list of taxable funds. Be sure to take the number from the column labeled "7-day average yield," not "7-day compound yield."

Even if your newspaper lacks the Donoghue's Money Market Funds table, it probably does report Donoghue's 7-day average (uncompounded) yield of taxable money market funds. (It may appear in a financial table or in an interest rate "roundup" article that is published on the same day each week.) *USA Today* prints Donoghue's 7-day average (uncompounded) yield of taxable money market funds every day Tuesday through Friday on the front of its business section. (Since the average is calculated only once a week — on Wednesdays — the number in *USA Today* changes only once a week, on Thursdays.)

But be extra careful if you take your data from a source other than the genuine Donoghue's Money Market Funds table. While most newspapers print the 7-day average (uncompounded) yield, as this is written the *New York Times* publishes only the 7-day compound yield. That is the yield you would achieve if you reinvested all your dividends for a year. It is useful for comparing money market fund yields to the compound yields of other investments. However, we have used the **uncompounded** 7-day average yield to calculate the Donoghue Signal Number because the uncompounded 7-day average yield is more widely available. So watch out. Do not use the compound yield. Switching to the compound yield for a week may generate a "sell" signal when you should be in a "buy" mode.

Some newspapers carry a money fund table from another source, the National Association of Securities Dealers (NASD). As a person who takes pride in presenting useful, accurate information, I find the NASD table inadequate in several respects:

1 The table is often published with an "average yield" that is the average yield of both *taxable* and *tax-free* money funds — a meaningless figure.

2 NASD's method of calculating yields is not in accord with generally accepted accounting principles, and has in the past indicated yields that no investor ever received.

You will do better to stick with our Money Market Funds table. It is usually published without the Donoghue name at the top, but you can recognize it because the word "Donoghue's" will always appear on the lines that list the genuine Donoghue's Money Fund Averages.

CONCLUSION

By riding interest rate movements intelligently, you can turn a treacherous era for investors into a period when investment success comes remarkably easily. Keeping track of the Donoghue Interest Rate Signal is easy, and it is a superb tool for investing in either the stock market or the long-term bond market. Moreover, as we will see in later chapters, it is likely to increase your returns on a very long-term investment such as an individual retirement account or a single premium variable life insurance policy as much as five- or tenfold.

Between them, the Donoghue Average Maturity Signal and the Donoghue Interest Rate Signal demonstrated that over the period 1981–87 they could have significantly **improved the long-term investment returns** on money market, stock market, and bond market investments (table 2.1) while significantly **reducing the risk**.

TABLE 2.1 *Sample results: stock market mutual fund performance over 8-year test (1980–87) of 46 funds*

Number of stock market funds tested: 46 funds

Number of funds on which yield was improved by trading: 46 funds

Average percentage improvement in 8-year return: 122.65%

Number of funds that earned more than 20% compound return without trading: 4 funds

Number of funds that earned more than 20% when traded following the Donoghue Interest Rate Signal: 40 funds

Number of funds that earned more than 25% without trading: 1 fund

Number of funds that earned more than 25% when traded following the Donoghue Interest Rate Signal: 14 funds

Number of trades Donoghue Interest Rate Signal indicated in 8 years: 16 trades or 8 round-trips
Number of losing trades in typical funds: 2 round-trips with minor losses

Total returns, 8-year test (1980–87) of 46 funds

	Total returns from a $10,000 investment			
	Buy/Hold	**Donoghue**	**Improvement**	**Percent**
Top performer Fidelity Magellan	$64,284	$94,460	$30,176	47%
Biggest improvement Axe Houghton Stock Fund	$8,990	$62,580	$53,590	596%
Smallest improvement Partners Fund	$37,230	$38,450	$1,220	3.2%
Average of 46 funds	$20,565	$46,174	$25,609	124%

See appendix 2 for compound rates of return achieved by each of the 46 funds.

3
GOALS: IF YOU CAN DECIDE WHERE YOU WANT TO GO, YOU CAN GET THERE

S etting investment goals is not a process of wishing but of negotiating with yourself.

You start by deciding what you want to achieve financially — first in the short term, then for the rest of your life. Then you look realistically at what it would take to accomplish these goals. You consider whether you have enough resources, savings discipline, and guts to do what is necessary.

Your next step is to readjust your goals to reality.

But at the same time, many of us decide that we just have to learn to do better and work smarter. That is what this book is all about — allowing you to live a fuller, more confident life. With a vision of where you are going, you can triumph.

THE THREE KEYS TO A DOABLE WISH LIST

Most of us can create a wish list. Few can acquire everything on the list, no matter how hard we try. Aside from your income, however, three factors determine the goals you can reasonably seek:

1 **What's the prize?** Can you envision your investment goals clearly enough so that you'll discipline yourself to save and invest?

2 **How much do you want to bet?** How much risk are you willing to learn to manage, to obtain maximum returns on your investments?

3 **Do you have time to win?** How much time are you willing to commit to managing your money?

If you approach these questions realistically and reach thoughtful decisions in answering them, you can set meaningful investment goals, achieve these goals, and *obtain most, if not all, of the things you'd like to include on a wish list.*

DECISION #1 — HOW CLEARLY CAN YOU ENVISION YOUR INVESTMENT GOALS?

The clarity with which you can envision your investment goals makes a big difference in whether you can apply the discipline to reach them.

Saving for retirement is an oft-mentioned goal. But a happy retirement is a difficult goal to envision. Who knows what kind of health you will enjoy after you retire? Who knows how much Social Security income or your company pension or savings plan will help? The uncertainties are enormous.

To get started, begin with something nearer at hand, something you can understand.

Also, start with the assumption that building wealth is building *choices*. Money will give you far better choices in life — choices like how you spend your leisure time and where you and your family live.

The first step — setting a short-term goal. To give yourself a clear vision of an investment goal, start by setting a numerical goal for one, three, or five years from now. For example, start by setting an arbitrary goal of adding $10,000 to your total savings pool in three or five years.

What do you have to do to add $10,000 to your savings in three years? Well, if you have $100,000 already in savings all you have to do is earn 3.2 percent interest a year. Not a very ambitious goal.

If you have only $10,000 in savings, you have to achieve returns of 26 percent a year to add another $10,000 in three years. That's a tough return to achieve consistently. Better seek to earn a 20 percent yearly return and save $50 a month.

If you have nothing to start with, you face a harder, but not impossible, task. You have to save $200 a month and earn 20 percent a year on it. Or you can save $230 a month and earn only 8.5 percent on it.

You will never get started if you cannot set a reasonable short-term goal. Then, as you gain confidence, you can start focusing more on longer-term goals. Walk first, then run. And don't get discouraged if you stumble a bit on the way — by learning from your stumbles, you can incorporate reality into your investment strategies.

The second step — building savings discipline. Probably the greatest single piece of investment advice ever is: *"Pay yourself first."*

Savings is personal. Start by saving what you can, and build up to a goal of saving 10 percent or more of your earnings as soon as you can. If you can barely survive on the money you make now, you can barely survive on 90 percent of it. Put 10 percent of your after-tax paycheck into your investment plan each payday and you will build up some savings quickly. Try it — it works. After a while you start spending less and saving more.

The third step — learning to keep your hands out of the cookie jar. The power of investment compounding is so great that I have long taught that *time* is the most important investment tool anyone will ever have.

Leave as much as you can of your savings to compound for you. If you must, draw on part of the profits (not the principal) for essentials. But to the extent that you can leave

TABLE 3.1 *The long-term yields of investing*
Devote the effort necessary to obtain a good return.

If you invest $1,000 today, you will have . . .

	After 5 years	After 10 years	After 20 years	After 30 years
At 20% returns	$2,488	$6,192	$38,338	$237,376
adjusted for 5% inflation	$1,950	$3,801	$14,449	$54,924
*adjusted for inflation and taxes	$1,733	$3,002	$9,011	$27,049
At 15% returns	$2,011	$4,046	$16,367	$66,212
adjusted for 5% inflation	$1,576	$2,484	$6,168	$15,320
*adjusted for inflation and taxes	$1,437	$2,066	$4,267	$8,813
At 8.5% returns	$1,504	$2,261	$5,112	$11,558
adjusted for 5% inflation	$1,178	$1,388	$1,927	$2,674
*adjusted for inflation and taxes	$1,115	$1,243	$1,545	$1,921
At 7.5% returns	$1,436	$2,061	$4,248	$8,755
adjusted for 5% inflation	$1,125	$1,265	$1,601	$2,026
*adjusted for inflation and taxes	$1,071	$1,147	$1,316	$1,509
At 5% interest	$1,276	$1,629	$2,653	$4,322
adjusted for 5% inflation	$1,000	$1,000	$1,000	$1,000
**adjusted for inflation and taxes	$935	$874	$765	$669

*Tax calculations assume a 28% bracket and tax sheltering for half the investment returns.
**The 5% interest example corresponds to a passbook savings account. Tax calculations here assume a 28% bracket and no tax sheltering.

your investment returns to compound, your money will make you money at an increasing rate.

Look how compounding returns will benefit you over the long haul. Suppose you put aside $100 a month. If you invest actively, you can expect returns averaging up to 15 to 20 percent a year. At 15 percent, compounded, a mere $100 a month will produce $27,900 in ten years, $151,600 in twenty years, and $701,000 in thirty years!

(Tables 3.1 and 3.2 can help you project how much different levels of saving and investing can produce.)

If you're self-employed, you may not be able to set aside a fixed amount each week. But you still need to establish a

TABLE 3.2 *The yields of saving AND investing*
You achieve real success when you wisely invest a consistent amount each month.

If you invest $100 a month, you will have . . .

	After 5 years	After 10 years	After 20 years	After 30 years
At 20% returns	$10,400	$35,600	$245,200	$1,573,500
adjusted for 5% inflation	$9,000	$25,900	$118,000	$470,800
*adjusted for inflation and taxes	$8,300	$21,900	$82,900	$264,400
At 15% returns	$9,200	$27,200	$133,800	$572,400
adjusted for 5% inflation	$7,900	$19,800	$66,400	$183,600
*adjusted for inflation and taxes	$7,500	$17,800	$52,100	$123,300
At 8.5% returns	$7,800	$19,200	$61,000	$158,700
adjusted for 5% inflation	$6,800	$14,400	$33,200	$59,900
*adjusted for inflation and taxes	$6,600	$13,500	$29,300	$49,300
At 7.5% returns	$7,600	$18,200	$54,100	$130,100
adjusted for 5% inflation	$6,600	$13,600	$29,900	$50,700
*adjusted for inflation and taxes	$6,400	$12,900	$26,900	$43,000
At 5% interest	$7,150	$15,900	$40,800	$82,600
adjusted for 5% inflation	$6,300	$12,300	$24,000	$36,000
**adjusted for inflation and taxes	$6,000	$11,300	$20,500	$28,700

*Tax calculations assume a 28% bracket and tax sheltering for half the investment returns.
**The 5% interest example corresponds to a passbook savings account. Tax calculations here assume a 28% bracket and no tax sheltering.

rule about what share of your income you'll invest when cash comes in — perhaps 10 percent of what you are able to draw from your business.

DECISION #2 — HOW MUCH RISK WILL YOU MANAGE TO MAXIMIZE YOUR RETURNS?

Smart investors deal with risks in two ways:

▶ First, they develop a healthy, reasoned fear of risk.
▶ Second, they carefully create strategies to manage risks.

Risk is uncertainty, and risks abound. No investment is free of them. Even insured bank CDs possess the risk that you will miss better returns on other investments because you have voluntarily tied up your money. In any investment strategy, the risk is that you may lose part of the value of your investments. In this book, however, we will be talking about well-diversified investments in carefully regulated institutions, so there will never be a risk of losing *all* your money. Moreover, the Donoghue Signals help you get out of risky markets when the risk is greatest.

To achieve high long-term returns we must manage probabilities. When you make decisions on the probabilities, you will, by the very nature of the markets, make some wrong choices. But by striking out a few times, you will develop the discipline to keep your eye on the ball when a home run pitch arrives.

It is wise to take prudent risks because, as we'll discuss in chapter 5, the very presence of risks necessitates that investors be rewarded with high returns. If you avoid all risk, you can't make much profit.

Often the worst strategies are practiced by those who say they will never take risks. They take the greatest risk of all — relying on the advice of a commissioned sales person to put all their marbles on one single long-term investment decision. As I see it, people who do that probably had lost all their marbles before they made the decision.

Let's decide on the risks we want to take

In order to average returns of 20 percent a year over time, you probably should be ready to allow your principal to decline as much as 10 percent once in a while. Investment success is seldom a straight road.

Given that the value of your investment can fluctuate with the markets, the risk you are willing to take should be related to the term of your investment goals. List your goals under three headings:

Shortest-term goals. If you are saving for a goal that is one year away, you probably should take very little risk.

If you need to reach your investment goal at a specific

point in time (such as the day your children's tuition is due), you had better not take the risk that your investment might be down 10 percent at that time. The market has a mind of its own, and investment losses can seldom be made up on your own schedule.

Intermediate-term goals. On the other hand, if tuition bills are five years away you might be wise to take a bit more risk. If, for example, you hit your investment goal a bit early, you'll have more for your family to enjoy.

Investment goals due to arrive in the three- to five-year range are best achieved by taking a middle-of-the-road investment strategy. Keep at least some of your money in stock market mutual funds when the Donoghue Signal says, "Buy," but consider using less-volatile funds such as those recommended for the "Lazy Person's Strategy" discussed in chapter 6. The odds of gaining greater returns by taking some risk are worthwhile since small losses can be made up over time. Nearly every five-year period offers one bull market opportunity. Patience pays off.

Long-term goals. Ah, here is the real wealth-building opportunity. Wise investors have always known that those who have risen to great wealth from humble beginnings had a long-term perspective.

Interestingly, the truly rich seem to come in two flavors: one, the hardworking entrepreneur who learns early to reinvest in his business; and two, the serious employee who never seems to have a penny to spend but moves to a grand home in Arizona or Florida five years before the rest of us retire.

Each has a simple long-term strategy. Invest as much as you can, nurture your money yourself in your business or your investments, reinvest your earnings into more of the same, don't get carried away by fads, gear down your risk as the time to cash out nears, and then maintain the same common sense in managing your money after retirement.

By taking a little bit more short-term risk (putting more of your money in the stock market, or putting more of your stock market money in volatile "aggressive growth" mutual funds), you can almost certainly add a few percentage points to your long-term investment returns if you follow the Don-

oghue Interest Rate Signal to buy or sell. And that can affect
your life dramatically. One thousand dollars will grow to
$4,248 in twenty years at 7.5 percent annual returns. But it
will grow to $16,367 at 15 percent returns and $38,338 at 20
percent returns. So taking a few risks is well worthwhile.

The test of your risk tolerance is coming soon. The "Donoghue Risk Test," later in this chapter, will help you more
clearly judge your risk profile.

DECISION #3 — HOW MUCH TIME WILL YOU COMMIT TO MANAGING YOUR MONEY?

Your next decision is how actively you will manage your
money. If you say you just don't want to be bothered, that is
a fair answer — though it is one that will cost you tens of
thousands of dollars over time. However, since you bought
this book, you are probably at least considering taking charge.

There are essentially three different approaches.

"I want to do it all myself." That's a brave choice, and
this book will help you make the most of it. Tens of thousands
of *Donoghue's Moneyletter* subscribers, and more tens of
thousands who subscribe to other investment newsletters,
seem to succeed at this task.

In ten minutes a week, you can monitor the Donoghue
Signal and the performance of your mutual funds. In thirty
minutes a week you can do even better.

"I'd like a little help with the discipline of investing." For
those with $25,000 or more, a number of money managers
systematically invest client money in no-load mutual funds.
(My own money management firm, W. E. Donoghue & Co.,
Incorporated [WEDCO], is one of them.)

Reasons frequently cited for hiring an investment manager
are: (1) "I can do it but I don't want to"; (2) "I travel too
much to keep a close eye on the markets, so I want a manager
to do it for me"; or (3) "I always seem to postpone making
investment decisions and miss the opportunities. I just don't
have the discipline."

"I'm going to manage my money myself, but I'm not sure

I will remember to check my investment every week." That's the voice of an individual who knows his or her limitations. You won't achieve the returns of the disciplined ten-minutes-a-week investor, but you can still do well. Read this book thoroughly. Then, one approach is to start out keeping the majority of your money in a well-managed money market mutual fund (see chapter 10). At a time when you're confident interest rates are moving downward, put a significant chunk of your money in one of the mutual funds we've recommended for the "Lazy Person's Strategy" of stock investing (see chapter 6). But remember, you won't achieve the returns that a more disciplined investor can produce, and you'll have to set your financial goals accordingly. *The choice is yours.*

WHAT'S WEALTH TO YOU? HOW BIG IS THE CARROT YOU ARE CHASING?

Now you understand the three factors that determine what your investment program can achieve — clarity about goals, willingness to take intelligent risks, and a commitment to investment management. And you've probably thought about adopting a short-term goal.

It's time to begin thinking about longer-term goals, too. Consider what you want your investments and wealth to do. What will it be? Growth to build security in your old age? Income to supplement or replace your paycheck? Or are you a person who's already accumulated considerable wealth and who's mainly concerned with protecting it from inflation and taxes?

Make a list of your goals. Consider including:

Financial independence. There are few goals that have the attraction of financial independence. For most of us, working for a paycheck is such a central part of our lives that we can feel independent only if we have the freedom to say no to an intolerable employer.

For younger investors, independence may mean having a full year's after-tax salary in the savings kitty. (I cannot say "in the bank"; four-letter words like "bank" stick in my throat.)

For others, financial independence has a larger meaning. It means that they will never have to work again. If this is your goal, you may be seeking an investment kitty large enough to produce returns equal to your current after-tax income.

A key element in determining how much you need is how much you feel you can average in investment returns. If you need, say, $25,000 to live on and expect you can earn only 5 percent on your investments, you need a $500,000 kitty. If you think that you can average 15 percent — a return that the Donoghue Stock Market Strategy can probably provide (see chapters 5 and 6) — you need only a $167,000 kitty.

The difference in these two examples is dramatic. If you have little investment confidence, the probability of raising the $500,000 is very small — you will probably never be financially independent. On the other hand, if you only need $167,000 to be financially secure and you have the confidence to seek Donoghue Stock Market Strategy returns, you will probably find ways to make it several times over.

Almost anybody can achieve key financial goals that are more than five or six years in the future if they'll just invest a couple of hundred dollars a month, protect an appropriate portion of their savings from taxes, take prudent risks, and manage well enough to achieve an average return of, say, 18 percent a year. And *you* can do that.

I have said before that financial independence is having choices. Financial independence also requires making choices, and this choice is up to you.

College tuition. Estimate the amount you'll need for your kids. Then subtract the amount you feel you'll be able to pay from your projected salary at the time they're in college and any loans or scholarships you think you can rely on.

Don't let the projections of $100,000 or more for college tuitions in fifteen years scare you off. Save all you can and expect that both you and your child will be able to earn and borrow more.

Second home, boat, or big vacation. Include a "treat" for yourself five or six years in the future as a key part of your financial plan. It will give you the incentive to stay the course.

Retirement. How much will you need to supplement Social Security and pension payments — and to give you a comfortable lead over inflation? A good rule of thumb is: seek retirement income (including Social Security, pensions, income from investments, etc.) equal to 70 percent of your current income.

Don't underestimate how much money you will earn on your retirement savings after you retire. Remember, after retirement you will have more time to attend to your investment strategies. To a large extent, the earnings can still be tax-deferred until you withdraw them. And your tax bracket could well be less — but don't count on it.

THE DONOGHUE RISK TEST

Unless you've already accumulated a pile of riches, you're likely to find when you add up all your desires that the total exceeds the amounts you're confident you can accumulate by "paying yourself first" every month and investing — especially if you aren't yet persuaded that you can achieve investment returns of more than, say, 10 percent a year.

The good news is that you're probably more ready to take an aggressive investing stance than you realize — and with a little bit of discipline you can probably build that nest egg faster than you expect.

Before you complete the process of negotiating your financial goals with yourself, take the following risk test. It will help you determine what kind of investor you are — and what kind of investor you may want to become:

1 You buy an investment based on the strategies in this book. But a month later, the entire stock market declines and the value of your investment goes down 15 percent. The fundamental reasons why you bought it still seem sound. Do you:

a Sit tight and wait for it to go back up?

b Sell it and rid yourself of further sleepless nights?

c Buy more — if it looked good at the original price it looks even better now?

2 Which would you rather have done?
a Invested in an "aggressive growth" mutual fund which failed to increase in value over six months.
b Invested in a money market fund, only to see an aggressive growth fund you had been thinking about rise 50 percent in value in six months.
3 Would you feel better if:
a You doubled your money in a stock market mutual fund?
b Your money market fund investment saved you from losing half your money in a market slide?
4 Which situation would make you feel happiest?
a You win $100,000 in a publisher's contest.
b You inherit $100,000 from a rich relative.
c You earn $100,000 by risking $2,000 in the options market.
d Any of the above — you're happy with the $100,000, no matter where it came from.
5 Your apartment building is being converted to condominiums. You can either buy your unit for $80,000 or sell the option for $20,000. The condo's market value is $120,000. You know that if you bought the condo, it might take six months to sell. The monthly carrying cost would be $1,200, and you'd have to borrow the down payment for a mortgage. You don't want to live in the building. So what do you do?
a Take the $20,000.
b Buy the unit and then sell it on the open market.
6 You inherit your uncle's $100,000 house, free of any mortgage. Although the house is in a fashionable neighborhood and can be expected to appreciate at a faster rate than inflation, it has deteriorated badly. It would net $1,000 monthly if rented as is; it would net $1,500 per month if renovated. The renovations could be financed by a mortgage on the property. You would:
a Sell the house.
b Rent it as is.
c Make the necessary renovations, then rent it.

7 You work for a small but thriving privately held electronics company. The company is raising money by selling stock to its employees. The managers plan to take the company public, but not for four or more years. If you buy the stock, you will not be allowed to sell until the shares are traded publicly. In the meantime, the stock will pay no dividends. But when the company goes public, the shares could trade for ten or twenty times what you would pay. How much of an investment would you make?

a None at all.

b One month's salary.

c Three months' salary.

d Six months' salary.

8 Your cousin, a biologist who has made large profits investing in the stock market, tells you that unusual gains can be expected in the stocks of certain small companies. He recommends a mutual fund that invests in them. You know nothing about publicly traded small companies, but you've heard they are risky investments. What do you do?

a Invest in the mutual fund immediately based on your cousin's recommendation.

b Send for the mutual fund's prospectus, and watch the newspaper for information to help you decide whether your cousin's suggestion is correct.

c Leave your money in a bank or money market mutual fund.

d Call a stockbroker for advice, and buy shares in IBM when the broker tells you IBM is less risky.

9 Your long-time friend and neighbor, an experienced petroleum geologist, is assembling a group of investors (of which he is one) to fund an exploratory oil well which could pay back fifty to one hundred times its investment if successful. If the well is dry, the entire investment will be worthless. Your friend estimates the chance of success is only 20 percent. What would you invest?

a Nothing.

b One month's salary.

    c Three months' salary.

    d Six months' salary.

10 You learn that several commercial real estate developers are considering purchase of undeveloped land in a certain location. You are offered an option to buy a choice parcel. The cost is about two months' salary and you calculate the potential gain to be ten months' salary. Do you:

    a Purchase the option.

    b Let it slide; it's not for you.

11 You are on a TV game show and can choose one of the following. Which would you take?

    a $1,000 in cash.

    b A 50 percent chance at winning $4,000.

    c A 20 percent chance at winning $10,000.

    d A 5 percent chance at winning $100,000.

12 It's 1992, and inflation is returning. "Hard assets" such as precious metals, collectibles, and real estate are expected to keep pace with inflation. Your assets are now all in long-term bonds. What would you do?

    a Hold the bonds.

    b Sell the bonds and put half the proceeds into money funds and the other half into hard assets.

    c Sell the bonds and put all the proceeds into hard assets.

    d Sell the bonds, put all the money into hard assets, and borrow additional money to buy more.

Scoring

Now it's time to see what kind of investor you are. Total your score, using the point system below for each answer you gave.

Your score

  ___ 1. a–3   b–1   c–4

  ___ 2. a–3   b–1

  ___ 3. a–2   b–1

  ___ 4. a–2   b–1   c–4   d–1

___ 5. a–1   b–2

___ 6. a–1   b–2   c–3

___ 7. a–1   b–2   c–4   d–6

___ 8. a–5   b–3   c–1   d–1

___ 9. a–1   b–3   c–6   d–9

___10. a–3   b–1

___11. a–1   b–3   c–5   d–9

___12. a–1   b–2   c–4   d–6

___Total

If you scored . . .

Below 18: You are a **conservative investor** who's allergic to risk. Stick with sober, conservative investments until you develop the confidence or desire to adopt more risky strategies. But when interest rates are falling and a bull market in stocks seems to be starting, don't eliminate the possibility of investing part of your funds in growth mutual funds. They offer opportunities too good to pass up.

18–32: You are an **active investor** who is willing to take calculated, prudent risks to achieve gains. You can consider all of the Donoghue investment strategies, and in the long run you'll achieve greater gains.

33 and over: You're a **venturesome investor**. Dynamic opportunities await you. Remember that the search for more return carries risks. If, however, you know you will not hit home runs all the time and are willing to strike out once in a while, *go for it*.

NOW, YOU CAN REALLY PLAN

Now that we have considered many of the choices, it is up to you to set your short-term and, if you feel you are ready for it, your long-term goals. You may want to reread this chapter and think about each issue.

Then sit down and think first about your short-term target. Set a savings program and decide how much of your existing savings you'll commit to your new investment program right away. Remember, if you start with a little, you first few mistakes will cost you little. Be prepared to commit more as you become more confident, and do not be embarrassed to reduce your exposure to the markets if growth begins to seem too easy. The crash of 1987 taught us all that a bird in the hand . . . can make a mess.

WHAT IS YOUR GOAL IN TERMS OF RETURNS?

If you're a conservative investor, you'll have to be satisfied with yields in the 7 to 13 percent range. In chapters 8 through 11 we'll show you how you can keep ahead of inflation without taking undue risk. But you can't expect profits that will make you rich, and you'll have to set your goals accordingly.

If you're an active investor but you don't want to spend much time managing your investments, you can expect to average perhaps 12 to 17 percent with only a small amount of effort.

Active investors can seek 15 to 20 percent or better returns if they'll regularly devote ten to thirty minutes a week to their portfolios. In some years, the value of a portfolio may decline, but if past experience is an indicator, the Donoghue Signal should keep those declines small. In other years, you may gain 30 percent or more, as many active investors did in 1985, for example. Over the long haul, you may average 20 percent or more. But since you have a streak of caution in your blood, you'll probably want to plan on a more modest return.

If you're a venturesome investor, on the other hand, you may want to set your goals on the assumption of 20 to 22 percent annual returns. You have a good chance of achieving or even exceeding these targets using the Donoghue Signals and aggressively employing the strategies in chapters 5 and 6. You'll be taking more risk than other investors, and you're more likely to lose money from time to time. Think a bit about what will happen if you actually make only 15 percent returns instead of achieving your target over time. But if you understand the markets, you'll do well in the long run. Invest with boldness.

NEGOTIATING WITH YOURSELF

Do your desires still exceed the results you can expect from a savings and investment program? Here's where the negotiating comes in. If you still come up short, you'll either have to put more aside each month or scale back your goals. But remember, a little bit of discipline and careful investment management can make almost anything possible.

First, can you turn yourself into a more aggressive investor? Can you move from the conservative toward the active category, or from active toward venturesome? Merely achieving 2 percent greater returns per year will yield dramatically more wealth over a period of ten or more years. If you're close to retirement and it seems like you don't have enough time ahead of you for your savings to compound, don't let that discourage you. Investing doesn't stop at age sixty, and you can keep your investment nest egg growing after retirement.

Second, can you find hidden assets you can turn into investable funds? Look at:

▶ Passbook savings accounts held for "emergencies."
▶ Money tied up in employer savings programs. Generally, unless you have control over the investment choices in the plan and are satisfied with the quality of the choices, don't keep all of your eggs in your employer's basket.
▶ Savings bonds or other low-yield investments Grandma gave to the kids "for their college education."
▶ The cash value of insurance policies. Many policies written before 1978 have loan provisions that allow you to borrow from them at rates of 5 percent or less.
▶ And don't forget that the interest on a home equity loan can be lower than interest on other loans, and it's still tax

deductible. If you can deal with borrowing on the equity in your home to invest, it may be worthwhile — if your investment system is sound and if you have the discipline to follow it.

At 15 percent returns, finding an extra $5,000 to invest assertively today means you can add $20,000 to your anticipated net worth ten years from now and $80,000 to your anticipated net worth twenty years from now. And if a real emergency arises, almost all the investments we'll discuss in this book are highly liquid. What kind of emergency would be so desperate that you couldn't wait twenty-four hours for your mutual fund to wire your money to your checking account?

Finally, can you tax-shelter a larger share of your investments? (See chapters 11 and 12.)

START SMALL AND START NOW

You don't become a millionaire using ordinary bank accounts unless you are Methuselah. (Only he had the time.) You have to make a commitment to take responsibility for your investments and to nurture them. You have to teach them how to grow, teach them the right things to do, let them teach you the wrong things to do (same as kids, right?), and get them back on the right path. But you can do it. Set your goals thoughtfully and you'll be on your way.

4
NO-LOAD MUTUAL FUNDS — YOUR ULTIMATE INVESTMENT TOOL

O ften, people ask me, "Bill, why do you recommend no-load mutual funds for just about every investment goal? Aren't there other investments just as good? How come you don't write more about other types of investments?"

My response is always the same. No-load mutual funds should be at the heart of any investment system. There are mutual funds designed for every investment goal. Carefully selected mutual funds can give you tremendous investment power, high liquidity, and great flexibility. And they avoid the unnecessary, expensive, and useless commissions stockbrokers charge. So they are the ideal investment.

INCREASING PROBABILITIES OF SUCCESS

Even more important, over the years I have developed strategies that, based on past experience, could earn you annual returns of 15 to 20 percent or more for the long term through investments in no-load mutual funds. No other investment can deliver such a high probability of a larger-than-average return, especially with safety and liquidity.

Other investments may offer the tempting *possibility* of high returns and great tax sheltering. But when you look for the *probability* of excellent performance over time combined with complete liquidity, mutual funds win hands down.

WHAT IS A MUTUAL FUND?

Perhaps the best way to define a mutual fund is to describe to you how one might have been organized.

If I wanted to sponsor a mutual fund, I would first have to determine if there was a market for the fund's services. Each mutual fund is designed with a specific investment goal.

If I sought to serve the many conservative investors who want an investment that keeps a constant principal value and pays a money market rate of return, I would create a **money market mutual fund**.

If I decided to serve aggressive investors who wanted a fund whose value would probably increase over time and who would not expect it to pay significant current income, I would probably create an **aggressive growth stock market mutual fund**.

Let's assume that we name our first fund "MoneyTree Money Fund."

Then let's name our aggressive growth fund, "MoneyTree High Roller Fund." (Both of these funds, I should note, are completely fictitious.) Now we have to find portfolio managers who can select the appropriate investments for our funds.

CLYDE CAREFUL'S CONSERVATIVE CACHES

The portfolio manager of our MoneyTree Money Fund — let's call him Clyde Careful — probably stays in his office all the time buying and selling (making and collecting) what are essentially short-term loans to the U.S. government and to the largest and safest banks and corporations in the world.

Short-term loans to the U.S. government are called Treasury bills. Short-term loans to the largest and strongest corporations are called commercial paper; to the largest and strongest banks are called negotiable certificates of deposit or, if used in international trade, bankers' acceptances. Short-term loans to U.S. branches of foreign banks are called Yankee certificates of deposit; to foreign (usually London) branches of U.S. banks, EuroDollar certificates of deposit; and so on.

These investments all pay regular interest and are considered among the safest investments that can be made. Essentially, these are viewed as no-risk investments. Nearly all are paid off within one year, most within a few months.

TOMMY TRAVELER'S TREMENDOUS TOMORROWS

The portfolio manager for our High Roller Fund, on the other hand — let's call him Tommy Traveler — will probably be searching the country for small growth companies that have great potential to increase rapidly in value. Tommy will see more off-the-beaten-track locations and forgotten corners of big cities than you and I can dream about. That's where tomorrow's best investments hide.

Tommy's type of company seldom pays current dividends since the managers usually think they can benefit their shareholders more by reinvesting in their own business. One of the firms Tommy Traveler might visit might be my favorite (fictitious again) speculative investment, Nocturnal Aviation Company, a fly-by-night deal if I ever heard of one.

A more typical potential (and this time real) investment might be Heidi's Frogen Yozurt, a new, expanding firm in Orange County, California, which serves a delicious brand of nonfat and low-fat frozen yogurt. (Believe me, this is a real company with publicly traded stock, and the spelling is correct.) My research on Heidi's Frogen Yozurt has been limited to trying several luscious flavors at a stand near my former home in Orange County. I have no idea whether stock in Heidi's Frogen Yozurt is a good investment. But it is typical of the investments our portfolio manager might seek out. With the renewed popularity of low-fat and low-cholesterol diets, yogurt could produce some unusually healthy financial returns.

No matter how well run it may be, a tiny company like Heidi's faces a far greater possibility of bankruptcy than big firms like General Motors. If yogurt sales take off like a rocket, however, the value of stock in Heidi's Frogen Yozurt is likely to soar far more rapidly than stock in General Motors. Aggressive growth mutual funds are looking for companies whose sales have a good chance of growing like that.

If Tommy Traveler buys stock in Heidi's Frogen Yozurt and the company, along with others in the portfolio, grows enormously, the value of investments in MoneyTree High Roller Fund will increase far more rapidly than the value of investments in MoneyTree Money Fund.

If Tommy Traveler's investments go sour, however, investments in MoneyTree High Roller Fund will do something that investments in MoneyTree Money Fund will never do: decline in value. Historically, though, stock market investments have gone up more often than down.

WHEN YOU PLAY, THE BANKERS MUST HOLD THE CARDS

Now we need someone to safekeep the money market instruments Clyde buys and the stock certificates that Tommy acquires. In reality, Clyde and Tommy probably never see the actual money market instruments and stock certificates they choose for their funds.

All of the investments purchased by America's mutual funds are kept in custodial accounts at trust companies or bank trust departments and stored in bank or trust-company vaults. The custodian is the organization charged with paying (only on delivery) for the fund's investments and collecting when the investments are sold.

Bruce Bent, the founder of Reserve Fund, the original money market mutual fund, told me that he once asked his custodian to send over a certificate of deposit included in his fund's portfolio.

A guard arrived, pistol in his holster and the CD in a

briefcase chained to his wrist. The guard opened the briefcase, took out the CD, and offered it to Bruce. Bruce re-
viewed it carefully and looked up at the guard. "I've bought
and sold billions of dollars' worth of these and I've never
seen one." The guard took the CD back, locked it in his
briefcase, and departed without a word.

THE TRANSFER AGENT KEEPS SCORE
FOR EVERY INVESTOR

Someone must also keep track of who owns the fund's shares.
That is the job of the transfer agent. A few major banks and
corporations dominate this business, including the Bank of
New York and Bankers Trust in New York, and the Bank of
Boston and State Street Bank and Trust in Boston.

REGULATIONS FOR YOUR BENEFIT

MoneyTree Money Fund and MoneyTree High Roller Fund
would both register with the Securities and Exchange Commission (SEC) as "regulated investment companies," corporations whose sole purpose is to invest to achieve stated
objectives. When you invest in a mutual fund, what you are
actually doing is buying common stock shares of a regulated
investment company.

The SEC regulates the mutual fund's operations: That is,
it sends in regular examiners, and processes the fund's filings
of regular reports.

"Regulated investment companies" registered with the
SEC can avoid paying any income taxes if they distribute to
shareholders each year 100 percent of the net dividends and
interest they receive and at least 98 percent (effectively 100
percent in most cases) of all of the realized capital gains they
achieve in trading their portfolio. Profits are taxable to the
shareholders (you), never to the fund or its management company. (If a fund invests in municipal bonds, its profits may
never be taxable to anyone.)

Let's be clear. The SEC does not "approve" any mutual
funds or render any opinion about their viability or ability to

manage your money. But the funds register with the SEC and the SEC makes sure that they fully disclose all relevant information in their prospectuses.

Now I have a tongue-in-cheek question: "What is brown and white and looks good on a lawyer?"

The answer is, "A pit bull terrier."

Perhaps lawyers are not our favorite people, but in mutual fund investing they are largely on our side. The mutual fund management team must include its share of lawyers to guide the fund managers through the maze of regulations set forth by the SEC and state regulatory agencies.

I love to kid securities lawyers. I call them mutual funds' "sales prevention departments" for their work in making mutual fund prospectuses totally unreadable. Compliance with the maze of securities rules is a major goal of a mutual fund manager.

"Mutual funds are the most heavily regulated financial institutions," was how one former SEC commissioner put it. I believe it. But the regulations benefit you as an investor far more than banking regulations benefit bank depositors. They ensure that the companies that sell mutual funds will:

▶ Fully disclose all charges and costs;
▶ Make no false claims about their performance records; and
▶ Manage themselves with such safeguards that a major fraud against investors is almost impossible.

I disagree with some SEC mutual fund regulations. But in general, mutual fund laws and SEC regulations give mutual fund investors some of the best legal support investors will find anywhere.

SOMEONE JUST HAS TO BE IN CHARGE

For mutual fund investors, the unsung heroes and potentially the most powerful champions are the "independent directors." They must make up at least 40 percent of any mutual fund's board of directors. (No-load mutual funds require only *one* outside director.) Legally, they must be completely independent of anyone doing business with the fund. (That means, for example, that they can't include the fund manager's uncle or anyone with a big contract to provide services to the fund.) A majority of the independent directors must approve any contracts the fund makes with the sponsor, portfolio manager, custodian, transfer agent, or lawyers or accountants of the fund.

By law, the independent directors represent the investors' interests, and little slips by the best of them. I have even seen them fire fund managers who did not perform up to standard. In 1979, the board of directors of a major institutional money fund family fired the sponsor and the investment advisor, which was forced to cough up $1,000,000 in back advisory fees. The board replaced them both with the investment firm of Goldman Sachs. The reason? Portfolio management had not been properly overseen and the fund nearly, by one account, had to reduce the value of a share from $1.00 to 99 cents. The dispute was about two-tenths of one percent of the fund's value!

Not all independent directors serve quite so conscientiously, but they do provide important investment safeguards.

WHAT ADVANTAGES DOES A MUTUAL FUND OFFER?

Mutual funds offer two major benefits:

Professional investment management. Easily the most popular benefit mutual funds offer is the professional management of the investors' money. Clyde Careful and Tommy Traveler may fail to perform as well as the money market and stock market averages. But the long-term records of some funds stand as a measure of the value that mutual funds can add to your portfolio.

Moreover, the investment clout of top mutual fund managers frequently allows them to gobble up hot investments before you as an individual investor would have heard of them, to demand and receive the best research, to analyze carefully many available investments.

The whole pool is managed for a single common goal, whether that goal is to provide income, to generate long-term capital growth, to generate tax-free income, or any of a number of other possible goals.

No mutual fund company will manage your money for your special individual needs. It is your responsibility, therefore, to choose the fund or funds that best suit your particular investment goals. But if you choose the right funds (and you know when not to invest in the risky types of funds), you'll get the best management anywhere.

Diversification to spread the risk. Mutual funds diversify their portfolio to maintain price growth or steady income with less risk than you'd face if you just bought a portfolio of a few stocks and bonds for yourself. The best "watch over their investments," as a Dreyfus ad says, the way "a lioness watches her cubs." Diversification carried out by skilled professionals at a low cost is a major reason investors choose mutual funds.

THE HIJACKING OF THE REVOLUTION

If we have successfully passed through the legal maze to establish MoneyTree Money Fund and MoneyTree High Roller Fund, we now have the problem of getting you to invest. A mutual fund without investors will accomplish very little. There are half a dozen ways to encourage people to invest, but they basically fit into two categories:

1 There is one way (or, for exceptionally well-run funds, perhaps two ways) to offer funds to investors for *their* benefit.
2 There are assorted dubious schemes dreamed up for the benefit of commissioned salespeople and their employers.

Unfortunately, over the past few years the schemes that benefit salespeople have been capturing some 70 percent of people's money. In the mid-1980s, stockbrokers and other overpriced "financial supermarkets" hijacked the financial services revolution. Let's review what happened and why.

The revolution had begun in the late 1970s with consumers — many responding to my appearances on television and radio — taking charge of their own financial affairs. They took their money out of banks where paternalistic bankers paid them rock-bottom interest rates. They put it in no-load money market mutual funds. To compete, even stockbrokers had to sell money market funds with no load.

Then in 1982, interest rates declined. My *No-Load Mutual Fund Guide* showed how investors could take advantage of the bull market that would inevitably follow by investing in stock market mutual funds without paying commissions to brokers, bankers, or anyone else. Hundreds of thousands of investors followed me and made enormous profits.

However, big-money firms that hadn't been able to find much profit in the switch to money market mutual funds found a vast array of ways to pick investors' pockets in the new, lower-interest-rate environment.

When interest rates on money market mutual funds fell to the 8 percent range, the big brokerage houses offered investors "something better" — better for them, anyway. Their something better was long-term bond mutual funds, especially funds that invested in bonds with U.S. government guarantees.

Long-term bonds offered higher yields than money funds. There was a good reason for that. As we'll show in chapter 7, investors in long-term bonds — even long-term bonds guaranteed by the U.S. government — faced a big risk. If interest rates rose, the value of the bonds would fall.

The big-money people discovered, however, that they could sell bond investments by implying that they were just like the money market mutual funds people like me had so carefully explained. Just teach your salesforce to use the words "U.S. government-guaranteed" in their spiel, the brokerage houses discovered. Customers would assume that bond funds were safe, just like money funds.

Customers had had such good experiences with money funds that they often wouldn't even ask about the exorbitant load that the bond funds carried. (A "load" is simply a fee paid to cover the cost of selling shares in the fund.) Total sales of load bond funds were $2.1 billion in 1980, when investors were using principally no-load money market funds. By 1987, load bond fund sales had risen to $55.8 billion!

Load mutual funds come in several guises. I'll give you a brief introduction to each type, and I'll try to strip off a few masks as I go.

FOOL-LOAD FUNDS

I call full-load funds fool-load funds. The rule of thumb in the mutual fund business is that "mutual funds are sold, not bought." In other words, the easiest way to bring investors into mutual funds is to hire well-paid salespeople to peddle them. Loads tacked on to pay the sales force can cost up to 8.5 percent of your initial investment.

That means that if you invest $10,000, you will have paid the stockbroker up to $850 for the privilege. Your $10,000 investment will instantly be worth $9,150 the day you invest. Now you have to earn 9.3 percent to break even. Some deal.

What did you get for your $850? Well, you might think that you got the benefit of your broker's expert investment advice. In reality, you probably bought the fund that came up at that morning's sales meeting, where the subject was "the fund that can generate the most commissions the fastest." "Sell 'em what they want, not what they need" is the theme of most brokerage sales meetings.

Throughout the greatest bull market we have seen in years, the easy sells were U.S. government and similar bond funds — which produced trivial profits or lost money when they were most widely sold! The facts are that in 1986 and 1987, most of the funds that stockbrokers recommended lost money for their clients. The top-performing stock market funds were generally not recommended and were missed by the clients. (Remember that even after the stock market crash of 1987 is considered, 1986–87 was on the whole a profitable period in which to invest.)

So remember, as millions of investors have learned painfully, to avoid stockbrokers' hype and learn to pick mutual funds yourself.

WHAT ARE WHOA!-LOAD MUTUAL FUNDS?

"Whoa!-load" is my term for what many call mid-load funds. These funds are most frequently offered by affiliates of savings and loan institutions, commission-based financial planners, stockbrokers, and insurance agents.

The story is that most of the clients of these establishments said, "Whoa! I won't pay 8.5 percent for a mutual fund"; so the fund salesmen started offering funds that charged 4 percent and 6 percent sales fees. Some break. You are still paying 4 to 6 percent for a one-time choice, and you are starting out your wonderful investing experience 4 to 6 percent in the hole.

Is mid-load better than fool-load? You bet, but nowhere near as attractive as no-load.

LOW-LOAD MUTUAL FUNDS

If you read the *Wall Street Journal* even casually, you have probably noted highly visible advertisements on the upper right-hand corner of the inside back page. The funds advertised are often the Fidelity Select Portfolios, a highly popular series of so-called "sector funds." (More on sector funds below.) Read the fine print and you will see there is a 2 to 3 percent load deducted from investments. These are low-load funds.

Until a few years ago, you could assume that loads or sales commissions were paid to a salesperson who "researched" the fund for you. Not this time. No broker is involved. You have to contact the fund company and open the account with their help — just as if you were investing in a no-load fund. "Hey," you say, "What is the load paying for?" Guess what it pays for. The ad you saw in the *Wall Street Journal*, of course!

If the public can be convinced to buy mutual funds by ads like this, who needs the stockbrokers? (Wait until the mutual funds discover the television shopping networks.) Why are they doing this? Think about it. If a no-load fund charges you 1 percent of your money to manage the fund and, say, 20 percent of that is profit, they make $2 profit per year on each $1,000 you invest. If a fund can get you to pay a 3 percent load in the first year, it will have taken in $40 in fees per $1,000 investment in the first year ($10 from the 1 percent management fee and $30 in load). Perhaps $25 of that $40 could be profit. That is more profit than they would have earned in twelve years under the no-load, management-fee-only system.

With that kind of money to be made, fund companies can spend a lot of money telling investors about their wonderful track records. That makes money for the fund managers.

Does it make money for investors? That depends on when you buy and when you sell. Does the extra load buy you good advice about buying? Nope. Does it buy you advice on when to sell? Nope.

What does it buy you? In many cases, the bottom line is that low-load funds are riskier than no-load funds, since they are easier to sell if they have hot track records. For example, the sector funds are basically undiversified mutual funds, a riskier proposition than even their managers thought. In the 1987 crash, some of those sector funds lost 30 and 40 percent of their value. If a new low-load fund does well, its performance will by hyped in newspaper ads. If it does poorly, its stockholders will bear the burden.

As I write this, each Friday I appear on Financial News Network's "Marketwrap" as their mutual funds commentator, and one feature of these weekly appearances is a discussion of the performances of the top five (numbers 1 through 5) and bottom five (numbers 30 through 35) performing Fidelity Select Portfolios. Before each week begins, I can usually tell which funds we will be talking about the following Friday; stocks in some industries (high technology, for instance) are sure to be extraordinarily volatile. But I cannot predict which list they will be on from week to week. Some weeks they'll go up a lot. If the trend continues for a few months, you can be sure that Fidelity Select Technology will be hyped in newspaper ads. In other weeks, however, the same sector will decline a great deal.

Some low-load funds are worth including in your investment strategies, and for that reason we have included several among the funds we follow in my *Moneyletter*. In a few cases, fund companies have attached low loads to their best-performing funds (Fidelity Magellan or Strong Total Return, for example) to take a well-deserved reward for their excellent management.

But in most cases, low-load funds perform no better than no-load funds and carry more risk. We can recommend them only infrequently. Never invest in a low-load fund based only on the impressive performance advertised in the newspaper.

THE SNEAKY SLO-LOAD FUNDS

Charge a small extra percentage each year on investments in a no-load fund, and what have you got? A slo-load fund. If you ever meet a fund manager, ask him if I am not right about this. In the bowels of some firms' marketing departments, I suspect people have been saying, "Bill Donoghue has told too many investors about no-load funds, and load funds are getting harder to sell. So let's charge nothing up front, but let's feed our marketing budget by charging a little fee on top of our usual management fee each year. We can make money and still call it a 'no-load' fund."

These firms use an obscure but now infamous section of the security law, Section 12b–1, to get the investor to pay their marketing bills. Section 12b–1 allows a fund to use its assets to pay marketing costs if the board of directors approves the plan. The board's independent directors are usually persuaded by explanations that somehow justify the payment as being in the best interests of the *existing* shareholders.

The fees on these 12b–1 funds are often between 0.25 and 1.25 percent per year. There is little an investor who objects to the plan can do except vote with his feet and leave the fund.

A better, more practical solution to this problem is continually to compare funds' performance and services and invest in the fund that suits you best. When considering a fund, check the prospectus for any indication that the fund plans to charge 12b–1 costs.

Also examine the fund's reported "ratio of expenses to average net assets." The lower this ratio is, the better. Of course, when funds report their performance, any profits they report are *after* deduction of all the fund's expenses. But while capital gains are likely to vary dramatically from year to year, a fund with high expenses and 12b–1 costs is unlikely to reduce them in the following year.

Thus a fund that achieved a 15 percent return last year by producing 15.5 percent in dividends and capital gains and keeping expenses to 0.5 percent of the fund's value is likely to be a better bet than a fund that achieved a 15 percent return last year by producing 17 percent in dividends and capital gains while spending 2 percent on expenses. (Generally, any fund that keeps expenses under 0.8 percent of average net assets is doing well. But expenses inevitably vary with the type of fund. Money market funds should be able to keep expenses under .7 percent. Some international funds have ratios as high as 2.8 percent even without 12b–1 plans.)

If the 12b–1 plan of one fund reduces its return so much that another fund suits you better, go for the better fund. If the fund with the "greedy" 12b–1 plan still is earning more than another choice, go for the higher-yielding fund; at least you are getting well paid.

And write the fund's independent directors (listed in the prospectus) with your complaints. Sometimes it just feels good to complain. Perhaps it might even have an effect.

THE SNEAKIEST — THE GO-LOAD FUNDS

The competition from real honest-to-goodness no-load mutual funds has gotten so heated that some fund sales geniuses have invented a new type of "no-load" fund. This one has no front-end load (one you pay when you invest) but does have a back-end "go load," which you pay when you leave the fund.

Remember. Stockbrokers and other commissioned salespeople *never* sell anything that is truly no-load. Everything has a load if your stockbroker recommends it.

"Go-load" funds and funds sold with a "contingent deferred sales charge" (i.e., you pay something like 6 percent if you leave in the first year, 5 percent in the second, and so on) are quite in vogue with brokers and commission-oriented financial planners. The bottom line is that the money comes out of your pocket any way you cut it. If you leave, the fees are charged. If you stay, the fees are added to the fund's management fees. (These funds will charge higher management fees to shareholders than other funds, both load and no-load.) Some way the salespeople must be paid, and the fund advances them fees up front. Then the fund collects from you.

For what it is worth — I have doubts about the effectiveness of enforcement of this regulation — the SEC says that calling a fund with a go load or contingent deferred sales charge a no-load fund is "misleading and fraudulent." There seems to be a lot of that going around. SEC take notice.

NO-LOAD FUNDS — IF NOT A FREE LUNCH, A VERY CHEAP ONE INDEED

Maybe there is no such thing as a free lunch, but there is a much cheaper way to eat than in a restaurant: shopping for food yourself and cutting out the middleman. That is essentially what happens with no-load mutual funds.

By dealing directly with no-load (no sales charge) mutual fund companies, investors can avoid the wasted money and questionable advice offered by brokers.

I always tell investors to compare whatever investment alternatives they are considering to a standard. If you beat the standard, you can declare the new system a standard. But at least you have shopped wisely. The Donoghue strategies, using no-load mutual funds as discussed in this book, are a standard you'll have trouble beating.

So, if you agree that avoiding the "Let's start your investment strategy off 8.5 percent in the hole" approach is a good idea, no-loads are the way to go.

DEALING WITH A NO-LOAD MUTUAL FUND

When you deal with no-load mutual funds, you can't expect a salesperson to call and tell you about the best deals. You have to find and choose a fund yourself. That's not too hard; appendixes 2–5 of this book provide useful lists to get you started.

When you've decided you are interested in a fund, call the sponsor's toll-free telephone number and ask for an information kit. It will usually include a prospectus (the legal document that describes the fund), a recent report to shareholders, and other information. If the material doesn't prominently display the fund's recent performance — how well investors have done compared to a gauge such as the Standard & Poor's 500-stock average — watch out. The fund may want to hide its recent performance.

If you decide you want to buy, you can simply fill in the form in the package and send in a check.

More astute investors will arrange for their bank to wire the money to the mutual fund to assure prompt investment. This also avoids a problem that individuals who invest by check can encounter: the inability to get their money, even in an emergency, until an initial waiting period of 14 to 30 days is up.

Sign up for the fund family's telephone switch, telephone redemption, and other privileges when you open your account. You can never tell when you might need them.

PROFESSIONAL TRANSACTION MANAGEMENT AND SERVICES

For many investors, the availability, convenience, and reliability of mutual fund transactions services is a welcome relief from experiences at their bank, especially when they discover that the services are free (or rather, included in the modest annual management fee, always deducted from the dividend income the fund earns).

You can invest conveniently by sending in a check, by wiring money from your bank, by electronically withdrawing

money from your checking account in an automatic investment program, or simply by switching your money from one
fund in the family to another via a toll-free telephone call.
Redemption is equally convenient; you simply reverse all of
the above.

Money market funds will even allow you to write checks
on your account. Some funds, such as those affiliated with
special stockbroker accounts like the Schwab One and Merrill
Lynch Cash Management Account, can make your mutual
fund family the answer to the "full-service banking" your
bank never seems to deliver. Fidelity Daily Income Trust
even offers no-minimum, unlimited free checking after you've
established your account with a $5,000 initial investment.

The bottom line here is that it is better to be paid for your
checking account (free checking and real money market interest) than to pay (banks pay low interest, if any, and charge
for every check, deposit, or balance inquiry unless you keep
a minimum balance). Even if you forget about the fact that
money funds pay higher rates, the savings in checking fees
could be significant.

Another of the important benefits investors receive from
mutual funds, especially no-load mutual funds, is that when
they call the funds' 800 numbers, they deal with federally
tested and licensed representatives who are not commissioned salespeople. If you deal frequently with banks, you
will be pleasantly surprised by the difference.

What services can you expect from a no-load mutual fund
customer representative? Investment advice? No, that is the
one thing you can expect not to get. But you can expect help
with opening an account, understanding the unique features
of each fund, getting performance information on your fund
and others in its family, getting money in and out of your
investments, and expediting the paperwork problems associated with retirement savings accounts.

MUTUAL FUND FAMILIES

Most mutual funds do not exist in a vacuum. They exist in
families. Mutual fund managers pride themselves on offering

many types of mutual funds. Fidelity Investments, for example, offers over one hundred choices.

A family may include stock, bond, and money funds; international stock and bond funds; gold-mining share funds; no-load funds and low-load funds. Investors may choose to invest only in the funds of a single family with an attractive set of choices. I would suggest that the T. Rowe Price funds in Baltimore, Maryland; Dreyfus funds in New York City; Vanguard funds in Valley Forge, Pennsylvania; and Twentieth Century Investors in Kansas City, Missouri would be excellent choices if you only want to use a single family.

Other investors like to use a few mutual fund families' funds in their portfolios and might add other choices like Columbia funds in Portland, Oregon; SAFECO funds in Seattle, Washington; Founders funds in Denver, Colorado; or Fidelity Investments in Boston, Massachusetts, to name some of our favorites.

Investors who invest in funds selected from several fund families frequently opt to deal with Charles Schwab's Mutual Fund Marketplace (1-800-526-8600) to trade multifamily portfolios. Schwab is a discount stockbroker, and it charges fees for buying and selling even no-load mutual fund shares. However, the fees are offset, in the minds of many active investors, by the advantage of convenience.

FRACTIONAL INVESTMENT

One nice additional advantage of mutual funds is that their price per share doesn't affect how much you can invest, since the funds sell fractional shares. So if you want to invest $1,000 and the fund offering price is $19.13 a share, you get 52.274 shares. If the price is $3.59 a share, you get 278.552 shares.

Occasionally investors tell me, "Bill, I invest in mutual funds with share prices under $5.00. They can go up a lot and can't fall far."

I am always flabbergasted. The price per share of a mutual fund is simply the fair market value of the fund's portfolio divided by the number of shares outstanding. A $50-a-share fund can go up by just as large a percentage as a $5-a-share fund, and a $5-a-share fund can decline by just as large a percentage as the $50-a-share fund. The price per share of a mutual fund should never be a consideration in your investment decision.

CONCLUSION: NO-LOAD MUTUAL FUNDS ARE "THE WAY"

Sometimes I wax a bit too poetic about the virtues of no-load mutual funds, but they are the best answer for most investors. Including the money funds, there are over a thousand no-load mutual funds to choose from. They are easy to use, convenient, well regulated, and well run. They offer awesome flexibility. A program of investing in no-load mutual funds can give you vast investment power.

5
COMING TO TERMS WITH THE STOCK MARKET

The stock market seems to many people — well, let's say it — a crapshoot. There are too many stock choices around, and too many stockbrokers chasing after your money, most of them providing the solidity of financial quicksand.

Yet surprisingly, stock market mutual funds are the easiest place to make big money over the long term if you know how to choose the best stock-pickers, how to invest confidently alongside them, how to recognize when they have gotten "cold" and move on, and how to get out of the market when it becomes especially risky.

Despite its occasional crashes, more people have made more money in the stock market than in any other publicly traded investment. (See figure 5.1.) And you have an advantage most investors don't. The Donoghue Signal tells you when you have the best chance to strike it rich in the stock market — and when to get out.

Despite the sensational stories about insider trading, program trading, and the like, if you want to make some **real** money on your investments you have to come to terms with the stock market. If you want to gain real financial security, send your kids to the best schools, live in a better neighborhood, retire comfortably, or whatever, you have to understand what drives Wall Street.

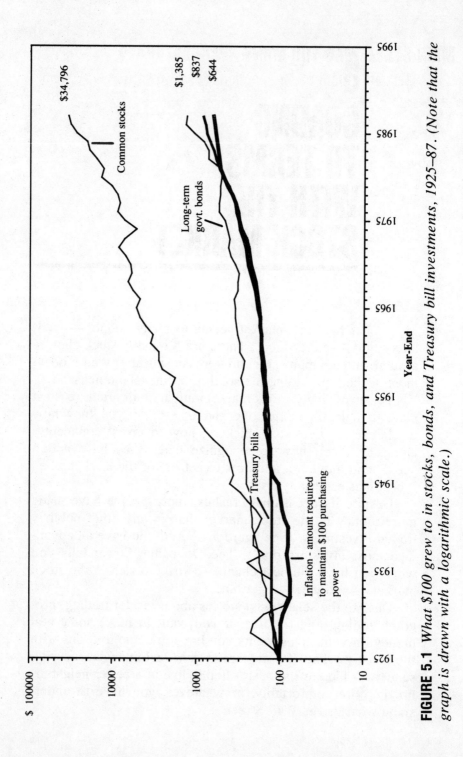

FIGURE 5.1 *What $100 grew to in stocks, bonds, and Treasury bill investments, 1925–87. (Note that the graph is drawn with a logarithmic scale.)*

MAIN STREET HAS TOO MANY SPECULATORS

"Hey, Bill, didn't you get that backward? Don't you mean that *Wall Street* has too many speculators?" you ask. No, folks, the sad fact is that most average men or women are speculators when they venture into the stock market. The fact that they make such horrendous investment decisions proves it.

Wall Street is a long way from Main Street, in many ways. Wall Street is playing a serious big-money game, taking much more risk, and losing big more often than Wall Streeters want us to believe.

Main Street is made up of two main groups of investors: those who are trying to play the game just like the big boys — but without the big boys' inside information, old-boy network, or high-tech computers — and those who are serious about their investments and about where these fit into their lives. The second group can be called prudent investors. But the first group should only be called speculators.

Think a bit about your investments. I define a speculator as someone who cannot differentiate possibilities (sales pitches) from probabilities (opportunities you understand). You call yourself a prudent investor, and then what do you do? You go down to your local stockbroker, who knows precious little about what investments are appropriate for you. You sit down. The broker tells you a story about the possibility that you will make money in the stock or bond markets, and you invest. Now you are in the hands of the gods.

The investors' quiz tells the tale

Here is a quiz for you. Think about your broker — let's call him Dave. Does Dave compare a recommended investment to other similar investments? No, if he's selling a stock he compares it with its track record in the past or its managers' track record somewhere else. Does he ever suggest something he doesn't sell, or on which he cannot get a commission? Your silence is thundering. Does he always make money on your business? You bet. Do you always make money on his recommendations? Answer that one for yourself.

When you leave Dave's office, could you answer the following questions from your spouse or a trusted friend? First, why did you buy *today*? (Do you notice Dave never says, "Buy this when such-and-such events happen." Heck no, that would blow the sale.) Why did you buy that investment instead of another? Why is it right for you? What else did you compare it to? Under what conditions will you sell the investment? Could you have earned the same after-tax return another, possibly safer, way? (After all, the return is what you wanted, not the specific type of investment, right?)

Getting uncomfortable? If not, you're a better-than-average investor. If this discussion does make you uncomfortable, answer another query: Do you think that the questions I'm asking are questions that would make a speculator feel uncomfortable? Now do you think you or your friends may be speculators?

The key to prudent investing is to conserve your capital while you are building it. Today, only investors who are willing to develop a well-thought-out, sound strategy for trading their investments qualify as truly prudent investors. The way to stop speculation and increase the odds of making money in the stock market is to build discipline in how you invest.

The Securities and Exchange Commission insists that mutual fund prospectuses state that "past performance is no guarantee of future results" (and then insists that past track records be spelled out in detail). Wise investors point out, "You have to make *your* profits in the *future*." And they are right. However, there is much to learn from the past relationships between the money and the stock and bond markets.

THE JOY OF STOCKS

Fundamental relationships continue over time in the stock market (and in the bond market, too). A strategy based on these fundamentals will make money in the long run. You can safely bet, for example, that over any long period the average

New York Stock Exchange stock will make more money for its owners than bonds or other fixed-income investments. Historically, stocks have kept investors *way* ahead of bonds, money market investments, or inflation.

Why? The very riskiness of the stock market in the short run is related to why it is, in the long run, a good place to invest. Companies sell stock when they need to raise capital but are unsure of the returns their investments will generate. To persuade investors to buy, they have to offer a promise of reward substantially greater than the rewards those investors could achieve by holding bonds or money market securities. In diversified portfolios, stock market investments that succeed have more than compensated for those that have failed.

If you had bought the average New York Stock Exchange stock in 1925 and reinvested all your dividends, today you'd have *nearly 348 times your original investment.* If you had bought long-term government bonds in 1925 and reinvested all your interest, today you'd have just over 13 times your original investment. That's a *big* difference. Figure 5.1 above provides further details of just how good stocks have been as investments over the very long haul. Note that the graph is drawn with a "logarithmic scale," which means that similar percentage changes produce the same slope at all points of the graph. (For example, an increase from $100 to $120 has the same slope as an increase from $10,000 to $12,000.) This makes a graph showing such dramatic growth easier to read. But the difference between stocks and other investments would be even more dramatic in an ordinary graph.

And you can expect to do even better than the graph suggests if you manage your money wisely — for example, by using the strategies in this book.

Other fundamental relationships also continue over time. For example, as we discussed in chapter 2, rising interest rates lead to falling stock prices. Declining interest rates lead to rising stock prices. After close study of this relationship, we developed the Donoghue Signals.

The calculation of the Donoghue Signal Number is explained in chapter 2. When the Donoghue Signal Number rises, that's a **sell** signal. When the Donoghue Signal Number falls, that's a **buy** signal. If you had followed the Donoghue Interest Rate Signal in the stock market in the 1980s, you would have had terrific returns. If you had bought shares in the large, well-managed Twentieth Century Select Fund on January 1, 1980, and simply held them continuously till December 31, 1987, you would have increased your investment by 345 percent. The fund's value at the end of the period was 445 percent of its value at the beginning. Pretty good.

Suppose you had followed the Donoghue Interest Rate Signal formula to buy or sell during that period, however. You would have switched sixteen times in eight years between Twentieth Century Select and a money market fund, probably switching into Twentieth Century Cash Reserves with a simple telephone call.

Following the Donoghue Signal, you would have increased your investment 710 percent. A $1,000 investment would have grown to $8,102. That is a terrific improvement. And following the Donoghue Signal would have improved the performance of many other funds far more than it improved the performance of Twentieth Century Select. In 1987, you would have sold on April 14, six months before the crash.

According to our "backcasted" analysis, when the Donoghue Signal told you to invest, it was right seven out of eight times. Once you were "whipsawed." You bought on a buy signal and sold on a sell signal a few weeks later at a lower price. But the loss was only 1.07 percent. The gains from the five successful in-and-out switches, on the other hand, averaged 38.3 percent each. On average, the funds in our 46-fund study were whipsawed slightly more than Twentieth Century Select. Some funds had losses on as many as three round-trips, and the average fund had losses on two — a total of four false signals, as discussed in chapter 2. But in every case, the losses were trivial.

Think about it. Returns in Twentieth Century Select totaled 710 percent during a period when a buy, hold, and pray strategy would have produced returns of 345 percent. And you would have been exposed to stock market risk far less than a buy-and-hold investor. But the *average* fund in our retrospective study, which would have produced buy-and-hold returns of 205 percent, returned 462 percent following the Donoghue Interest Rate Signal. That's why I am convinced that the Donoghue Interest Rate Signal turns the stock market from a pretty good but fairly risky opportunity into an excellent, low-risk opportunity.

NOW THAT YOU HAVE A HANDLE ON THE MARKET, HOW DO YOU BUILD A WORKING STRATEGY?

The next step in building an investment strategy is to find an efficient way to choose the stock market mutual funds in which you want to invest. Making the actual investments — and switching when the signal says, "Sell" or "Buy" — will be easily done by toll-free telephone call to a mutual fund family. With over 2,000 funds of all types to choose from, you have the right to be choosy. We cover all these funds in *Donoghue's Mutual Funds Almanac* each year, and we have developed a list of the most important, useful stock market funds. They are listed in appendixes 2 and 5 of this book and covered regularly in *Moneyletter*.

We have chosen the following criteria to select the funds we think most appropriate:

1. No unnecessary sales charges. As a rule, the fund should be no-load. If you already know how to select a mutual fund or will trust us to recommend one, why should you pay a middleman? Occasionally we will list a low-load fund (one with a load of 3 percent or less) if it has an outstanding record.

2. Competitive performance. The performance of the fund should be competitive with similar funds. We have selected stock market funds that have matched or beaten the Standard & Poor's 500 over the past three to five years. That excludes some funds that are widely advertised but did not perform consistently, some funds that are new and exciting but unproven, and some funds whose brief success turned out to be a flash in the pan. Most importantly, this selection process eliminates the underperformers. (Note that appendix 2 lists only funds for which reliable week-by-week performance data since 1984 are available. Thus, not all stock funds in the Donoghue fund universe are listed.)

3. Telephone exchange convenience. Each of the selected stock market funds — and their fund families — provide the "exchange privilege" that allows you to exchange shares of one fund in a fund family for shares of another fund. I call funds that offer this privilege "switch funds." Each provides an 800 toll-free phone number so that you can call the family to switch your money into or out of its funds at your pleasure. This is particularly important when the Donoghue Interest Rate Signal says, "Sell." You can move your money to a completely safe money market mutual fund without any sales commissions or delays.

You, on the other hand, will have agreed to play by their rules, as spelled out in the fund prospectuses. Most funds offer unlimited free switching, but some limit the number of switches to six a year. Some charge a nominal fee of perhaps $5 a switch, or expect you to stay for thirty days or so before your next switch. Most of these limitations do not really intrude on the Donoghue strategies. But it is wise to ask about the limitations of each fund you choose and to make a note to conform to them.

4. Available money fund "home base." Occasionally I find a fine family of mutual funds with excellent stock funds and telephone switching privileges among them, but no money market mutual fund in the family. We have eliminated from our list (appendix 5) any families that do not have a money fund you can dive into for absolute safety in a financial storm.

The only exceptions are a few families that have no money fund but from which you can switch by telephone using other mechanisms:

▶ In a few cases, a family has an arrangement with a money fund in another family.
▶ Other mutual funds are available through the nationwide offices of the discount broker Charles Schwab & Co. If you buy a fund through Charles Schwab, you can switch into other fund families by telephoning Schwab. Schwab's Mutual Fund Marketplace is used by many active inves-

tors who do not want their investment choices to be limited to a single mutual fund family and who want the full run of the mutual fund world. To trade mutual funds through Charles Schwab, you set up a Schwab One asset management account. Then you can buy no-load mutual funds from most of the major fund families for a fee — a fee that is not insignificant, but is not prohibitive, either. Note that you can use the Schwab One account to switch out of a fund by telephone only if you put your fund into your Schwab One account in the first place, either by buying it through Schwab or by filling in a form to transfer it there.

5. Minimum fund size. We have restricted our listed funds to those with at least $50 million in assets, for two reasons. First, we want to make sure we are dealing with funds sufficiently large to be making enough money to enable their managers to afford a full array of services. Second, we do not want Donoghue subscribers, readers, and managed account clients to control so much of a fund's assets that changes in our recommendations would be disruptive to the fund's management. We desire strongly to be good citizens in the mutual fund community.

6. No extreme volatility. Some funds are highly leveraged and extremely volatile. They are not suitable for prudent investors. They have been eliminated from our lists.

CHOOSING THE RIGHT FUNDS

The above criteria do not mean that none of the funds we recommended were on the hit list in the crash of 1987. All stock market funds are vulnerable to cataclysmic events like that. While some stock market funds, such as T. Rowe Price Capital Appreciation, will shift much of their assets into money market investments when they fear a decline in the market, many excellent stock funds have a policy of remaining fully invested in the market all the time. You have to do your own switching.

Q So the funds in the appendixes are the funds you recommend? Any one of them is good enough for me to invest in, right?

A No, those are the funds from which our recommendations are drawn. At any time, we publish in *Moneyletter* a much smaller list of specific "buy" recommendations. We seldom recommend more than a handful of funds, all of which have performed consistently well over the last year or so.

Q Why Charles Schwab & Co. and not other discount brokers?

A Because only Charles Schwab & Co. among discount brokers offers a full range of some 270 no-load mutual funds (albeit at a fee). The major convenience of this service is that maintaining the fund investments through Schwab makes trading among mutual fund families much simpler, with less paperwork.

Q Why is *my* fund, the one my advisors recommended, not listed?

A This is the most common question asked by new *Moneyletter* readers. The answer is simply that the fund did not meet our selection criteria. The most probable reason is that your advisors recommended a fund which paid them a load, a sales charge. For example, Franklin, Putnam, Merrill Lynch, American Capital, and other load funds are obviously very widely held, but are not on our list.

You should compare your fund's performance with those of the funds featured in the appendixes and in *Moneyletter*. If it suffers by comparison, sell yours and buy recommended funds. You will then be "in the system."

You should be aware that if you have a gain in a fund, selling it will trigger a taxable event and you will have to pay taxes on the profits. If you have a loss, of course, sell the fund immediately before you have additional losses. List the loss on your tax return and save money on taxes.

HOW DO I GET STARTED?

Don't jump the gun. Did you check the Donoghue Interest Rate Signal? Does it say, "Don't invest"? Then don't invest in any stock market fund. Park your money in the money fund of the family that houses the stock fund you would most like to buy.

If the signal says, "Buy," then to guide you in choosing your first fund investment, I can give you two ways to proceed. Below are five favorite no-load stock market funds that I have found to be excellent over the long term both under a buy, hold, and pray system and under the Donoghue Stock Market Strategy utilizing the Donoghue Interest Rate Signal. These funds' managements could have changed by the time you read this. But if you're desperate to go out and invest without any more current information than is in this book, these funds are unlikely to do badly by you. (Note that the performance statistics below are for 1984–87, not 1980–87 as in our full eight-year study. We find recent performance statistics are often a better guide to the future than older performance statistics.)

		Performance 1984–87	
Fund name	Toll-free phone	Buy, hold, & pray	The Donoghue Stock Market Strategy
Twentieth Century Select	800-345-2021	12.02%	21.06%
Scudder Capital Growth	800-453-3305	10.63%	20.06%
Founders Blue Chip	800-525-2440	14.18%	19.57%
Evergreen Fund	800-235-0064	10.43%	18.36%
Partners Fund	800-367-0770	15.10%	19.02%

Your second way to proceed is to consult the latest issue of *Moneyletter* for my current recommendations. (You can ask for a free copy by calling 1-800-445-5900, or in Massachusetts, 508-429-5930.) Note that the Donoghue Stock Market Strategy generally performs best when used with volatile small-company stock funds like Hartwell Emerging Growth, Axe Houghton Stock Fund, and Stein Roe Capital Opportunity. However, I'm reluctant to give a flat recommendation of this kind of fund here because conditions involving them change so much from period to period. To trade them, you should follow an investment publication like *Moneyletter* regularly.

If you've decided to commit yourself to the Donoghue Stock Market Strategy, you'll be interested in table 5.1, which lists the funds that ranked in the top ten in both four-year and eight-year performance in our tests when traded following the Donoghue Interest Rate Signal. All are no-load except for Fidelity Magellan, which carries a load of 3 percent.

WHAT IS THE *BEST WAY* TO PICK THE *BEST* STOCK FUNDS?

So you have a choice. Once you have determined that it is time to invest in a stock fund (the Donoghue Signal Number is declining, signaling a "buy" for stock market mutual funds), you can pick a few likely-looking funds from this book, call the fund families' 800 numbers for prospectuses and annual reports, and try to decide which seem best.

Or you can consult us for our current recommendations. We rank the recent performance of the 78 general-purpose U.S. stock market funds and 25 special-purpose funds by carefully calculating the performance of the funds each week. The performance statistics for the past 4 weeks (one month), 13 weeks (three months), and 26 weeks (six months) are determined weekly; we then use a weighted average of those three statistics as our ranking system.

This identifies the funds that have the most consistently excellent recent performance. All the general-purpose U.S. stock market funds in our system are growth or growth-and-income funds, all investing in the same stock market. We recommend those whose performance over these three past periods is best and most consistent. The top funds faced the

TABLE 5.1 *Successful funds under the Donoghue Stock Market Strategy*

Funds ranked in the top ten in both eight-year and four-year performance when traded following the Donoghue Interest Rate Signal.

Fund name	8-year period, 1980–87 (46 funds)				Most recent 4 years, 1984–87 (48 funds)			
	Trade following Donoghue Signal		Buy and hold		Trade following Donoghue Signal		Buy and hold	
	Rank	Annual return	Rank	Annual return	Rank	Annual return	Rank	Annual return
Fidelity Magellan	1	36.3%	1	28.3%	4	21.6%	21	10.6%
Hartwell Emerging Growth	2	33.3	31	12.4	1	24.6	47	0.2
Scudder Capital Growth	3	31.5	2	23.7	9	20.1	29	10.6
Twentieth Century Select	4	30.2	17	20.6	5	21.1	18	11.4
Stein Roe Capital Opportunity	5	29.1	26	14.1	8	20.2	39	7.1
Twentieth Century Growth	7	28.9	11	17.6	2	22.2	17	12.5
Axe Houghton Stock	8	28.1	46	7.6	6	20.9	57	3.7

same choices of investments and the same market conditions as all the others. So the best *are* the best.

Consistent top performance in the recent past increases the probability that a fund will outperform its peers in the future. The cream rises to the top of the peer group, and our evaluation techniques indicate when a fund's management seems to have lost its touch.

TO SUMMARIZE

All you need to know to make big profits on your investments can be summarized in a few points:

1 Historically, the stock market has produced far greater earnings for investors than any other publicly traded investment, and over the long run it is likely to do so in the future as well.
2 You can't expect maximum returns from the stock market if you rely on recommendations from a broker or other commissioned salesperson.
3 The best no-load stock mutual funds can give you all the benefits of investing in the stock market without high fees or pressure.
4 Stocks tend to *rise* when the interest rate trend is *down* and *fall* when the interest rate trend is *up*.
5 You can follow the current interest rate trend by tracking the Donoghue Signal Number. When it falls, that's a "buy" signal. Invest in stock market mutual funds that allow convenient switching to a money market mutual fund and that have consistently performed well over the past year or so. Then continue to watch the Donoghue Signal Number, and bail out when it rises, saying, "sell."

6
THE SIX SMARTEST STOCK MARKET INVESTING STRATEGIES

Just as you can choose to live your life in many ways, you can build a personal approach to the stock market in many ways as well. For this chapter, I have chosen six different approaches. Each is based on the basic Donoghue Stock Market Strategy outlined in the last chapter. So each allows a high probability of success.

It is up to you to recognize which best suits your situation. Decide where you feel the most comfortable. With responsibility comes wisdom — both new insight from setbacks and delight in success.

Stock Strategy #1 — The lazy person's strategy

If all you want to do is to buy a few mutual funds, hold on for dear life, and pray they go up, at least we can significantly reduce the risks of this dangerous strategy. If this is your approach, your choice of a day to invest is the riskiest investment decision you will make. (After that you are at the mercy of the markets.) We can help you pick the day to start and suggest some funds that are appropriate for the buy, hold, and pray approach.

Stock Strategy #2 — The basic Donoghue stock market strategy

This is the crucial high-power strategy that will produce the best shared profits over the long term. I say "shared profits" because the government is going to want its share of your gains.

Stock Strategy #3 — The Donoghue strategy for income

This strategy is for folks who look to their investments to increase their income. No, it is not a strategy for investing in bonds; it is a strategy for investing in stocks for growth plus a predictable cash flow to keep the creditors at bay.

Stock Strategy #4 — A strategy to counterbalance your investments for crashproof returns

For those who don't quite trust the Donoghue timing system, we have an answer. It will still take you just ten minutes a week, but it involves no predictions and no economic analysis.

The returns under Stock Strategy #4 are surprisingly good and the operation amazingly simple. The real benefit from this system is the opportunity to earn profits no matter what happens in the economy. In 1987, the year of the crash, this strategy would have returned 13 to 15 percent.

Stock Strategy #5 — A tax-sheltered strategy using retirement programs

Self-directed retirement savings programs such as IRAs, Keoghs, 401(k)s, 403(b)s, and the like are probably the greatest investment tools in America. Too many investors see retirement accounts as "money on which I should not take any risks" and avoid tax-sheltered stock market returns that could compound tax-free for decades, building up serious riches.

We will show you how to build a strategy around retirement programs.

Stock Strategy #6 — The all-purpose tax-deferred Donoghue stock market strategy

"Tax-free" . . . the words trip on the tongue and visions of tax-free profits dance through the mind like the legendary visions of sugar plums. The reality can be *almost* as good.

Still, perhaps a little cold water is needed. We will be talking about tax-free investing run by the insurance companies under rules established by the IRS. And Congress got into the act recently and changed the rules. Sorry for the letdown.

Don't fret — it's still likely to work well, but only if you know how to make it work well. If you're the sort of person who hires an accountant just to make sure the dividends from the stocks you own are deposited in your bank account, perhaps this is not your cup of tea. If you can deal with a little insurance company bureaucracy and some significant service charges, however, the opportunities will more than reward you over the long term.

Now, are you ready for the details?

STOCK STRATEGY #1 — THE LAZY PERSON'S STRATEGY

Are you a person who loves to read about investment strategies, absorbs every detail, and yet never feels sufficiently confident to put all you've learned to work? You're looking for a system that will allow someone else to do everything.

If you are willing to do just the smallest smidgen of work, we can help. The following lazy man's (or woman's) strategy is a sophisticated, lower-risk variant on the most popular investment strategy in America — that buy, hold, and pray we have noted so often. The differences between the Donoghue Lazy Person's Strategy and the traditional buy, hold, and pray strategy are two: (1) We are going to consider carefully each step along the way; and (2) we are going to use the knowledge we have acquired about timing the stock market.

The "buy" decision

The "buy" decision is the crucial decision. It can haunt investors for decades, especially if they decide wrong.

Four critical points can help you with your buy decision:

1. Stick with no-load stock market mutual funds.

2. Buy at the right time. Follow the Donoghue Interest Rate Signal to assure yourself that interest rates are declining. If you are not going to keep current with the system, at least get started at the right time. But suppose you order your free Donoghue Signal worksheet, you keep track of the Donoghue Signal Number for a few weeks, you find the Donoghue Signal Number is saying, "Sell," and then, being lazy, you fail to keep up your records? There is still hope; I can't send you a new worksheet every time your interest in investing revives, but I *can* send you a free sample issue of *Moneyletter* as often as every three months.

3. Dollar-cost-average your way in. As an alternative to doing all your buying at once (after checking that the Donoghue Interest Rate Signal is saying, "Buy"), you can use a tried and true technique that "blind" investors — those who have no idea where they are in the investment cycle — have found helpful. The technique is called dollar cost averaging.

You invest a fixed amount of money per period for a number of periods. If you have, say, $10,000 to invest, you might invest $1,000 each month for ten months, or $100 a week for a hundred weeks. (You may already be using this technique inadvertently if you are buying a mutual fund on a payroll deduction basis.)

The advantage of dollar cost averaging is that you buy more shares when the price is lower and fewer shares when the price is higher. Thus, the average *cost* per share of your investment will be less than the average *price* per share over the entire period you were investing.

Dollar cost averaging does not insure that you will make

money on your investments, only that the average per-share cost will be less. You may lose profits by leaving some of your money in the bank while you are waiting to invest, at a time when the Interest Rate Signal might have said, "Buy." But dollar cost averaging does guarantee that your losses will be less should you start investing at a bad time, and that you will make at least some money if you start investing at a good time. At a minimum, it keeps you from making a totally disastrous investment.

4. Minimize downside risks. Choose a mutual fund that has a good track record of losing little in bear markets. You'll avoid part of the risk of the "hold" decision.

A fund that loses less in a bear market is also likely to make less in a bull market. You could probably do significantly better over the long run by purchasing other funds and following the Donoghue Signal. But if you want to buy and hold, here's a list of funds that have done well for investors following this strategy.

Five good funds for lazy investors

Fund name	Telephone	Performance 1984–87 (buy, hold, & pray)
Partners Fund	800-367-0770	15.10%
Financial Industrial Income Fund	800-525-8085	14.91%
Evergreen Total Return	800-235-0064	12.68%
Founders Blue Chip	800-525-2440	14.18%
Acorn Fund	312-621-0630	13.19%

Since the performance above is for a period that ended December 30, 1987 — right after the 1987 crash — the returns indicate that these funds held up well during that trying period. But note that even the best performer, Partners Fund, produced far poorer returns than even an average fund would have produced if investors traded in accord with the Donoghue Interest Rate Signal.

The "hold" decision

You will enjoy your investing experience more if you are an active buy, hold, and pray investor — that is, if you remember that you can always take steps to control your destiny. Here are two steps that will make holding less worrisome and more worthwhile:

1. Diversify among a few recommended funds. Consider including in your portfolio small investments in an international stock fund and in a fund that invests in things that do well in hard times, such as gold stocks.

2. Consider switching part of your holdings to a money fund when you're worried about stock market trends. Remember that, if you have chosen funds from the Donoghue fund selections listed in appendix 2, you have the ability to sell your holding easily by using the telephone switch privilege.

Never switch your entire investment to a money fund without first monitoring indicators such as the Donoghue Signals. If you switch the whole of your portfolio just because of some comments you hear from economists on television, you can miss big upward moves of the market. The biggest upward moves often occur when economists are most nervous.

Switching part of your investment when you feel worried can be a good idea, however. It reduces your risk, and the experience of making or losing money on a switch will help you gain the confidence to be a more assertive investor. You simply make an 800 toll-free call and say "put part of my money in your money fund."

The "pray" phase — giving yourself more than a prayer

Finally, remember that *good information is insurance*. As insurance that you have not made a bad investment decision and that trends are not moving so powerfully against you that you should change your plans, you might keep an eye on the average maturity of taxable money funds (as detailed in chapter 2) or some other indicator of interest rates, or you might also subscribe to a publication such as *Moneyletter* that will alert you to important "sell" signals. This strategy is, after all, for lazy men and women. Stay awake during the day and you can sleep well at night.

STOCK STRATEGY #2 — THE BASIC DONOGHUE STOCK MARKET STRATEGY

Just a little bit more work is likely to produce significantly better returns — that is, make your money grow significantly faster — than even a well-executed version of the buy, hold, and pray strategy.

Just build on the tactics outlined in chapters 2 and 5:

1 **Watch interest rates.**
2 **Watch the Donoghue Signal Number.**
3 **Remember that UP interest rate trends mean DOWN stock trends.** If the Donoghue Signal Number is increasing, stock market mutual fund investing is *not* recommended.
4 **DOWN interest rate trends mean opportunity.** If the magic number is decreasing, interest rates are falling. Invest immediately in stock market mutual funds.
5 **Swing every time; you may hit a homer.** We want to increase the probability that we will succeed. We understand that like any indicator, the Donoghue magic number may not be so magic all the time. To gain its benefits, however, we have to follow its advice every time. Patience will allow us to win larger when we win, lose smaller when we lose, and win more often than we lose.
6 **Use the best.** Choose top-performing, no-load, telephone switchable stock funds, either as listed in the back of this book or as the list is updated in *Donoghue's Moneyletter*. Generally, only these funds fit the dynamics of this strategy. The specific funds most attractive at a given point in time are listed as "buy" recommendations in *Moneyletter*.
7 **Remember the tax man.** Understand that each sale or telephone switch of a mutual fund is a taxable transaction, with taxes payable if the sale generates a gain and losses

deductible if the sale generates a loss. Dividends and other distributions from funds must also be reported as income even if your fund automatically reinvests them for you in your account. Keep track of capital gains distributions. If you later sell shares in a mutual fund for an amount that is less than the price you paid plus the capital gains distributions on which you paid taxes, you can deduct the difference as a loss. Such fine points are worth noting.

These simple suggestions can constitute an excellent growth-oriented strategy. You'll pay more taxes than if you carefully used retirement savings plans and insurance-investing strategies, as discussed below. But you'll come out way ahead of people who leave their money in the bank or just entrust their decisions to their brokers.

STOCK STRATEGY #3 — THE DONOGHUE STRATEGY FOR INCOME

The basic Donoghue Stock Market Strategy is an excellent plan for growth. But some readers need income. "I want income from my investments," they are saying. "I need a check a month to pay my bills. How do I adjust the Stock Market Strategy to fit my needs? Should I invest in bonds rather than stock market mutual funds?"

I thought you would never ask. Of course you can get a regular cash flow. You will notice I did not say "income" but "cash flow." You pay bills with cash, not income.

A check a month is a request away

Many people buy long-term bonds because they want to receive good interest rates and a check every month. However, that is the *wrong* way to invest. As we will see in the next chapter, long-term bonds are not like money market investments or bank accounts. They can decline in value, leaving your principal sharply reduced.

The Donoghue Stock Market Strategy, however, can give you a check a month almost as easily as if you invested in bonds, and you should be able to spend the money with more confidence.

If you are following the Donoghue Stock Market Strategy exactly as described so far, you are investing most of your money in one or more stock market mutual funds when the Donoghue Interest Rate Signal says, "Buy," and in a money market mutual fund when the Donoghue Interest Rate Signal says, "Sell." Each time you enter a new fund, you should ask the fund family to reinvest all dividends and capital gains distributions for you. You will probably be achieving returns averaging anywhere from 15 to 20 percent or more per year.

The mutual fund company will be happy to establish a "systematic redemption plan" at your request. It will redeem an exact dollar amount you specify (usually a minimum of $50 or more) from your account each month on the same date. It will send you a check or transfer the money electronically to your checking account. Just keep the amount you withdraw each month below the long-term growth rate of your portfolio, and you'll have a far better cash flow than from a bond portfolio. Your portfolio's value will dip occasionally, but in the long run it will keep growing.

You will face only one problem. Your switches between funds when the Donoghue Interest Rate Signal says, "Sell" can mess up the systematic redemption system.

To keep up your cash flow, you will have to choose one of three courses of action:

1 First, you could instruct the fund family to create a new systematic redemption plan each time you switch. But this might mean filling out a new form, and a check could fail to arrive on time while the systematic redemption system was being established on the new fund.

2 Therefore a more practical choice may be: Do all your systematic redemption from a single fund, the money market mutual fund in the family. When it's time to switch from the money fund to a stock market fund, leave enough in the money fund to cover all withdrawals for a certain period. (A year is convenient.) Many fund families will require a minimum balance in the designated fund for

systematic redemption (usually $10,000). Redeeming from the money fund also minimizes bookkeeping for tax purposes. Money funds always maintain a constant price of $1 per share, so you don't have to keep track of capital gains and losses on each redemption.

3 If the required minimum balance is too large to be comfortable for you, you may write your own monthly checks from your fund family's money market fund. Most major money market funds will gladly establish check-writing privileges for their investors. They will send you a checkbook, and you write checks just as you would on a bank checking account. (Sometimes checks must be written in certain minimum amounts; $200 minimums are common.) Many funds require lower minimum balances for checking privileges than for systematic withdrawal, and a few require no minimum at all. Thus you can leave only enough cash to cover six months' worth of redemptions in the money fund, write the checks yourself, and have a good deal more cash available for stock market funds. Replenish the money fund twice a year from the stock fund with a toll-free phone call to the fund family — unless, of course, you get a "sell" signal in the meantime.

The choices are yours. Discuss the options with the fund family so there are no surprises. You will find them very cooperative.

Ten percent is a good starting point

Why do I say you can take a check a month from a portfolio managed with the Donoghue Stock Market Strategy with *more* confidence than if you invest in bonds?

The answer is simple. Over the long run, stocks produce better returns than bonds. Moreover, bonds are only slightly less likely than stocks to decline in price, and if you watch the Donoghue Interest Rate Signal and switch to money market mutual funds when it says, "Sell," you will minimize the chance of significant losses. Your portfolio is likely to increase in value faster over the long haul if it is invested in stocks than if it is invested in bonds. Thus you can better afford to take out a check a month if you are following the Donoghue Stock Market Strategy than if you are investing in bonds.

Now comes the obvious question: "How much should I withdraw so I don't take too much out each year?"

Only you can answer that. No one can tell you exactly how much you will make in the stock market or promise that you will never lose anything. But there are some useful guidelines:

If you are conservative, you may want to start out taking perhaps 6 to 8 percent.

However, if you are sticking closely to the Donoghue Stock Market Strategy, your returns are likely to exceed that level considerably. Thus, drawing out 10 percent of your money each year should not turn out to be a problem over the long term.

If you are retired and living off your savings, drawing off your money at 10 percent when you are earning 15 percent or more means that you will enjoy the comfortable situation of my mother. She uses this strategy and says it makes her confident she will "never run out of money before I run out of life." We jokingly call it "Mom's Double-Digit-Returns-Forever Investment Strategy." The growth potential of the Donoghue Stock Market Strategy tied into the check-a-month convenience of systematic redemption is a real winner.

STOCK STRATEGY #4 — A STRATEGY TO COUNTERBALANCE YOUR INVESTMENTS FOR CRASHPROOF RETURNS

One of the joys of my life is the friends I have discovered over the years. As I was finishing this book, my old friend Dr. Chuck Chakrapani visited me at my new home. Chuck is the founder of the Investors Association of Canada and publisher of *Money Digest*.

He has been studying mutual fund trading systems for years and has developed a strategy that involves no predictions, no forecasts, and no trend following. Yet it actually forces investors to buy low and sell high. It provides excellent safety. Thus it is ideal for safety-conscious investors who know that leaving money in a bank will cause losses to inflation, but who don't quite trust an interest rate signal such as we have been discussing to switch them out of stocks before market declines.

It deals with the challenges of **Recession**, **Inflation**, **Growth**, and **Safety** — **RIGS**. We call it the CounterBalance Strategy.

The system is simple to follow. The basic approach is to invest *equal amounts in each of four sectors* to meet each of the four RIGS challenges: **bond funds** to protect against Recession, **gold funds** to protect against Inflation, **stock funds** to take advantage of Growth in the economy, and **money funds** for absolute Safety. At least one of those sectors will make good money in just about any economy.

As the investment program progresses, the equal amounts will become unequal. Periodically (for example, once a year), you adjust the amount of money in each investment so you again have an equal number of dollars invested.

The mechanics are fairly simple. At the end of each period, you simply add up the total value of your investment and divide by four. That is the average value of your four portfolios. One, two, or three of your portfolios will then be worth more than this amount; one, two, or three of your portfolios will be worth less. You now sell off the part of your most successful investments that exceeds the average amount. In doing so, you are selling part of your holdings in the investments that have performed best. Then you reinvest in the sector or sectors that have performed worst. That process is called, with great reverence, "selling high and buying low."

The plan intrigued me, so I asked Dr. Chakrapani to test the system for the eight-year period we have been investigating in this book. So he tested the system with several of the funds we had studied over the period from January 1980 through December 1987.

The system worked well (though its long-term returns

were not as great as the long-term returns of trading growth stock funds on the basis of the Donoghue Interest Rate Signal). Assuming you had traded annually and you had put your **R**ecession investment in the bond mutual fund Dreyfus A Bonds Plus, your **I**nflation investment in U.S. Gold Shares, your **G**rowth investment in Columbia Growth Fund, and your **S**afety investment in Kemper Money Market Fund, you would have achieved an annual yield of 13.9 percent for the period.

A slightly more aggressive version of the strategy might have invested only in the bond, gold, and growth stock funds, leaving out the money market investment. It would have produced a return of 14.6 percent for the period. This approach would probably have worked best if you had used the most volatile funds in each category:

a Zero-coupon bond funds like Benham Target Maturity 2015, a smallish and very volatile fund, seemed to be the best choices after they came into being in 1985.
b Gold funds are volatile by nature, since they are actually stocks in small mining companies and the impact of rising or falling gold prices will cause their value to change much more rapidly than the price itself changes.
c The most volatile stock funds are those that invest in small growth companies.

STOCK STRATEGY #5 — A TAX-SHELTERED STRATEGY USING RETIREMENT PROGRAMS

As you will read in chapter 11, tax-qualified retirement programs offer special advantages. Sheltering allows you to defer taxes on profits from "switches," and in many cases you can deduct your contribution on your tax return. Tax deferral allows much more rapid buildup of earnings, so that even after payment of taxes when you withdraw the money (usually after age 59½), you'll have far more than you would have had otherwise. Thus, you can use retirement savings programs as an extremely powerful component of an overall wealth-building strategy.

What's unique about tax-deferred investing?

The advantages of tax-deferred investing are manifold. You probably know about the tax deductions and the tax-free compounding of interest (and if you don't, chapter 11 will fill you in).

The special advantages of tax-deferred investing are important in creating a strategy, however. Ordinarily, every sale of a mutual fund other than a money fund (which will maintain a fixed $1 price per share and therefore won't create capital gains or losses) is a taxable event, and that includes every telephone switch out of a stock or bond fund. At minimum, a sale produces paperwork; often, it means increased payments to Uncle Sam. But in a tax-deferred account, you could trade your portfolio daily if you wanted and never be constrained by tax consequences. You can reinvest profits and the money you would have paid in taxes, and as you invest your tax-deferred money, your profits compound faster and faster. That is the true investment power of tax-deferred retirement plans.

Full-force investment power

Some people invest ordinary savings in mutual funds but put their individual retirement accounts in a bank because they "don't want to take any risks with retirement money." That's a big mistake. Keep money you expect to need over the next four years in riskless bank money market accounts if you want. But use your most assertive tactics with your retirement money. If you lose money one year, you can make it up the next. Remember that over all long periods, stock market investments have outperformed bank accounts and bonds for generations. The only time you really need to move to no-risk investments (other than when the Donoghue Interest Rate Signal says, "Sell") is when you think that a bout of ill health might keep you from attending to your investments and cause you to miss a "sell" signal.

Your retirement account is the place to take managed
risks. Think about it. Suppose you invested $1,000 in a no-
load stock market mutual fund on January 1. Nine months
later, after a burst of energy in the stock market, your investment had grown to $1,300. Now suppose that interna-
tional investments were heating up over a falling dollar. You
switched to an international fund, and you earned another 20
percent over the next five months, at which time you switched
your money back to a money market fund. If your investment
were tax-deferred, it would grow another $260 to $1,560,
giving you a return of 56 percent in fourteen months. Outside
your tax-deferred account, however, your gains would be
taxed at every stage. If you were in, say, a 28 percent bracket,
you'd end up with $1,391.10 — $248.90 less than you'd accumulate in a tax-deferred account.

You can see that over the long term, the investment power
of a tax-deferred investment can significantly improve your
returns. Thus it is wise to manage the money in tax-deferred
accounts much more assertively. This is where your investment power is on full blast.

How do we maximize tax-deferred investment power?

The guidelines to choosing retirement accounts and integrat-
ing them with the rest of your finances are simple:

1. Invest first in the most attractive plans. First, make sure
that you make maximum contributions to any plans in which
you get employer-matching contributions. Next, invest in a
plan that allows you to deduct the contributions on your tax
return. Finally, make sure that all your plans allow you suf-
ficient flexibility to practice the Donoghue Stock Market
Strategy. Your employer or mutual fund family may have
several such programs available, and choosing how to allocate
your money for best advantage is an important strategic decision.

**2. Define what goals you need to reach through savings
apart from your retirement kitty, develop a strategy to meet
them, then invest as much as you can afford in tax-advantaged
plans.** If you're accumulating a down payment for a home or

a tuition fund for your kids, you probably won't put all your savings into tax-advantaged retirement plans. Invest what you must to achieve these goals outside your retirement plan. Then invest the balance in the tax-advantaged vehicles. Don't worry about falling a bit short on your other needs because of retirement investments. Tax-advantaged investments will accumulate rapidly, and you'll find they make you feel more comfortable about borrowing to cover any shortfalls that occur in other areas.

3. If YOU make the decision, choose the most flexible place for your tax-deferred account. Most employer-sponsored plans will give you a narrow range of choices. But you can choose from thousands of institutions for your IRA or Keogh plan, and the decision will make a big difference in the long run. A large no-load mutual fund family such as T. Rowe Price, Vanguard, or Fidelity is excellent. A Charles Schwab account that allows you to deal with dozens of mutual fund families is ideal. Banks and full-commission brokers shouldn't even be considered. Fund families with just a few funds may be poor choices in the long run.

Stick to your guns, maintain the discipline of your strategy, and keep the faith. You will win over the long term.

STOCK STRATEGY #6 — THE ALL-PURPOSE TAX-DEFERRED DONOGHUE STOCK MARKET STRATEGY

"What about me?" says Joe Prosperity. "My retirement plans will allow me to invest no more than $2,000 a year. I have $100,000 I just inherited [or I just got from selling my business or some real estate]. How can I tax-shelter the income from that money?"

That's a good question. After all, almost everyone has money they can't tax-shelter through retirement plans.

The answer to your heart's desire is single premium variable life insurance, and you can use it as the centerpiece of a superior strategy for untaxed returns.

A *superior strategy for untaxed returns*

I know you don't want to hear about insurance. I used to hate to talk about insurance. In fact, if I wanted to sit alone on a plane, I would tell the person next to me that I was an insurance agent. He'd be gone in no time — even in midflight! I recently took the test to be an insurance agent myself.

Don't worry this time. We are going to make it fun. In chapter 12 we will fill in the details, but let's do some strategic thinking now.

Most life insurance policies have always been a mixture of insurance and tax-free investment. They built up a cash value tax-free. Generally, they were not good investments, but that's not the point here. The point is: The U.S. tax code has always allowed life insurance companies to invest people's money for them tax-free.

Over the past decade, life insurance companies have taken this idea a few steps farther to create truly attractive investments. They've created policies under which you pay a single premium ($5,000–10,000 minimum) and the policy is paid up for life. These policies are perfect opportunities to play the stock market tax-deferred. Or if you choose, you can use much of your money while you're alive — simply by "borrowing" against the policy.

Your single premium is invested in a family of mutual funds. A small portion of the income the premium earns pays for a modest amount of insurance. (For example, at age fifty a $30,000 premium might buy $60,000 worth of life insurance.) The insurance cost and other fees charged by the insurance company (and the associated mutual fund management company) amount to 2 to 3 percent of the premium per year.

Everything else the mutual funds earn is added directly to the insurance policy's cash value. Under current law, no taxes are payable as long as the policy remains in force, except if you "borrow" some of the cash value. If you don't borrow the cash value, or if you borrow and then repay all your borrowings, the cash value goes to your beneficiary when you die. However — and here's the best part — you also have the choice of borrowing most of the cash value at any time in your life *and you never have to repay the loan.*

In other words, single premium variable life insurance (SPVL) — at least under the laws in force as this is written — is a way for *anyone* to invest in mutual funds for *any* purpose with access to their money *at any time*, and they'll *pay no taxes* until and unless they take the money out of the policy. I call it "**Investment Life**."

Suppose you have $100,000 to invest. (You can invest as little as $5,000 to $10,000.) Once you have found a knowledgeable insurance broker — our referral service has screened a few independent brokers — the process is simple.

1 You invest by paying a *single premium*. Think about this as an investment rather than an insurance policy. It helps.

2 You choose which of the mutual funds available with the policy you want to invest in at the start. How do you make your decision? By following the basic Donoghue Stock Market Strategy, of course, and looking at the trend of the Donoghue Signal Number. Your choice will probably be a stock or money fund or perhaps a combination. Most of the policies offer enough mutual fund choices that you should be able to pursue the Donoghue Stock Market Strategy over the long term.

3 You manage your money by watching the Donoghue Signal Number. One beauty of the Donoghue Stock Market Strategy is that you don't even need to know the performance trend of the specific funds in the policy. All of your "buy" and "sell" signals come from the Donoghue Signal Number, which you can calculate from the newspaper, not from the funds themselves. No adjusting for dividend payments. No worrying about days when the fund doesn't report to the newspapers. Nothing to worry about; you are only following one number each week.

Triple tax-free returns

From here on, it gets really good.

The profits you make on single premium variable life insurance are tax-deferred.

What if you want access to your money? That's easy. You "borrow" the money. You have to take the initiative and ask for a "loan" when you want money, but if you take the initiative, you can borrow *what you want* up to 80 or 90 percent of the policy's cash value.

If you are looking for a wealth-building tool and you don't want current income, on the other hand, you will love SPVL, since your money accumulates *tax-free* and you don't have to take distributions as you would from an annuity. Still sound good?

Suppose you die. The "loan" will be paid off at your death. Only then do any payments have to be made. And the life insurance company distributes the proceeds of the insurance policy — certainly more than you put into it — to your heirs after deducting the loan balance, free of all income tax.

Trouble in paradise

What can go wrong with such a great deal? You need to know the downside risks.

1 The laws can change. Until the second half of 1988, single premium insurance profits were totally tax-free. But then Congress passed the present rules, which made single premium insurance resemble a super all-purpose IRA. (Like an Individual Retirement Account, your money earns money tax-free and you can spend it without penalty taxes starting at age 59½. But there's no limit to the amount you can contribute.) Congress could change the laws again. However, most additional proposed restrictions are not very dangerous to policy owners. Whatever the outcome of proposed changes in variable insurance between the writing and the publication of this book, you can order our latest "Single Premium Update Report" by writing us at "Single Premium Update," 360 Woodland Street, P.O. Box 6640, Holliston, MA 01746.

2 If you cash in the policy, you trigger current taxes on all profits you have made. So in general, you can't get at more than 80 or 90 percent of your money during your lifetime unless you cash in the policy and pay taxes, *or* convert it to an annuity.

But why cash in the policy if you can get most of the cash out of it by borrowing it? No good reason.

3 The mutual funds available through a particular policy could perform less well than other funds. But if you see this occurring, you can transfer your money to another policy with better-performing funds by filling out a Form 1035, available from many insurance brokers (see appendix 1).

4 When you reach the age of ninety to one hundred, depending on the plan, the policy will be paid off to you rather than your heirs, and your distributions become taxable, since you have outlived the policy. The good news is that the tax-deferral benefits have probably earned you more extra money over time than the taxes you will have to pay. But who wants to pay taxes?

Well, you got the benefits of an IRA-like account (tax-deferred buildup until withdrawal). Nevertheless, the tax on the distributions can be a real shock to a ninety-year-old. By selecting a policy with the latest possible date for this process, you can avoid the likelihood that it will occur. Also, you can avert the process by rolling the policy into an annuity before the trigger date arrives.

5 If you need to take out all available cash in the first four years or so, you may wind up doing worse than you would have if you had invested outside the policy.

6 It's conceivable — though highly unlikely — that if the stock market plummeted catastrophically you would either have to put more money into your policy to keep it in force or else close it out at a loss. But if you follow the Donoghue Signal, it's unlikely that you would be invested in stocks at the time of a major decline like this.

7 Choosing a policy can be confusing. See chapter 12 for further details.

Using variable insurance strategically

Don't put your whole portfolio into single premium variable life insurance, especially if you are less than 59½ years old. (Under the government's rules, you pay a 10 percent penalty tax on any money you take out of a single premium insurance policy before age 59½.) Keep some investments outside the policy, if only for possible use in the policy's first few years, when borrowing is not advantageous.

Keep an IRA or other retirement plan that is separate from the variable insurance policy, too. Contributions to most retirement plans produce immediate tax deductions, while purchases of variable insurance do not. Also, keeping some assets outside the policy avoids turning your whole future over to the one or two mutual fund families that are associated with your one or two variable life policies.

But variable insurance is a great strategic opportunity. If you're willing to take the time to understand it and use it together with the other elements of the Donoghue strategies, and if you double-check the policy's tax-deferred status just before you buy, you should have an investment program that can't be beaten. Variable insurance is simply too good to ignore.

FINDING A STRATEGY THAT'S RIGHT FOR YOU

Where do *you* fit into all these opportunities? In the end, that's for you to decide. But whether you're a lazy person or a tax-shelter wheeler-dealer, you'll find that a little bit of know-how and strategic thinking can make you a whole lot richer.

7
UNBLEST BE THE BONDS THAT TIE

"Want to make more income from your investments? Have I got a deal for you!"

Who wouldn't react to that pitch? Our jobs pay us a regular income. Bank accounts pay regular interest — in effect, a regular "rent" for our money — and guarantee we get our money back. That is how Americans start out thinking about investing. So when brokers offer high yields from seemingly secure bond investments, Americans quickly respond.

Unfortunately, there's trouble ahead.

INVESTING FOR INCOME — THE GREAT AMERICAN PASTIME

"How much will it pay me?" is on the lips of millions of investors looking to supplement their income. It is also on the lips of many people investing for the long term who do not particularly care about current income. They are all looking for safety, liquidity, and guarantees of high yield. So of course, their broker, financial planner, or insurance agent recommends "the proven safety of investing in **bonds**."

WHAT ARE BONDS SUPPOSED TO DO FOR US? — WHAT WE EXPECT

Can you blame them? Bonds look really good. They are long-term commitments, generally from well-established borrowers: major "household name" corporations; major cities, counties, and taxing authorities; and even the federal government itself.

Bonds offer higher returns than short-term money market accounts, a promise to repay at maturity, and a locked-in return for decades if you wish. And they seem to give you a chance to make a one-time investment decision. Many investors desperately want to make a one-time decision so that they will never have to worry about their investments again.

This is why bonds are an easy sell. Tell people they can get a large check each month and forget about their investments forever, and you can sell a lot of bonds.

WHAT ARE THE PROBLEMS WITH BONDS? — WHAT THEY DO TO US

But what brokers do not tell you is the most important thing to know: Bonds can be riskier investments than stock market holdings unless you know how to *actively manage* your portfolio.

The only thing safe about bonds is that you will get your money back at maturity. That could be in twenty or thirty years. For many bond investors, this length of time might as well be forever. If inflation rears its ugly head, the cash you get back may have lost most of its value by the time you get it. But long before the cash became worthless you would probably become disgusted with the returns you were receiving. You'd decide to sell. And you'd be surprised to discover you could sell only by taking a big loss.

If you bought a bond mutual fund, of course, there would be no such thing as "maturity" for the fund as a whole. A managed mutual fund simply reinvests the proceeds of matured bonds into new bonds. The fund's *average maturity* is an important statistic, and we will discuss that below, but a managed bond mutual fund does not mature, only its investments do.

BONDS CAN BE SAFE — BUT ONLY IF YOU DON'T NEED THE MONEY

Think about it. With bonds, if inflation and interest rates rise, that guarantees two things: Your current yield is not competitive and you have lost money. It doesn't matter that you bought "U.S. government guaranteed" bonds. If the market turns against you, your portfolio will show a loss.

If you have ever considered investing in bonds, you should understand the following risks.

1. Market risk: interest rate fluctuations. In recent years the risk that interest rates would rise and wipe out much of your investment has been very real. As we've said before, as interest rates rise, the market value of your bond falls. Let's see how this works. If you're a bond investor and last year's long-term interest rates were 8 percent, you would have paid roughly $1,000 for a bond that yielded $80 a year. Now suppose interest rates rise to 9 percent. Your $1,000 can now buy a bond that pays $90 a year. You would no longer be willing to pay $1,000 for a bond issued last year that yields only $80 a year; nor would others, so that bond's worth in the bond market declines significantly. Thus, the bond you bought last year for $1,000 will have been a bad investment.

Let's take a specific example of how you can be hurt. Suppose you bought a thirty-year bond guaranteed by the U.S. government with a 10 percent yield. Then interest rates in the marketplace rose just a bit. Now a new thirty-year bond is being issued at 11 percent. *You lose 8.7 percent in market value.*

If rates rise to 12 percent — *you lose 16.2 percent in market value.*

If rates rise to 14 percent — *you lose 28.1 percent in market value.*

Consider a dramatic example from the real world. Suppose you bought Franklin U.S. Government Fund, a very popular bond mutual fund sold by brokers, in July 1979. By September 1981, you would have lost 37.8 percent of the value of your investment, assuming that you took the dividends and did not reinvest them. That's a lot of money to lose in a "conservative" government investment.

Of course, if interest rates had *fallen* four percentage points on a thirty-year bond, *your investment would have gained 55.4 percent in market value.* And interest rates have declined that much, producing this kind of profit in bond investments, at least once in the past decade.

Thus, *when you buy and when you sell* are critical decisions in today's highly volatile bond markets.

Why be concerned now? Because today's interest rates are among the lowest of the last decade, and it is more than likely that they will rise in the next few years. They have a lot more room to rise than to fall. Therefore buying bonds in a rising interest rate environment is especially fraught with risk.

2. Market risk: maturity risk. The longer the time period between now and the bond's maturity, the greater its sensitivity to swings in interest rates.

In our previous example, we talked about the effect of interest rate swings on a thirty-year bond. Let's compare that to the effect of the same interest rate movement on a one-year bond.

	Change in market value, 10% bond	
Interest rate movement	30-year maturity	1-year maturity
Increase 1 percentage point	− 8.7%	−0.9%
Increase 2 percentage points	−16.2%	−1.8%
Increase 4 percentage points	−28.1%	−3.6%

That is why you want to know the "average maturity" of any bond mutual fund in which you invest. The longer the maturity, the better in a falling interest rate environment. When rates are rising, the shorter the better. But in fact, when interest rates are rising you're almost always best off in a very-short-term money market mutual fund, not in a bond fund.

The following types of portfolios are arranged in sequence of increasing risk:

	Rising rates	Falling rates
Money market portfolio (maturities under 1 year, often under 60 days)	Safe	Safe
Short-term bond portfolio (1 to 3 years)	Small loss	Higher profits*
Intermediate-term bond portfolio (3 to 10 years)	Larger loss	Still higher*
Long-term bond portfolio (10 years or more)	Biggest loss	Highest profits*

* Profits are defined as total return, i.e., dividends plus increase or decrease in market value. You must, however, sell to capture these profits or losses.

3. Credit risk. "Credit risk" is the risk that you won't get your money back. Not all bonds are certain to repay you at maturity. The following types of funds are listed in order of increasing exposure to risk of default.

U.S. government bonds are sure to repay you. They have no credit risk because they are backed by the full faith and credit of the U.S. government. If under pressure, the U.S. Treasury could simply print money to repay you.

Insured bonds are bonds insured by a private insurance company as to payment of interest and principal (but not, of course, as to risk due to interest rate fluctuations).

High-grade corporate bonds are issued by corporations and often secured by a claim on the corporation's property.

Municipal bonds are issued by tax-exempt authorities, which rarely default. The major recent exception was Washington (State) Public Power Supply System (known in the investment business as WPPSS or, more informally, "Whoops!"), which defaulted in 1983.

High-yield or "junk" bonds are bonds used for many purposes, including corporate acquisitions (such as the "corporate raids" you've heard about). Defaults in payment of high-yielding bonds are not uncommon. For this reason they are normally sold in mutual funds or unit investment trusts (see discussion below) so that the investor has the benefit of a diversified portfolio.

Credit risk is normally a very real risk in higher-yielding bonds, but in recent years it has rarely been as significant as market risk due to interest rate fluctuations — the risk that the bond's price will fall because of interest rate increases.

4. Commission and expense risk is a risk you seldom see mentioned in the financial press, but it is very real and can eat into your returns significantly.

Suppose I were your broker and I came to you at the beginning of 1987 and said, "You asked me to find you a safe investment that pays about 10 percent and I found one. Buying into this fund will cost you 6 percent of your money up front."

You might have been wise enough to reply: "That means that I only earn 4 percent in the first year [10 percent minus 6 percent]. I can get that in a passbook savings account."

I, as your broker, would answer: "But next year you'll get to keep the whole 10 percent." So, not knowing what else to do, you sign on. Now you are 6 percent in the hole. Some strategy.

Now it's the end of the year. You look up your fund in the paper, and it's lost 10 percent in value because interest rates have risen. Now you are 16 percent in the hole for taking my advice. Oh yes, you do have the 10 percent yield — but you have to pay taxes on it! If you are in the 28 percent bracket, you pay 2.8 percentage points of your yield in taxes. Now your losses total 18.8 percent (6.0 percent + 10.0 percent + 2.8 percent = 18.8 percent). The net "income" you've received is only 7.2 percent by the most generous calculation possible (10 percent − 2.8 percent = 7.2 percent).

Never ask a barber if you need a haircut.

A few hardy souls will argue: "My broker sold me a no-load bond fund." Try to redeem your shares and you will find the load. It is a "redemption fee" of 1 to 6 percent depending on how long you have been in this trap. The broker got paid up front by the fund manager.

If you had bought a no-load bond fund on your own, you could have sold your shares, taken the 10 percent loss as a tax deduction, and been only a little worse off than you started. But you'll lose big if you do that after paying a broker's commission.

As you can see, bonds can be a real can of worms.

A REAL CAN — MAKE THAT A CASE — OF WORMS

Let's talk briefly about some of the varieties of bonds and their individual problems.

Savings bonds. Yes, you could invest in **U.S. Savings Bonds**, and many do. Most U.S. Savings Bonds are sold through payroll savings plans, often at defense plants, where employees are pressured to do their patriotic duty and sign up. Many of those bonds are redeemed as soon as they are delivered. Who can blame the purchasers? These are ten-year bonds which must be held to maturity to produce maximum interest; redeem in less than five years and you get less than the guaranteed minimum rate (which is 6 percent or 85 percent of the average yield on five-year Treasury securities during the most recent five-year period — whichever is higher). These are the current rules; the rules change regularly.

Forget 'em. Savings bonds are for kids and patriotic financial fools. Stick with me. We will show them that richer patriots can be much more effective.

Municipal bonds. These are the highly popular tax-free bonds. All the warnings that apply to ordinary bonds also apply to municipal bonds: Buy only when interest rates are high and likely to fall; avoid broker commissions by buying no-load municipal bond funds; be willing to sell if interest rates begin to rise. Your tax bracket is a factor in determining whether municipal bonds may make sense for you; see table 9.1 on page 140.

Note, however, that municipal bonds also involve some special problems.

As a result of the Tax Reform Act of 1986, certain of the so-called tax-free bonds held by municipal bond funds have become subject to the alternative minimum tax. They are not tax-free as you thought. What is more, you cannot find out exactly what share of the income from a "tax-free" bond fund will be subject to the alternative minimum tax until the end of the tax year. The taxability of some portion of your profits could make a taxable fund a better deal for you.

The highly popular double and triple tax-free (state, local, and federal tax-free) mutual funds declined sharply in value as interest rates rose in 1987. This revealed that they were working in very thin markets. Many of these issues had been created in the expectation that mutual funds would buy and hold them to maturity. Suddenly funds had to sell to expedite redemptions. There were few buyers, so prices dropped far more than funds expected. The losses were shared by the shareholders who sought to redeem.

Zero-coupon bonds (and "target maturity" bond funds). Bonds that do not pay interest until a future maturity date are the latest fad investments. They are sold at a discount and pay off at a much higher value in the future. Investors are encouraged to use them in their IRAs and to invest for a far-off "target" like college tuition or retirement.

These bonds and the mutual funds that invest in them are worse than a can of worms. They are a can of snakes in ways that few anticipated, because they have proved to be among the most highly interest rate–sensitive funds ever created. This is particularly true of the longer-term ones. For example, Benham Target Maturity 2015, a no-load zero-coupon U.S. Treasury bond fund, lost 20 percent of its value in the week before the crash of October 1987 and gained a similar amount in the following week. Now that's volatility!

Because interest rates have fallen more quickly than they have risen in recent years, it is only a very lithe and courageous investor who can take advantage of profit opportunities in these highly volatile funds. Meanwhile, the dollar amount you'll need when your target arrives is difficult to forecast because inflation is unpredictable. Invest with great care.

BOND MUTUAL FUNDS: THE OKAY AND THE AWFUL

Two structural types of mutual funds invest in bonds: open-ended funds and unit investment trusts (UITs).

Open-ended bond mutual funds. These are the most popular types of bond mutual funds. They are managed portfolios, which means that as their bonds are sold or mature, they are replaced with other bonds. Because the fund stands ready to buy back shares from those who wish to redeem them, or to sell new shares to those who wish to invest, this type of bond investment never matures or pays back your investment unless you request it.

When brokers sell bonds, they like to gloss over the risks by assuring you that you'll get all your money back "at maturity." That does not hold true for a bond mutual fund. There is no "maturity," and the fund can lose money as long as interest rates rise. But a no-load open-ended bond mutual fund can be a good investment when interest rates are stable or declining.

Unit investment trusts. UITs are *un*managed mutual funds. The sponsor invests a fixed amount all at one time and then sells investors shares of the fixed fund, usually charging a big commission. As the fund's bond portfolio matures or its bonds are redeemed by the issuer, the proceeds are returned to the investor as a nontaxable "return of principal" and the investor assumes the responsibility of reinvesting the proceeds in some other investment. High broker commissions make unit investment trusts expensive to buy and even more expensive to sell. Don't touch them.

MARKET SPECIALS

Either of the above two structural types of bond funds can invest in plain government or corporate bonds, or in some specialty markets. The following specialty bond funds demand a few words:

Ginnie Mae funds. "Ginnie Mae" — what a sweet and gentle name. To many investors who have plowed billions into Ginnie Mae funds in recent years, the name is reminiscent of a kindly aunt who doles out double-digit yields backed by a federal government guarantee.

Well, Ginnie Mae is not a lady but is a corporate instrumentality of the federal government. It (she?) is GNMA, the Government National Mortgage Association, which buys mortgages from America's banks and thrift institutions, "pools" the mortgages, and then sells "participation certificates" to private investors, including mutual funds. GNMA guarantees the payment of interest and principal.

The government will not guarantee any protection, however, from the massive refinancing of mortgages that occurs when interest rates are at the bottom of one of their cycles. People like you and me take advantage of interest rate dips to pay off our existing mortgages and take out new ones at lower rates. For the Ginnie Mae investor, that means the promised "high yields" simply disappear. Ginnie Mae funds also have to write off the premiums they paid for the high-yielding mortgages. Thus investors lose part of the market value of their funds, since the value of the investments they bought must be written down as the refinancings occur.

Just when you think you have a nice high-yield investment, borrowers repay their mortgages and you have to figure out where to reinvest the money. If rates rise, however, borrowers will hang on to their relatively low-interest mortgages and the value of your investment will decline just like the value of any other long-term bond fund.

Very simply: Ginnie Maes are not the high-yielding, government-guaranteed, low-risk investments that brokers imply they are. Invest with care. Or avoid them entirely.

High-yield "junk" bond funds. Surprisingly, these funds' per-share prices have held up very well relative to U.S. government bond funds, Ginnie Mae funds, etc. A recession could break this type of bond fund out of the pack — it could be eaten alive by defaults. But many argue that over the long

term these junk bond funds more than repay the investor for
risks through higher yields.

You will feel much more comfortable holding these funds
if you have a "stop loss" trading strategy. That is, if you own
one of these funds, sell it at the first indication of a decline
in value (perhaps at a 2.5 percent loss), then buy back when
you see it has recovered 2.5 percent from its low. That way,
you can avoid the wildest swings by watching from the side-
lines.

To do this, you have to know when the fund pays its
dividends, because funds normally decline in price right after
the dividend distribution and you don't want to sell in reaction
to one of these normal declines.

If you own a loaded high-yield bond fund you bought
through your stockbroker, the broker will probably allow you
to shift commission-free from the bond fund to their money
fund and back.

International bond funds. These funds have been very
attractive in recent years, especially as a way to invest at
times when foreign bond rates are falling and the dollar is
falling against foreign currencies. You win both ways.

In 1987, T. Rowe Price International Bond Fund (one of
my favorites because it has traditionally maintained a more
conservative, shorter maturity than many of its peers) returned a total of 26 percent on each dollar invested! And that
was in a year of crash in the U.S. markets.

As with any type of bond fund, of course, if conditions
reverse themselves, you can lose money. In 1988 they did,
and we recommended our subscribers sell international bond
funds.

SOME FINAL THOUGHTS ABOUT BOND FUNDS: THE PRO, THE CON, AND THE BOTTOM LINE

The advantages of bond mutual funds are those of all mutual
funds: professional management, diversification, the ability
to buy fractional interests (you can invest any dollar amount
above the minimum in any fund), and the comfort of easy
liquidity.

The big disadvantage is the market risk: You can lose a significant amount of money in rising interest rate periods. Of course, you can lose money in stocks, too; but bonds just don't offer the same long-term upside potential as stocks.

Two types of creature mature faster than your bond investments: your children, who need money to go to college, and *you*, who need money to buy a new car or a new home, or to pay for emergency medical expenses. Most investors are more likely to sell at a loss than to be lucky enough to sell at a profit. Experience shows that interest rates rise over longer periods than they fall.

In my opinion, bonds are mediocre investments when interest rates are falling (stock funds will beat the pants off them in a falling interest rate market) and they are a *disaster* in a rising interest rate market (they lose money). Nonetheless, if you manage your portfolio in the ways shown in the next chapter, bonds can play a useful role. But don't tie — or let a broker tie — your whole financial future to a bunch of bonds.

WHAT HAVE WE LEARNED?

The story of bonds can be summarized simply:

1 When interest rates rise, bonds decline in value.
2 When interest rates rise, longer-term bonds decline in value more than shorter-term bonds.
3 Credit risk (the risk that you won't get your money back) is zero in government and insured bonds; but market risk (the risk that the price will decline when interest rates rise) is significant.
4 Credit risk can be very real in individual junk bonds and municipal bonds.
5 Paying a commission to a stockbroker does not guarantee that you will get good advice, only that you will pay an unnecessary commission.
6 Savings bonds are poor investments.
7 Municipal bonds are wholly or partially tax-free, but it may still be better to make a taxable investment.

8 Zero-coupon bonds are exceptionally volatile investments.

9 No-load bond mutual funds do not charge commissions.

10 Unit investment trusts are expensive to buy and even more expensive to sell.

11 Junk or high-yield bond funds and international bond funds can be useful. (More on junk bonds in the next chapter.)

8
THE *ONLY* SAFE WAYS TO INVEST IN BONDS

L et me restate my position on investing in bond funds using the buy, hold, and pray system (*buy* a bond fund, *hold* on for life, and *pray* your account will increase in value): **If you make only one decision in your life, don't make this one.**

Buying a bond fund to hold indefinitely is so dangerous that no intelligent investor should ever do it. First, you are likely to buy at the wrong time, and second, you are likely to sell at the wrong time.

Why are you likely to buy at the wrong time? Simply because that is when brokers sell the most bond funds. They can truthfully tout rising yields, but that is exactly the moment when bond funds are losing money for investors.

Why are you likely to sell at the wrong time? Because, as stated before, many bond investors will need their principal before they anticipated, and that is liable to mean cashing in when interest rates are high. (Of course, you can be hurt if you have to sell stocks when interest rates are high, too, but the stock market investor is usually better prepared for the risks he takes and more likely to pull his cash out before a disaster destroys his nest egg.)

If you want to put all your eggs in one basket, learn to love omelettes. An investor who makes just one big investment decision in his or her life is never properly prepared for that decision. Millions of investors thought they were making a safe decision investing in long-term bond funds in the past few years. Many of them lost money.

IS THERE ANY WAY TO INVEST IN BONDS WITH CONFIDENCE?

You've heard the bad news. Yet long-term bonds do produce higher returns, on average, than money market investments. Many people feel comfortable investing in bonds, and that comfort can be based on a realistic understanding of the facts. Bonds are seldom susceptible to the abrupt crashes the stock market occasionally suffers. And nearly all bonds eventually pay off at maturity or a call date.

How can you invest in bonds with confidence? You can start out by taking a minute, imagining looking at yourself in the mirror, and deciding clearly what you are trying to accomplish. (Don't close your eyes, of course. You will need them to read the book.)

YOU CAN ALWAYS GET WHAT YOU WANT — IF YOU KNOW WHAT IT IS

Ms. IncomeSeeker says, "I wanted a higher cash flow. I wanted to get a check a month." She wanted the check to replace a paycheck after retirement, to supplement another income, or whatever.

If that sounds like you, let us restate the problem: You want a predictable additional income. You want an investment that will provide reliable interest with safety, just like your bank savings account interest except at a higher rate.

Bonds cannot do that. Bond mutual funds will send you a dividend check every month or every quarter if you wish, but they cannot protect your principal like a bank account. The check may make you feel good, but you'll feel bad the next time you get a statement from the fund that shows a rise in interest rates has caused your account's value to *decline by more than the amount of the check.*

If you want a check a month, there are ways to get one with safety. But you have to take some action to **protect your principal yourself.**

Mr. AssetBuilder says, "I went into bond funds just because I thought I'd build wealth for my retirement more quickly in something that paid 10 percent interest than in something that paid 7 percent interest."

If you're like him, bond funds seem to make sense (though stock funds may make even more sense). But they have drawbacks. Aside from producing long-term returns inferior to those of stocks, bonds force you to accept currently taxable income. (Much of the profit from stock market investing will consist of capital gains, which are not taxable until either you sell the security or the mutual fund's trading activity forces the fund to declare the gains as "distributions.") Currently taxed income is anathema to wealth building. Finally, you still have to find a way to limit the market risk — i.e., the risk that bond funds will decline in value.

Still, with careful management, bonds can produce substantially more income over the long haul than bank accounts or money market investments.

HOW CAN YOU PROTECT YOUR PRINCIPAL?

If you are going to invest in bonds, you need a strategy to protect yourself when interest rate increases cause price declines. How can you protect your principal from the volatility of the bond market?

Very simply. You can sell your bond fund holdings when they are likely to decline significantly in value. You wait out the decline in a safe money market fund. Then you repurchase when bond prices are on the way up.

THE SIGNAL IS THE TRICK

To do this, you will use the very same Donoghue Interest Rate Signal that helps you enormously increase your returns in the stock market. Review the directions for tracking the Donoghue Interest Rate Signal in chapter 2. You will keep track of interest rate trends, and you'll change from long-term bond investments to risk-free money market investments when the trend shifts against you.

The significance of the Donoghue Interest Rate Signal arises from the fact that when interest rates develop a clear trend, more often than not *the trend continues for a while*. If the trend is up, it has a high probability of producing significant declines in the prices of bonds (and eventually, stocks). If the trend is down, it has a high probability of generating significant increases in the prices of bonds and stocks.

Let's look at how trading on the Donoghue Interest Rate Signal would have affected a program of bond fund investing over the last eight years. If you chose Fidelity Government Securities Fund, a mutual fund that invests in government bonds, and held it from January 1, 1980, to December 31, 1987, you would have achieved a total return of 132 percent, equivalent to about 11.1 percent per year compounded. Not bad, but only a little bit better than you could have achieved with a money market fund. (And your returns would have varied enormously depending on when you bought and when you sold. If you had bought in June instead of January of 1980, for instance, and sold that October, you would have *lost* 8 percent of your money.

If, however, you had watched the Donoghue Signal, you would have sold Fidelity Government Securities Fund early in all its major downward moves. You would have missed a little bit of some upward moves too, but all in all you would have made a total return of about 200 percent — about 14.7 percent a year.

You would have achieved *better* returns with vastly less risk! During all the most dangerous times to own bonds, you would have been invested in totally riskless money market funds.

About the only way you can lose big money with this system is if the bond market crashes dramatically in a few weeks, moving too fast to give you a signal. And that has never happened in the last fifty years. You can lose a few percent by missing the first part of a move, but the bulk of your funds will be safe.

WATCHING FOR THE DONOGHUE SIGNAL

As we showed in chapter 2, the Donoghue Signal is easy to use. Just follow the directions in chapter 2 to get the current Donoghue Signal Number and a free workbook. Then check the current 7-day average yield of taxable money funds from the Donoghue Money Market Funds table in your local newspaper, and calculate the Donoghue Signal Number (a 25-week moving average of the yield of taxable money funds) once a week.

Suppose you calculate the Donoghue Signal Number for three weeks. Suppose it is 6.25 percent, 6.21 percent, 6.20 percent. That tells you that interest rates show a falling trend and it's OK to be invested in long-term bonds.

(Hint: As a moving average, the Donoghue Signal Number will usually fall when the current week's Donoghue's Money Fund Average (DMFA) taxable 7-day average yield is *below* last week's moving average. The moving average will usually rise if the current week's DMFA taxable 7-day average yield is *above* last week's moving average.)

Interest rates can often rise a bit without triggering a "sell" signal from the Donoghue Signal Number. Suppose last week the DMFA taxable 7-day average yield was 6.10 percent and the Signal Number was 6.20 percent. This week, the DMFA taxable 7-day average yield rises to 6.18 percent. Leave your money in bonds. The Signal Number will be stable at approximately 6.20 percent. (A key function of a moving average like the Donoghue Signal Number is to keep you from panicking or making unnecessary moves because of minor variations within an overall trend.)

Now suppose that in the next week, the DMFA yield is 6.27, giving you a Signal Number of 6.20525, which rounds off to 6.21.

The Donoghue Signal Number has moved **up**. It's time to sell *all* of the bonds and bond mutual funds you own. Keep calculating the Donoghue Signal Number each week, and remain invested exclusively in money market mutual funds and other **short-term** investments until your calculations show the Signal Number is going **down**.

THE RIGHT NUMBER

You could also use moving averages of other interest rates as your "buy" and "sell" signals. Our research shows that they might also work. But Donoghue's Money Fund Averages are easier to obtain in a standard form each week than many other interest rates, and they are less volatile than most other rates, so they will give you good results with less trading.

Act immediately when a signal is generated. Don't pay any attention to economists' pronouncements on television. Bond market crashes often occur exactly when economists are most confident. Only by sticking with the system religiously can you minimize your risk and get the system's long-term benefits.

A FALSE SIGNAL

Now you've made your first trade, and your money is in money funds. Suppose the next week the DMFA taxable 7-day average yield is 6.13 percent. The Donoghue Signal Number will move back down to 6.204, which rounds off to 6.20. Interest rates have taken another turn downward. It's okay to buy back into the bond market fund of your choice.

You have just experienced a false signal. You may have to buy your bond fund back at a price slightly higher than the price at which you sold it. If so, you have been fooled — in the parlance of the trade, whipsawed.

Don't be dismayed. This will happen occasionally. Every two or three years the Donoghue Signal will tell you to buy one week and sell a few weeks later. After a while, the temptation is to second-guess the system. *Don't*. It will cost you in the long run.

WHERE DOES YOUR CASH FLOW COME FROM?

Now, suppose you are Ms. IncomeSeeker. You have thought about what I've said. You've recognized that you can't expect to utilize this system and live off the dividends that a bond fund sends every month. Where do you get the cash to live on?

The best way to create a regular, predictable cash flow is to reorganize your investment portfolio *as a whole*. As we discussed in chapter 6, you can set up a "systematic redemption" plan on one of your mutual fund accounts, so that the mutual fund family sends you a check every month. But that can produce complications when you switch funds.

So always keep some cash in a money fund. Use that account for your monthly withdrawals.

WRITE YOUR OWN DIVIDEND CHECK

Let's say you own just two investments, a bond fund and a money market fund.

1 Tell the bond fund managers to reinvest all of your dividends in the bond fund.
2 Establish check-writing privileges on your money fund. (Most money funds make this easy; just call the 800 telephone number of your money fund for details.)
3 Decide how much cash flow your investments can support over the long term and how large a cash flow you want to take.
4 Write your own budgeted check each month from the money fund.

If past trends continue, investing in bonds and money funds and switching based on the Donoghue Signal will probably produce returns in the 9 to 13 percent range over the long run. If you're a bond investor, you are conservative by nature, so you'll probably want to limit the cash you draw to 5 to 8 percent of your principal every year. That way, you can still expect your principal to increase a bit over time to compensate for inflation.

Thus if your total portfolio is worth, say, $100,000, you can confidently take $5,000 to $8,000 a year, which works out to checks of $420 to $670 each month.

(If you want to spend more than 8 percent of your principal every year, the best move is to invest some of your money in the stock market, where you can, over the long term, expect a higher return than in bonds and money market funds. See chapters 5 and 6.)

If you invest only in bonds and money funds, always keep at least 10 percent of your money in the money market fund on which you will write your monthly check. If the Donoghue Signal tells you to sell bonds, your money fund will be replenished. If the interest rate trend is down for a full year and you never have occasion to switch your assets from your bond fund to your money fund, your money fund will become depleted. But your bond fund will have increased significantly in value. So once a year, move money from the bond fund to the money fund.

Finally, if you're afraid of possessing a checkbook on which you could write a far larger check than you budgeted, you can still ask your mutual fund family to establish systematic redemption for your budgeted amount. See chapter 6 for details and pros and cons of this procedure.

WHAT KIND OF BOND FUND SHOULD YOU USE?

You can manage an investment in any bond fund as described above. Let's compare the results obtained with a few different funds, however.

"High-yield" funds, such as Fidelity High Income Fund, have traditionally produced the best yields using the Donoghue switching strategy. They not only start out with higher-yielding bonds, but they swing in price more widely and you benefit more from the switching strategy.

Of course, these are the high-yield funds investment professionals traditionally call "junk bond" investments (see chapter 7). The market is young and may not be as immune to sudden crashes as the market for higher-quality bonds. Nevertheless, I would put at least part of my bond portfolio in high-yield bond funds. Although some high-yield bonds may default, the higher yields of the bonds that do pay off will probably more than compensate.

Fund name and system used	Number of round-trips	Total return	Average annual return
Fidelity Government Securities			
Buy and hold	0	132.2%	11.12%
Follow Donoghue Signal	8	200.0%	14.72%
Dreyfus A Bonds Plus			
Buy and hold	0	146.7%	11.95%
Follow Donoghue Signal	8	208.7%	15.13%
Fidelity High Income			
Buy and hold	0	197.8%	14.62%
Follow Donoghue Signal	8	261.9%	17.44%
Fidelity High Yield Municipals (tax free)			
Buy and hold	0	94.7%	8.68%
Follow Donoghue Signal	8	161.6%	12.77%

All comparisons are for the eight years from January 1, 1980, through December 31, 1987.

Moreover, switching to money market funds following the Donoghue Interest Rate Signal will give you considerable protection. (Defaults are most common in periods of rising rates.) And you can add an extra layer of protection by also using the 2.5 percent stop-loss rule I discussed in the last chapter. In other words, sell your junk bond fund *either* if interest rates rise and trigger a Donoghue Interest Rate "sell" signal *or* if the price of the fund drops 2.5 percent from its high. Then buy again only when the Donoghue Interest Rate Signal is in a "buy" mode *and* the price of the bond fund has risen at least 2.5 percent from its low. If you follow these rules, then investing your *entire* bond portfolio in junk funds is not excessively risky.

WHAT ABOUT MY BROKER?

For those who have paid a commission to a broker as an "opportunity fee" to take advantage of his or her advice, I have good news (maybe). You need not end your brokerage relationship unless you want to. Most load fund groups offer unlimited free switching between money funds and bond funds. Few will charge you for the privilege of reinvesting in the bond fund when you've already paid the commission once.

The only necessary change of strategy if you're dealing with a load fund is that if there is a commission on dividend reinvestment, instead of having all your dividends automatically reinvested in the bond fund you may want the dividends paid to your money fund account.

On the other hand, if you're sick of loads and fees, you can make your next shift from your broker's funds into a no-load mutual fund family, where all of these issues are irrelevant. Just call up your broker and tell him you want him to send you a check.

CONCLUSIONS

A few clear conclusions turn bond investing from a dance with disaster into a waltz toward wealth:

1 The only safe way to invest in bonds is to trade them occasionally to avoid the risk of a big decline.
2 The Donoghue Interest Rate Signal provides an easy and generally profitable trading system.
3 The best way to get a regular cash flow from a portfolio that includes bond fund investments is to keep some money market investments in the portfolio, have the mutual fund company reinvest all distributions for you in your bond fund, and take your monthly cash flow from your money fund.
4 If you insist on investing in bond funds, reread this chapter until you fully understand it — it's worth your time and will probably buy you many a good night's sleep.

9
THE MONEY MARKET: THE ULTIMATE IN CRASHPROOF INVESTING

Let's face it. The stock market can earn you a lot of money, but it can and it does crash (at least once every fifty years). Long-term bond markets can crash, too — a bit more slowly, perhaps, but you can still lose a lot of money.

There has to be a safe harbor somewhere — and there is.

Wisely chosen money market investments never crash. Investors in money markets, both the consumer money market (which serves folks like you and me) and the "institutional" money market (for organizations that can invest $1 million at a shot) do not and should not tolerate risk.

When you understand the money market, moreover, you can squeeze significantly more return from it with little effort — while achieving maximum safety.

THE SAFE CRASHPROOF HARBOR

The Donoghue Signals will protect you from most investment risk, but that's not enough for some people. They want absolute safety. Others need a secure place to hide when indicators like the Donoghue Signals say, "Sell." The money market is the place.

THIS LITTLE DOLLAR
WENT TO MARKET

The money market is people lending money at interest to other people. Borrowers simply pay for the use of your money. They don't offer long-term interest rate guarantees, capital gains, or anything else — just free market fair returns.

If you play by the rules and keep your eyes open, you will not be asked to take risk. (If you are dealing with a bank or thrift institution, "playing by the rules" means never allowing your accounts to exceed $100,000 at any single bank or thrift institution and never depositing in any institution unless it is federally insured.)

Money market investors don't even risk losing money to inflation. All true money market investments must be repayable in a year or less. If inflation roars up, interest rates will rise, and so will returns in the money market. When inflation even threatens, money market rates rise to reflect those concerns.

Moreover, the money market differs from the bond market (where obligations can run for twenty or thirty years) in that, as we have noted, people are making very short-term (1-day to 365-day) loans. In the money market there is virtually no "market risk" from the danger that a higher interest rate will produce a lower price. Your money always comes back in full within a few months.

Nothing remains certain forever. More than eight hundred banks and savings and loan institutions have failed over the past few years. Those collapses have cost so much money that today the government's deposit insurance agencies cannot afford the costs of closing down "walking dead" institutions which should be out of business. So you have to keep awake to be sure that any investment — even insured deposits

— doesn't suddenly turn risky. Remember: No place for your money is so safe that it doesn't need to be watched.

IF I AM LENDING, WHO IS BORROWING?

When you deposit money in a bank you are, in effect, lending in the money market to your bank. The bank, in turn, lends your money out to others at a profit.

Sometimes consumers lend through middlemen — money market mutual funds and deposit brokers. These middlemen can often get you higher interest. A money market mutual fund lends to the largest corporations and banks and to agencies of the federal government. A broker places your deposit in a bank or savings and loan institution that offers a high rate, often in another part of the country.

Finally, consumers sometimes lend directly to the federal government. (These loans are called savings bonds, Treasury bills, or Treasury notes.)

CREDIT RISK SHOULD *NEVER* BE AN ISSUE IN THE MONEY MARKET...

The money market is a very exclusive club. Consumers should always deal exclusively with federally guaranteed, insured, or regulated money market institutions.

Securities and Exchange Commission (SEC) mutual fund regulations make money market mutual funds essentially as safe as banks. All investments by money market mutual funds must be kept in a bank trust department. No money fund manager has access to the investments, so no one can run off to South America with the money.

The SEC also regulates money funds' investment practices. No money fund has ever invested in anything that did not pay off as agreed at maturity.

... IF YOU WATCH OUT FOR THE FAKERS

If a deal in the money market looks too good, however, it just may be too good. The exclusivity of the money market club occasionally tempts those who can't get in to stretch the truth a bit.

I am constantly amazed, especially in traveling in the Midwest, to read ads for finance companies and other non-banks offering CD-like accounts. These are just companies' unsecured IOUs — uninsured, uncollateralized, and unsafe.

Folks, if it is not a federally insured bank or thrift institution, or a money fund regulated by the SEC, or a genuine obligation of the federal government such as a Treasury bill, don't touch it. Never take the risks of a fake money market instrument just to receive 1 or 2 percent more than money market rates.

And note that we said *federally* insured. *State* insurance of a savings and loan institution is almost as bad as no insurance at all. The only reason an institution would choose state insurance rather than federal insurance is that for some reason it does not qualify for federal insurance. If you doubt my advice, ask the folks who invested in state-insured savings and loan associations in Ohio and Maryland and state-insured banks in California. There are even a few *uninsured* credit unions still around. Avoid them!

WHAT ARE OUR CHOICES — ONES THAT MAKE SENSE?

Understanding your choices can make a big difference in yield in the money market. Frequently the yields offered by the best money market opportunities exceed the worst so-called "money market rates" by more than the difference between the worst "money market rates" and old-fashioned passbook savings accounts. (And as you now know, "investing" in a passbook savings account is almost as bad as putting money in a mattress.)

USE THE BEST AT YOUR LOCAL BANK

Local banks and thrift institutions offer the most convenient money market investments. Their three most popular investment programs are:

1 Money market deposit accounts (MMDAs),
2 Six-month certificates of deposit (six-month CDs), and
3 One-year certificates of deposit (twelve-month CDs).

Money market deposit accounts

Federally insured money market deposit accounts are banks' answer to real money funds. They often require fairly high ($1,000–$2,500) minimum balances, but they are insured to $100,000 per person per bank. You can generally write up to three checks each month. If you want safety, liquidity, and yield and federal deposit insurance, this is your choice. Money market accounts are best used, however, as a "parking place" between certificates of deposit.

Banks often call these accounts by confusing names, so be sure that the account you open is what you think it is. (One Maryland bank called an account an "Insured Silver Money Fund" when it was not related to silver, not a money fund, and barely fully insured.)

Look for accounts that pay returns comparable to those of good money market mutual funds. (Check Donoghue's Money Market Funds table in your newspaper.) Never invest in a money market account that yields less than Donoghue's Money Fund Average.

When bankers say money market deposit accounts pay "money market rates," however, they usually seem to be at least half joking. The rates on money market deposit accounts are set by the bank; they can change daily and, as you will see, are usually about half a percent or more under the rate on real money funds.

As I write this, really broad-based money funds are paying 28 percent higher returns than bank money market deposits.

 **MONEY MARKET DEPOSIT ACCOUNTS**

Advantages

1. MMDAs are the only bank accounts that usually offer safety, liquidity, and money market yields.
2. They are insured and easily accessible.
3. If you regularly buy certificates of deposit or Treasury bills from a bank, keeping your liquid funds in its money market deposit account will put all your accounts conveniently at the same bank.

Disadvantages

1. These accounts usually earn less than real money market mutual funds — usually 50 to 80 basis points (hundredths of a percentage point) less. For example, if money funds are paying 6.80 percent, the banks are paying 6.00 percent.
2. A money market deposit account will usually allow only three checks a month, while many money market mutual funds will allow an unlimited number.

Certificates of deposit

Certificates of deposit are your bank's other most popular investment choice. The six- and twelve-month maturities are most widely sold, but if you need your CD to mature in, say, eight months and thirteen days, your banker should be able to accommodate you.

CDs carry, of course, those ever-unpopular "substantial penalties for early withdrawal." The bank can set the penalties pretty much at will. And while the bank probably has a well-defined policy, the officer you meet at your branch is not required to know what it is.

Consider twelve-month (and longer) certificates of deposit when interest rates are declining. Stick with shorter-term CDs

⇨ **BANK CDs**

Advantages

1. You know exactly how much you will earn and when you will get it.
2. CDs are federally insured to $100,000 per bank per person.
3. There are no sales charges.
4. CDs are available in any amount.

Disadvantages

1. If rates go up, you have locked in a low yield for the term of the CD.
2. You are committed to the bank CD until it matures, so if rates go down, you cannot sell at a profit as you could a CD purchased from a broker.
3. If you find out later that a higher yield is available elsewhere, you will have to find some other money to take advantage of it. Your CD money is not going anywhere else, at least before its time.

and money market accounts when there is a danger that rates may rise. (More on that in the next chapter.)

Invest in the best and forget about the rest

Do not invest your money in any bank account other than an MMDA or a short-term CD.

Ordinary savings accounts are an out-and-out ripoff. As I write this, they average only 4.8 percent nationally; and many require minimums below which the banks will charge all kinds of fees for deposits, withdrawals, and even mere account maintenance. (Consumers are losing $50 million *a day* in interest just by leaving cash in passbook savings and other liquid bank savings accounts instead of using broadly based money funds.) Christmas clubs are another — and even poorer — version of this old-fashioned account, but they frequently pay no interest at all.

Long-term bank CDs (bank certificates of deposit with terms of over one year) are rarely worthwhile. Below, I'll discuss a way to get a better deal on this kind of investment than your local bank is likely to offer.

"Specialty CDs" are the latest fad. You can buy "Stock Market CDs" and "Gold CDs" whose returns are tied to stock and gold price movements. These make no sense for investors who understand no-load mutual funds, however. CDs will rarely offer a return comparable to a mutual fund's if prices rise, and they give you no chance to get out if prices start to fall.

In some areas you can even buy a CD that will pay you a bonus if the local baseball team makes it to the division playoff. This is just a form of gambling. If you want to bet on baseball games, stick with your bookie.

MONEY MARKET MUTUAL FUNDS — THE ORIGINAL FAIR DEAL AND THE STANDARD FOR ALL TO SEE

The standard of excellence in the consumer money market is a well-run money market mutual fund (money fund, for short). Nearly every mutual fund family and every stockbroker offers a money fund.

Money funds have been around since 1970 and have an unblemished track record for safety, liquidity, and competitive yields. Their returns are determined by the earnings on their portfolios.

Perhaps the best part of the deal is that managers obtain high yields while taking only 0.7 percent, on average, of the funds' assets per year in management fees.

Money funds are not insured as are money market deposit accounts, but while eight hundred banks and savings and loans have failed since 1982, no money fund has ever failed or is ever likely to fail. Federal regulations have worked better to preserve investors' money in money funds than federal insurance has worked in banking. In any case, *no one has ever lost money in either a money market fund or a federally insured money market deposit account of $100,000 or less.*

The chance of losing even one dollar of a $1,000 money

⇨ **MONEY FUNDS**   *Advantages*

1. They offer the best combination of safety (a perfect track record while eight hundred banks have failed), liquidity (ready when you are), and yield (as I write this, 1.74 percent over banks' MMDAs).
2. They are easy to shift from if you want to invest in another, related mutual fund.

Disadvantages

1. You do not know exactly how much you will earn. (But if interest rates are rising you will probably earn more than a bank CD would offer, and if they are falling, you will of course be off elsewhere making a killing in bonds or stocks.)

market fund deposit is probably one in one hundred thousand. It may be less than that. It has never happened. So why give up 1 percent or more in interest to invest in a bank money market account? *That would be like paying an insurance premium of one hundred thousand times the risk!*

And as we have noted, money funds can offer benefits that money market deposit accounts do not. Some even offer unlimited free checking privileges, and most offer free wiring of money to a bank account, and convenient access to other investments in a mutual fund family.

YOU CAN EARN TAX-FREE RETURNS AS WELL

Tax-free money funds are an exciting development of the 1980s. These funds operate much like taxable money market funds, but they invest in short-term money market instruments issued by municipalities, state governments, and government authorities. The interest payments are exempt from federal income tax.

You can decide whether a tax-free money market fund makes sense for you by converting a tax-free money fund's yield to its "taxable equivalent." You do this by multiplying the tax-free fund's yield by a factor derived from your tax bracket and then you can compare it with a taxable alternative. If you are in the 28 percent federal tax bracket and the investment you are considering is not exempt from your state's taxes, for instance, the conversion multiplier is 1.389. If you are in the 33 percent federal tax bracket, the conversion multiplier is 1.493.

In several states with high state income taxes, such as New York, California, and Massachusetts, double tax-free money funds have been offered. These funds invest in in-state tax-exempt instruments, so their income is exempt from state taxes as well.

Triple tax-free money funds are available to New York City residents. These invest in New York City tax-exempt issues and are triple exempt from state, local, and federal taxes.

Table 9.1 will help you compare taxable and state tax-free yields based on your federal tax bracket.

BROKERED CDs: STOCKBROKERS OUTDO THE BANKS AT THEIR OWN GAME

When sold through a stockbroker, bank and thrift institutions' certificates of deposit are called "brokered CDs." They are insured just as if the bank or thrift institution had sold them to you directly, and of course, their interest is fully taxable.

Merrill Lynch Money Market Instruments Inc. helps federally insured banks and thrift institutions develop a truly national base for their business. When an institution has a special need for money, Merrill Lynch will market its CDs nationwide. Many local brokerage firms can sell these CDs to you, and discount brokers may even be able to get them for you at a lower commission. But Merrill Lynch is the major

⇨ **TAX-FREE MONEY FUNDS**

Advantages

1. Income is exempt from federal income tax, and some funds offer returns exempt from specific state and local taxes.
2. All of the same benefits of money market mutual funds.

Disadvantages

1. Low yields. Unless you are in a high tax bracket you may earn less than you would after paying taxes on your taxable money fund.
2. Unless you are in a high tax bracket and/or live in a state with a high state income tax, such as California, New York, etc., you may be better off most of the time in a taxable money fund. Invest with care.

broker — the firm that pioneered the market and that works directly with most of the banks who participate.

The differences between brokered CDs and regular CDs are that:

▶ The broker has to convince the bank or thrift institution to offer a highly competitive rate so the CDs will be saleable, and

▶ Merrill Lynch maintains a "secondary market" for the CDs. Other brokers do not necessarily do so. A secondary market means that if you wish to redeem your CD before maturity, you can go to the broker and he will buy it back at today's market value.

Most brokered CDs have longer maturities than those at your local bank. Maturities range from six months to ten years, and certificates with maturities of more than one year

TABLE 9.1 *Is tax-exempt investing for you?*

Special mutual funds provide income free of both federal and state taxes for the residents of some states. Here is how to decide whether you should utilize these funds. (1) Find out how much they yield by calling their managers (double tax-free money market funds appear in appendix 3; for information about tax-free bond funds, consult a publication such as *Donoghue's Mutual Fund Almanac*). (2) Multiply the double tax-free fund's yield by the appropriate factor, below. (3) The result is the amount that a comparable taxable investment would have to yield to produce the same after-tax income. Don't forget, however, that while tax-exempt *money market* funds involve little risk, investors in tax-exempt *bond* funds face all the risks of bond funds outlined in chapter 7.

If an investment is not exempt from your state's taxes, it makes no difference where you live: If you are in the 28 percent bracket, the conversion multiplier is 1.389. If you are in the 33 percent bracket, the conversion multiplier is 1.493.

	Conversion factors			Conversion factors	
	28% federal tax bracket	33% federal tax bracket		28% federal tax bracket	33% federal tax bracket
Arizona	1.513	1.626	Minnesota	1.510	1.631
California	1.513	1.646	New York	1.550	1.665
Colorado	1.458	1.567	North Carolina	1.493	1.605
Connecticut	1.578	1.696	Ohio	1.492	1.603
Delaware	1.505	1.617	Oregon	1.526	1.640
Florida*	1.389	1.493	Pennsylvania	1.419	1.525
Georgia	1.472	1.582	South Carolina	1.493	1.605
Kentucky	1.479	1.590	Tennessee	1.478	1.588
Maryland	1.502	1.614	Texas*	1.389	1.493
Massachusetts	1.543	1.658	Virginia	1.474	1.584
Michigan	1.511	1.624	West Virginia	1.485	1.596

* Florida and Texas do not levy income taxes; however, tax-free securities issued in those states may produce other benefits on state and local personal property or other taxes.
Source: E. F. Hutton. Information correct as of 1988.

⇨ **BROKERED CDs** · *Advantages*

1. Competitive yields above national averages for similar investments.
2. You can choose from many federally insured institutions screened for credit quality by the research department of a major firm, such as Merrill Lynch.
3. Very long maturities are available (five to ten years), which increases the profit potential of buying when interest rates are declining.

Disadvantages

1. Maturities may be longer than you might prefer. Brokered CDs carry significant market risk if they are bought at the bottom of an interest rate cycle and a need arises to sell (at a loss) in a higher interest rate environment.

make up the majority. Longer-term certificates possess the risks of short or intermediate-term bonds, discussed in chapter 7. But because brokers try to help you sell certificates when you desire, even a certificate with a maturity of more than one year can be a sensible choice for some of the cash you would otherwise invest in the money market. Just remember to avoid long maturities when interest rates are rising.

If rates fall after your CD is issued, you will make a profit when you sell. That is a lot better than the "substantial penalties for early withdrawal" the bank itself will impose. If rates have risen, your loss will still probably be less than a bank would charge in penalties.

There is no absolute guarantee of a secondary market.

But Merrill Lynch, the biggest player, assures me that to date it has always been able to find a buyer.

ASSET MANAGEMENT ACCOUNTS: WORTH CONSIDERING

Central asset management accounts (or "cash management accounts") like Merrill Lynch's Cash Management Account, Charles Schwab & Co.'s Schwab One, and Fidelity's USA Account provide a convenient way of keeping track of a large portion of your assets and maximizing your money market returns. (See appendix 9 for some details of top cash management accounts.)

An asset management account is not itself an investment, but rather a convenient one-statement accounting of all the investments you've made through a particular brokerage firm. Any free cash will be "swept" into the money market fund periodically, usually weekly, so you'll never lose interest. Many brokers charge no fee for maintaining an asset management account if you have a minimum amount of cash or securities on deposit. You also receive unlimited free check-writing privileges.

Be careful about establishing an asset management account with a full-service broker, however. The more assets the broker knows you have, the more telephone calls you'll receive advocating "great opportunities," which are mainly opportunities to generate commission revenue for the broker. Learn to say no gently but firmly. Why pay someone to sell you something when you know how to buy?

AT YOUR LOCAL FEDERAL RESERVE (OR EVEN THROUGH YOUR BANK OR BROKER)

The "full faith and credit" of the U.S. government, the highest guarantee of repayment on the face of the earth, backs U.S. government Treasury bills. In addition, Treasury bills often pay higher interest than bank certificates of deposit or money market deposit accounts, and they are exempt from state and local income taxes. The government issues three-month

T-bills due in 91 days, six-month T-bills due in 182 days, and twelve-month T-bills due in 364 days.

Treasury bill investing doesn't offer the flexibility of investing in bank accounts or money market funds. They come in $10,000 minimums and $5,000 increments. (You can buy one that will mature at $10,000 or $15,000 but not one that will mature at $12,000.) So you must figure out where you want to invest any extra odd amounts.

There are two ways to buy Treasury bills, directly from the Federal Reserve or indirectly through your stockbroker or bank.

You buy Treasury bills at auction at the Federal Reserve bank in your district every Monday. Don't get excited; you don't have to stand around and shout out bids. As a private citizen you have to put up your money first. You go to your local Federal Reserve bank, tell them you want to make a "noncompetitive" bid, and give them cash or a certified check for $10,000 or a higher multiple of $5,000. You will pay the average price of all bills sold that week — which will be less than the T-bill's face value — and the bank will return you your change the week after.

Treasury bills are sold "at discount." That is, you pay the auction price and they mature at $10,000 or some other multiple of $5,000. The interest rates quoted on Treasury bills are "discount rates," and if you are comparing them to bank CDs or money fund interest rates, you must find out the "annualized yield" and compare it with the bank's "annual effective yield."

For example, a 12-percent discount rate means that you can buy a $10,000 twelve-month T-bill at $8,800 (or 12 percent less than the face value). Your return will be 13.64 percent ($1,200 divided by $8,800), and the real annualized yield will be 13.69 percent, since twelve-month T-bills are for 364 days and a full year is 365 days. (Forget about leap years, for now.) Confusing, isn't it? A broker or bank can help you with the annualized yield calculation, however.

One of the advantages of T-bill investing is that you can sell your T-bill before maturity if you wish. If you think you might want to do that, buy through a bank or broker, since

⇨ **T-BILLS**

Advantages

1. You know exactly how much you will get at maturity and when that will be.
2. Repayment is guaranteed by the federal government.
3. You lock in a yield. If rates go down, you may be able to sell at a profit.

Disadvantages

1. You must invest in $10,000 minimums and $5,000 increments. If you buy directly from a Federal Reserve bank, you will get back part of that money (your change) after the auction. You must find a place to invest that difference.
2. A locked-in yield means that if rates go up, you are committed to the lower yield.

that will make the T-bill easier to sell. (It will be registered in the bank's or broker's name.) Buying through a bank or broker could cost you $25 to $50 per transaction — but this is a fee that is well worthwhile if you think you may need their services in selling.

If you do business directly with a Federal Reserve bank, and many people do, plan on holding each bill to maturity, and figure out what to do with the uninvestable excess over the auction price.

IN SUMMARY

When we survey the money market (fixed-income investments with maturities of one year or less), we find eight investments around which we can form investment strategies.

Our investment "hit list" is as follows:

► Money market deposit accounts
► Six-month CDs
► Twelve-month CDs
► Money funds
► Tax-free money funds
► Brokered CDs
► Three-month T-bills
► Six-month T-bills
► Twelve-month T-bills

Now we need to formulate strategies to earn high, safe returns.

10
THE THREE BEST MONEY MARKET INVESTMENT STRATEGIES

Now that you understand the best and most convenient money market instruments, you are halfway to becoming a savvy money market investor.

If you're serious about low-risk money market investing, your goal should be to develop a strategy that will reduce the small risks that do exist, maximize liquidity, and yet increase — dramatically — the yield from your money market investments.

"Why do I need a strategy to invest in the money market?"

People ask me that question *a lot*. I think it has never occurred to them that they have a choice in money market investments or that their decisions could make a difference in their lives.

Bankers and brokers, who sell most money market investments, obviously focus on selling only what their institutions offer. It pays to remember that you do have choices and to know some commonsense strategic rules for money market investing.

THE WORST ARE REALLY BAD AND THE BEST ARE REALLY BETTER

The differences between the yields of the worst money market investments and the yield of a coherent program of money market investing can be 2 or 3 percent a year or more. If that doesn't sound like much to you, remember that in a 6 percent money market, that can be a 33 to 50 percent greater interest check.

Long-term investors: Consider how much an additional 3 percent can give you if you allow it to compound for you. Over ten years, for example, $10,000 invested at 6 percent a year will turn into $17,908. That increase probably won't keep up with inflation and taxes.

But a 9 percent yearly return will produce $23,674, an extra profit of $5,766 over that same decade. That amounts to 73 percent more interest. A little goes a long way.

WHAT ARE THE BASIC RULES OF THUMB FOR MONEY MARKET INVESTING?

Every investor should keep some cash in the money market part of the time. So you should understand the following basic rules of money market investing.

1 Always compare alternative money market investments before you invest. The facts are easy to find. The tables in the newspapers will tell you a good deal — if not in your local paper, then in *Barron's*, the national financial weekly. If these are virtually no-risk investments, why shouldn't you get the highest yield?

2 When interest rates are **rising**, invest in the shortest-term investments, such as money market mutual funds. (Then you will see your returns rise with the tide.)

3 When interest rates are **falling**, money that stays in the money market should be invested in longer-term money

market investments such as six- or twelve-month certificates of deposit and Treasury bills. That way, you will
"lock in" today's rates for the term of the investment.
(You should, of course, also consider investing where the
real profits are, in the stock or bond markets, when the
interest rate trend is down.)

4 When you know which way interest rates are moving, you
can make the right choice at the right time.

5 When you do not know which way interest rates are
moving, you are better off staying liquid (i.e., keeping
much of your money in money market funds).

6 Never take unnecessary risks in the money market at any
time for any reason.

WHAT DO YOU LOOK FOR WHEN YOU DEVELOP A MONEY MARKET INVESTING STRATEGY?

Different kinds of investors will choose different strategies.
But it's important to **think** about your money market investments. Then you can avoid tying up your money, taking
unnecessary risk, and discovering unpleasant surprises about
the investment you chose. You should look for the same
things that you seek when you develop any other investment
strategy: How safe is the strategy? How big a risk is it if I
am wrong? How easily can I get out of the investment if the
market turns on me? How much additional yield will I earn?
And how convenient is each alternative?

We call this the SLYC analysis. In the money market,
SLYC stands for Safety, Liquidity, Yield, and Convenience
and is pronounced "Slick."

THE BEST SOURCE FOR MONEY MARKET INFORMATION

Your most basic source of money market information, as
explained in chapter 2, will be Donoghue's Money Market
Funds table, which appears every week in most major re-
gional newspapers (usually on Thursday, Friday, Saturday, or

Sunday). Even the Federal Reserve Board consults our data base every week. (See appendix 8 for a list of newspapers that carry it.) You can choose a few top performing funds from the list in appendix 3, watch the Money Market Funds table in your newspaper for a few weeks to choose the fund with the best current performance, then call its 800 telephone number, always available from Information: 1-800-555-1212. Or you can use the Money Market Funds table to monitor the performance of a fund you already own.

THE INSIDE SCOOP ON INTEREST RATES

As we've noted, you can forecast interest rates by looking at the real world as indicated by the Donoghue Signals.

The Donoghue Average Maturity Signal indicates what "the smart money on Wall Street" really believes when money managers put the funds entrusted to them on the line. We must look at what they **do** and **not** at what they **say**.

As we noted in chapter 2, Donoghue's Money Market Funds table not only includes the recent yields of both taxable and tax-exempt money market funds, it also lists the "average maturity" of the securities these funds hold. The average maturity tells you what the Wall Street professionals who manage these funds think about future interest rates.

When they expect interest rates to rise, they will buy very short-term investments, and the average maturity of their portfolios will often be 30 days or less. Often they will invest only overnight. Then as rates begin to fall, they shift to longer-term investments to lock in today's rates, and the average maturity of their portfolios moves up toward 50 days.

Sometimes they have jumped the gun, but on the average they are pretty savvy. Our research has shown that if you follow their lead, you'll do better most of the time.

MONEY MARKET STRATEGY #1 — THE LAZY PERSON'S STRATEGY

You'll invest most successfully if you work at it, and I ask only ten minutes a week. But if you don't want to work at money market investing, you can adopt my "lazy person's strategy."

The lazy person's strategy is: Pick a money market mutual fund that has consistently performed well over a period of twelve months or more and leave your money in it.

Why not leave your money in a bank that offers a comparable return? First of all, banks paying competitive rates are hard to find. But even if you find one, a bank money market account is a bad investment for a lazy person. Banks must be constantly watched. The bank controls how much it will pay on its "money market accounts," and for as long as money market accounts have existed, banks have tended to pay as little as they could and to sneak in hidden fees when they thought no one was watching.

Money market funds, on the other hand, pay you all the income your money earns minus a small management fee proportional to the amount invested (generally in the range of 0.7 percent of your money per year). All yields are quoted with the fee already deducted.

Generally, the fund managers can't quickly change their fee even if they want to. The only way the managers increase their own earnings is to attract more investors to the fund. Attracting new investors, in turn, depends on achieving a good return.

Therefore this year's top-ten money fund is often next year's winner as well. Once a fund's management develops a good investment strategy, investors' money comes in. The fund achieves economies of scale and its managers can actually charge a lower percentage fee than the managers of less successful (and therefore smaller) funds. A fine example of this virtuous cycle is Kemper Money Market Fund, which has been a top-ten fund for over a decade. Kemper's Cash Equivalent Fund is another excellent example. For the past two-and-a-half years, Vanguard Money Market Reserves' Prime Portfolio and Flex-Fund Money Funds have been consistent yield leaders as well.

Thus, choose a fund that has shown a high yield for at least a year or so, and you're likely to achieve better-than-average returns over the long term.

MONEY MARKET STRATEGY #2 — THE CLEVER PERSON'S STRATEGY

Many money market investors aren't satisfied with better-than-average returns, however. They want to achieve excellent returns.

The best way to do that is by switching your money occasionally as interest rates rise and fall between *short-term money market investments* (such as money market mutual funds) and *longer-term money market investments* (such as six- or twelve-month certificates of deposit). Bond mutual funds and CDs due in more than a year can also be added to the mix when you "go long."

To execute this strategy, you closely watch an indicator such as the Donoghue Average Maturity Signal — the average maturity of money market mutual funds as shown in Donoghue's Money Market Funds table.

When the average maturity is **more than 40 days**, money market fund managers are locking in the high yields of longer-term securities because they expect interest rates to remain stable or decline. That benefits you.

But money market fund managers can't give you as much benefit from the higher rates on longer-term securities as you would like. They are not permitted to move to longer-term investments such as bonds because these investments violate two money market rules: They lock up money for a long time and they have too much market risk. If you want to take advantage of long-term investments in a falling rate environment, you have to do it yourself.

If you don't need your money in the next three months, you can invest it in something longer-term and lock in returns that are likely to be higher than those money fund managers will achieve. Certificates of deposit and Treasury bills are typical examples (see chapter 9).

Let's review the implications of the Average Maturity Signal for you, the clever money market investor. First, when the average maturity of money market funds is stable (or rising) at **more than 45 days**, fund managers are convinced that interest rates are stable or falling. It is worthwhile to buy certificates of deposit that mature one year or more in the future. This would be a good time to invest in a longer-term brokered CD through Merrill Lynch. If you buy a longer-term, say five-year, CD, then when interest rates threaten to rise again, you can sell the CD back to the broker, usually at a profit.

When the average maturity of money market funds is **between 40 and 45 days**, money managers are investing in longer-term securities, but they still see some danger that rates may rise. It is safe to buy certificates of deposit, but wise to limit yourself mainly to certificates that mature in six months or less.

An average maturity of **less than 40 days**, moreover, is a danger signal. Portfolio managers are seriously concerned that interest rates may rise. Consider keeping all your money in money market accounts and money market funds **unless you have evidence that interest rates have begun to fall**.

Recognizing when interest rates have begun to fall

The best indicator of whether interest rates have begun to fall is the Donoghue Interest Rate Signal (see chapter 2). However, if you haven't been keeping track of the Donoghue Interest Rate Signal, you can still obtain a clear enough idea of interest rate trends to decide when to lock in a high CD yield. If the average maturity in the Money Market Funds table is 40 days or more, you can always feel confident in buying a certificate of deposit.

If the average maturity is less than 40 days, watch the Money Market Funds table for about four weeks.

If the smart money believes interest rates have turned around, the average maturity will rise. Leave your money in a short-term investment **until you see the average maturity rise at least three days above its most recent low**.

For example, if you checked the average maturity in the newspaper a few weeks before your certificate of deposit matured and it was 32 days, that would warn you to be cautious in renewing.

If the average maturity remained steady at 32 days until

your certificate matured (or if the average maturity declined to 30 days), you should put your money in a money market deposit account, or better yet a money fund. If, however, it increased to 35 days, you would conclude that interest rates were probably falling again, and you could buy another certificate of deposit.

Before buying a longer-term CD

If the average maturity is over 45 days and you want to buy a 12-month (or longer) certificate of deposit, you should also watch the Money Market Funds table each week for about four weeks.

It's okay to buy a one-year or longer certificate of deposit if the average maturity is 45 days or more and if, over a period of at least four weeks, the average maturity either shows continued increases or declines by no more than one day. If, however, the average maturity declines by two or more days in a period of four weeks, interest rates may be rising somewhat, and you're better off tying your money up for no more than six months.

A strategy for all seasons

Let's recapitulate our strategy:

If the money fund average maturity (the Donoghue Average Maturity Signal) is:

Over 46 days		Buy a one-year or six-month certificate of deposit
46 days		Buy a one-year or six-month certificate of deposit
45 days		Buy a six-month certificate of deposit
44 days		,, ,, ,, ,, ,, ,, ,,
43 days		,, ,, ,, ,, ,, ,, ,,
42 days		,, ,, ,, ,, ,, ,, ,,
41 days		,, ,, ,, ,, ,, ,, ,,
40 days		,, ,, ,, ,, ,, ,, ,,
39 days	**Danger!**	Stay liquid till evidence shows rates are falling
38 days		,, ,, ,, ,, ,, ,, ,, ,,
37 days		,, ,, ,, ,, ,, ,, ,, ,,
36 days		,, ,, ,, ,, ,, ,, ,, ,,
35 days		,, ,, ,, ,, ,, ,, ,, ,,
34 days		,, ,, ,, ,, ,, ,, ,, ,,
33 days		,, ,, ,, ,, ,, ,, ,, ,,

32 days	Stay liquid till evidence shows rates are falling
31 days	" " " " " " " "
30 days	" " " " " " " "
Less than 30 days	" " " " " " " "

MONEY MARKET STRATEGY #3 — THE RICH PERSON'S STRATEGY

Are you in a tax bracket where the IRS would take much of your money market returns? Then consider tax-exempt money market funds.

First, look over your income tax return or consult your tax preparer to determine your federal tax bracket. You won't benefit from any tax-free fund unless your federal tax bracket is at least 28 percent.

As mentioned in chapter 9, if you live in a high state income tax state like Massachusetts, New York, or California, you should check out a double tax-free money market fund to see if it is paying high enough yields to make it worth your while. Don't confuse double tax-free *bond* funds with double tax-free *money market* funds, however. Double tax-free money funds invest in short-term securities issued in your state and present no risk of price declines if interest rates rise. Double tax-free bond funds generally pay higher rates, but they invest in longer-term securities and suffer from all the market risks of ordinary bond funds outlined in chapter 7. In some states, tax-free bond funds are available but tax-free money funds are not.

Remember, moreover, that just because a fund is exempt from state and federal taxes does not mean that you will make more money in that fund than from a fully taxable fund after paying taxes. Multiply the yield you can get from the fund by the factor in table 9.1 to determine the "taxable equivalent yield."

When the Donoghue Average Maturity Signal exceeds 40 days, consider investing in tax-free bond funds. (But only after reading chapters 7 and 8 on bond investing.) Note, however, that any extra profits you make because the price of tax-exempt municipal bond funds rises will be *taxable* capital gains.

11
THE BEST RETIREMENT SAVINGS STRATEGIES

The greatest investment secret in America is right beneath your nose: the self-directed, tax-sheltered retirement programs available to you and your employer. These investment tools can take your annual contribution of a couple of thousand dollars and multiply it a hundredfold or more.

In this chapter I'll show you some new ideas about retirement accounts. Sadly, people take them for granted. They shy away from them if, for example, the government refuses to allow them to deduct their investment. But after all, who ever heard of a tax-deductible investment before IRAs were introduced? Don't be too blasé and spoiled to appreciate these exciting opportunities.

THE GLORIES OF SELF-DIRECTED RETIREMENT INVESTING

Uncle Sam offers a great variety of tax-sheltered retirement programs. Individual Retirement Accounts (IRAs) are for everyone; 401(k) savings programs require employer sponsorship; Keogh plans benefit the self-employed; 403(b) programs help teachers and other employees of nonprofit organizations. And traditional pension programs are available for large organizations.

If you are selecting an employer and one of your criteria is retirement programs, I would suggest you look for **self-directed** programs with enough choices to make the Donoghue strategies, especially the Donoghue Stock Market Strategy, work.

A self-directed retirement program is a plan in which *you* choose how your money will be invested. Self-directed plans include most 401(k) retirement savings plans, some 403(b) nonprofit organization savings plans, all IRAs and all Keogh plans.

THE PAIN OF BUREAUCRATIC MONEY MANGLERS

No bureaucracy will manage your money better than you yourself, especially if you practice the strategies in this book.

Some people seek employers with traditional company-funded pension programs. As recently as a decade ago, that strategy might have made sense: Big organizations often provided good benefits. But programs were often structured to provide a far better deal for the top managers (the guys who chose the pension consultants) than for ordinary people. In other cases, programs that looked good at first wound up leaving employees in near poverty after retirement as inflation eroded benefit checks.

The economic shocks of the 1970s and 1980s have left everyone more cautious and careful, and big organizations' bosses are no exception. They've cut back on commitments to today's employees. And institutionally managed pension programs *can't* produce the returns that a self-directed retirement program can produce. Even smart pension managers must worry more about meeting government regulations than about maximum performance. So don't expect a cornucopia from an employer-paid pension plan today.

A "defined contribution" pension plan — a plan into which the company contributes a specified amount of money, and whose benefits vary with the returns the money achieves —

is a pot of money with no one watching the pot. After the company makes its contribution, it feels that its job is done. A Wall Street firm manages the money and there's no telling how much you will receive at retirement.

"Defined benefit" plans can be even worse. In a defined benefit plan, a complex formula determines in advance how much each employee will receive. Often the company officers ask the accountants to design the formula to favor themselves. And even when they don't, the benefits may be defined without taking adequate account of inflation.

The IRA surprise is coming. Starting in the 1990s, thousands of Americans who put a few hundred dollars a year into mutual fund Individual Retirement Accounts are going to discover that they're richer than friends who worked for thirty years at big corporations and thought that corporate pensions would take care of them.

EMPLOYERS' HELP IS NOT ALWAYS WORTH A LOT

Many supplemental employer programs provide little help. For example, you may have invested in a program that helps you buy your company's stock or in a company savings program that provides no tax shelter. If so, consider taking at least some of the money out and managing it yourself.

Consider some of the sad stories about investors who never invested on their own in the stock market but had all their savings tied up in the stock of the company they worked for when the company's business failed. Too many eggs in one basket often means too many smashed eggs.

TAX BENEFITS FOR ALL

Yet no one need face near poverty in retirement. Retirement tax benefits leave no one out. Most people don't realize that the biggest benefits from retirement programs come not from the immediate tax deductions, but from the tax-free compounding of investment returns.

Did you stop contributing to your IRA because Congress "ended the tax deduction"? Watch out. Unless your boss

offers a good self-directed retirement program such as a
401(k) plan, you could be making the biggest mistake of your
financial life.

Sure, some retirement tax benefits aren't quite as juicy as
before the 1986 Tax Reform Act. But consider this: While
many people lost a tax break worth perhaps $560 a year when
Congress ended their IRA tax deduction, they can still get
tax breaks worth tens of thousands of dollars for each year
that they contribute to an IRA, because the compounding
income the IRA earns is tax-deferred. Moreover, millions of
people who think they've lost the IRA tax break could still
be taking one.

Suppose you can't take an IRA tax deduction. If you're
forty and you deposit $2,000 into an IRA today and achieve
returns of 15 percent, that $2,000 will turn into about $65,000
by the time you're sixty-five — a substantial contribution to
a secure retirement.

If you invested the money outside an IRA, and achieved
a 15 percent return but paid 28 percent of that return in taxes,
you'd achieve an after-tax return equivalent to only 10.8 percent. Your $2,000 will turn into only about $27,000 by the
time you're sixty-five — less than half as much as you could
produce by investing through an IRA. With an IRA you'll
pay tax after retirement, perhaps at a lower rate than you're
paying today. Even if you pay at the full 28 percent rate,
however, you'll wind up with $46,800 after taxes. If you pay
at 10 percent, you'll wind up with $58,500 — still more than
double what you'd accumulate by investing outside the IRA.

The kicker is that if you did not put the money in your
IRA (where you'd have to pay a penalty and taxes if you took
it out) you probably would neglect to invest the money anyway. That money would probably walk out of your wallet
when you weren't looking. And you'd wind up later in your
life with nothing.

A TIME FOR BOLDNESS

Moreover, most people can shelter their returns, and also
receive at least some tax deductions. So why doesn't every-

one retire a millionaire? In part, it's because people postpone saving for retirement, and thus enjoy far less compound returns than they should. If you deposit $2,000 into an IRA at age fifty-five and achieve returns of 15 percent a year, you'll have only $8,000 at age sixty-five.

But at least equally important, people manage their retirement money timidly — or they don't manage it at all.

Give me a break. Putting your IRA in a bank is like buying a Jaguar and towing it with a mule. Don't tell me you don't like risks. Leaving your IRA money in the bank is the riskiest thing you can do! What will you do when inflation returns in force? What if the bank, taking advantage of the knowledge that it's difficult to move your IRA from one institution to another, pays returns even worse than the average for bank certificates of deposit?

Will banks' poor interest rates really protect your old age? If at age fifty-five you put $2,000 of IRA money in bank certificates of deposit earning 7 percent, it would come to only $4,000 ten years later — not much of a contribution to your retirement.

THE RIGHT TIME FOR THE DONOGHUE STRATEGIES

The right attitude to retirement investing is to recognize that your retirement funds are **long-term money**, and you can afford to put up with the bumps of market fluctuations far better with long-term money than with money you intend to spend in the next five years or so. As I explained in chapter 6, even the most conservative investor should put at least some retirement savings in fairly assertive investments such as stock market mutual funds when the Donoghue Signal says, "Buy."

So practice the Donoghue Strategies with extra assertiveness in managing your retirement account. No-load mutual fund families are ideal vehicles for retirement investing. So is a self-directed account with Charles Schwab & Co., which will allow you to switch freely among all of the leading no-load fund groups.

"Low-load" mutual funds like Fidelity Magellan are also

a reasonable choice for IRA accounts. Most fund families will allow you to switch within the family without paying a load.

If you switch from a low-load stock market fund to a money fund when you get a "sell" signal and then from the money fund back to another low-load fund on a "buy" signal, keep an eye on the fund company statements, however. Mutual fund companies have been known to forget that you already paid the load. (Note: the Fidelity family in Boston has a good computer system that remembers. On the other hand, the T. Rowe Price family in Baltimore never charged you the load in the first place.)

As discussed in chapter 6, you can also trade more freely with your retirement money than with your unsheltered savings because you don't have to worry about the tax consequences of every purchase and sale.

IT'S ALL IN THE FAMILY

Many husbands and wives can choose among several retirement investment plans. And if they coordinate planning with their children, things can get really good. Consider the Investor family.

Sam has a small-business Keogh

Sam Investor is fifty-six years old and runs an auto repair shop. Sam has established a Keogh plan which allows him to put a bit more than 13 percent of his gross income aside for retirement. He set up his plan with the discount broker Charles Schwab & Co. so he can invest in a vast array of mutual funds and also purchase other investments if he feels they meet his needs. Sam puts aside the full amount allowed because he sees retirement as his key goal. Keogh plan rules also require that he make contributions on behalf of Joe, his longtime employee; but those contributions help keep Joe loyal, and Sam considers them well worthwhile.

Sally has a 403(b)

Sam's wife, Sally Investor, age fifty-three, is a teacher. Her school district offers a 403(b) retirement savings program that is pretty liberal on how much she can contribute but pretty unimaginative on the choices: a "guaranteed investment contract" (something like a certificate of deposit) and an annuity.

Sally is going to talk with the benefits manager about getting some mutual funds into the program. Meanwhile, she contributes only $500 a year. From a tax-sheltering point of view, the 403(b) plan seems superior to Sam's Keogh. It doesn't require any contributions for other employees. But the unexciting investment choices mean that the value won't increase like the value of the investments in Sam's Keogh.

Therefore, Sally, who files taxes separately from Sam and whose adjusted gross income is $32,000 a year, has also set up her own Individual Retirement Account, and she makes nondeductible contributions of $600 a year.

Sam and Sally have a stash

Sam and Sally also have a $150,000 portfolio of nonretirement investments they manage using the Donoghue Stock Market Strategy. It increased at an average of 25 percent a year from 1982 through 1986 and even rose a bit in 1987, the year of the crash. But Sam and Sally aren't directing their retirement savings into this portfolio. As Sam asked Sally, "Why should we struggle to save outside the Keogh plan when the IRS is just going to take a chunk of everything?" He's a smart man.

Sue has a SEP

Sally and Sam's daughter Sue, age thirty-one, works for a small business and has a Simplified Employee Pension–Individual Retirement Account (SEP–IRA). That means her employer contributes in Sue's case some $400 a year directly to Sue's IRA. Since Sue knows already how to invest, she has set up an IRA at the Vanguard Group of mutual funds in Valley Forge, Pennsylvania. She uses *Moneyletter*'s advice and her own intuition to manage her employer's contribution plus the monies she contributes.

Sue is anxious to add to her employer's contribution because she knows that with the returns she can expect to achieve, an investment at her age can be multiplied more than a hundredfold by the time she reaches retirement. She also knows that if she had to pay taxes on the income her investments achieved, she could expect far less gain in the long run. (Perhaps a thirty-fold increase between age thirty-one and retirement; see table 3.1 on page 34 for details on tax-free and after-tax compounding of investment returns.)

But Sue also has other goals she must handle before retirement — like buying a house and educating her own daughter, who is now four years old. So Sue contributes only $600 a year to her individual retirement account. (With her employer's contribution, that makes $1,000 a year, which should be equal to $100,000 or more by the time Sue is ready to retire — a respectable step toward a secure life.) Sue also puts aside another $1,800 a year outside her IRA in a portfolio she invests using the Donoghue Stock Market Strategy.

Sam, Jr. has a 401(k) and loves it

Sam, Jr., age twenty-eight, works for a large company which offers a 401(k) savings program. He can contribute up to $7,000 or 25 percent of his pay per year, with his employer matching part of his contribution (in Sam's case, 40 percent of the first $1,600). On top of this, Sam can exclude his whole contribution from his taxable income.

Sam wins several ways. The 401(k) program offers him several investment choices, and he is allowed to change where his money is invested as often as four times a year. Sam, who isn't yet married, cares even less about retirement than Sue. But he makes the full contribution every month to his employer's savings program. Where else can he get an immediate 40 percent return on an investment? Admittedly, he'll have little opportunity to touch the money for the next thirty-seven years without paying considerable tax. But the existence of such a comfortable nest egg will allow him to use other assets, such as home equity and even borrowings, for other expenses. Meanwhile, his savings fund will be growing.

Since Sam, Jr. knows that the Donoghue Signal recently issued a "buy," he has his savings plan money in stock market mutual funds. They usually charge a load, but one nice feature of employer savings programs is that load mutual funds will waive their loads when employers offer them to plan participants.

Moreover, you can use the Donoghue Signal to manage even mutual funds that are not listed in this book since it is a *market* timing signal, not a fund timing signal, and applies to *all* stock funds. Sam, Jr. knows it will be time to switch from the stock market portfolio to his savings plan's money market portfolio the next chance his 401(k) program gives him after the Donoghue Signal says, "Sell."

IF YOU HAVE THE CHOICE . . .

As you can see, you and your family are likely to have several different self-directed retirement programs to choose from. Which should you choose first? And how is the management of tax-sheltered programs different from that of taxable investing programs? Those are very important questions.

If your employer offers it, the best retirement program is a 401(k) retirement savings program with employer matching contributions. Everyone who has access to this program should take advantage of it, no matter how far he or she is from retirement.

Under a 401(k) program, you must agree to allow your employer to put aside a portion of every paycheck. In most cases, the employer then matches a part of your contribution, typically adding thirty to fifty cents for every dollar you've contributed. Your contribution doesn't count as taxable income and so is, in effect, tax deductible. Your employer's contribution and the earnings your account accrues do not count as taxable income. The employer usually offers an array of investment vehicles that's well suited to the strategies we've recommended in this book.

A 401(k) plan makes your savings grow dramatically. It's a great bet even if you're in a very low tax bracket. Say you let your employer withhold $100 a month from your paycheck. You tell the investment company to invest your money in a stock market mutual fund when the Donoghue Interest Rate Signal says, "Buy," and you direct it to switch to a money market fund after the Donoghue Signal says, "Sell."

Then suppose your investments produce returns of 15 percent a year. If you had just put the money in a mutual fund yourself, paid taxes on it, and also paid taxes on the earnings, after four years you would have $5,507.02 — even if you're only in the 10 percent tax bracket. But if your employer matched 30 percent of your contribution and you sheltered the mutual funds' profits in the 401(k) plan, you would wind up with $8,191.46. Sound good?

And unlike IRAs, 401(k) plans can offer "hardship" withdrawals and some loans to participants.

IF A CHANGE IS IN ORDER, DO IT CAREFULLY...

Now suppose you quit this employer. You can either take your 401(k) money immediately and pay taxes on it, roll it over into an Individual Retirement Account, or roll it over into your next employer's 401(k) plan. If you retire with money in a 401(k) plan, you may benefit from five- or ten-year forward income averaging.

Many nonprofit organizations offer 403(b) programs, which resemble corporations' 401(k) programs but rarely offer matching contributions. Sometimes they also fail to offer mutual funds as possible investment choices.

If your employer has a retirement savings program that doesn't allow you to invest in mutual funds, ask your boss or your personnel department to add mutual funds. If they neglect to do so, consider an employee petition or a union demand. Over a period of a decade or more, having mutual funds in the retirement savings program could mean hundreds of thousands of extra dollars for you.

THE INS AND OUTS OF IRAS

So your employer doesn't offer either a 401(k) or a 403(b)? Then your key tool for self-directed, tax-deferred savings is an Individual Retirement Account (or perhaps a Keogh plan if you're self-employed).

The basic mechanics of IRAs remain relatively simple:

You set up an account with a financial services organization such as a no-load mutual fund family or a discount broker.

You can contribute up to $2,000 a year to your IRA, and the investment grows tax-free. You can't touch the money before age 59½ without paying income tax on the money you withdraw and also a penalty tax of 10 percent of the money withdrawn. But don't let that hold you back. If your account grows an average of 15 percent a year and you keep your money in the account more than four years, the taxes you save through tax-deferred compounding are likely to exceed the taxes you pay in penalties.

Most of us qualify

Most Americans — more than 80 percent by some estimates — can still deduct at least part of their $2,000 a year from their taxable income for contributions to an Individual Retirement Account.

Anyone who is not covered by an employer's plan can deduct the full $2,000 a year. *Anyone* can deduct the full $2,000 if he or she is single with adjusted gross income under $25,000 a year. *Any couple* can deduct the full $2,000 if they are married and filing jointly with an adjusted gross income under $40,000.

Even if you don't fit in any of these categories, don't give up hope. Let's say your adjusted gross income is greater than $25,000 a year (or you're married and your adjusted gross income is greater than $40,000 a year). You're covered by an employer-sponsored plan but it's a conventional pension plan or a 403(b) without the mutual fund option, and you don't believe you can count on the plan for security in retirement. There's *still* a good chance you can take a significant tax deduction.

Individuals with incomes over $25,000 a year (and couples with incomes over $40,000 a year) lose $1 in potential tax deduction for every $5 in additional income. Thus, individuals with adjusted gross incomes of $30,000 and couples with adjusted gross incomes of $45,000 can still make deductible IRA contributions of up to $1,000 — enough to build a great deal of wealth over time. The IRA deduction doesn't disappear completely until adjusted gross income reaches $35,000 for individuals and $50,000 for couples.

If you REALLY can't take a deduction

What do you do if, after reviewing the rules, you *still* can't take a worthwhile tax deduction, but you're not satisfied with your employer's retirement plan? First, see if you can persuade your employer to offer a worthwhile plan. If your boss is paying you well, maybe he or she trusts you enough to change the company's retirement plan on your recommendation.

Is any of your income from self-employment? (That includes consulting on the side, fixing the neighbors' plumbing, etc.) If so, you are entitled to establish a Keogh plan. For most people who are self-employed on a full-time basis, Keogh plan contribution limits are more generous than Individual Retirement Account limits. A self-employed person can typically deduct a bit more than 13 percent of his self-employment income. If he has any full-time employees, he may be required to make contributions for them too. (Those rules are complex.) But the rules for taking money out of a Keogh plan resemble those for an IRA.

If your only self-employment income is a few thousand dollars a year for plumbing work on the side, however, your maximum Keogh deduction may be small. Two thousand dollars of self-employment income will permit a deduction of about $260.

If all these tricks still don't give you an adequate retirement program on a tax-deductible basis, another option is a variable insurance policy. (See chapter 12.) If you don't purchase one of those, consider a nondeductible IRA contribution. It won't cut your taxes this year, but it will still leave you far better off in the future because of tax-deferred compounding.

GIVE IT AWAY AND KEEP IT UNDER YOUR CONTROL

There is one more way to arrange your finances that you should consider if you have a substantially appreciated asset such as real estate or a business and you want to turn it into a source of tax-deferred income.

Suppose you have a business you are about to sell. (It could also be a house, some raw land that has been in the family for generations, or whatever.) The value of this asset is $1 million, and that is the price you have negotiated with a knowledgeable buyer.

Before you put the sale in writing, you transfer the ownership of the assets into a Wealth Accumulation Trust (WAT) or, technically, a "charitable remainder trust." Why? Because instead of selling, you are going to *give* the asset to a charity of your choice through the trust. The charity will then sell the property. (The charity could be the American Red Cross, a private foundation, or your favorite college. It's your choice.)

Why should you do that? Because giving your property away can actually make you richer than selling it.

Save taxes on capital gains and get a big deduction

First, giving your property away makes the sale tax-free. You have saved $280,000 or more in capital gains taxes (taxes which under the 1986 Tax Reform Act are now levied at the same rate as on ordinary income).

You also have the good feeling that you have donated a significant sum to a fine charity. You get a deduction on your tax return for the value of the contribution.

So, so far, you have avoided the capital gains tax on the sale, earned a deduction for the value of the contribution, and helped out the charity of your choice.

"But," you say, "I have lost my money."

How to ensure a generous income for life

Let me respond by asking you a question: While you're alive, who do you think gets the income from that WAT? You do. In fact, if you hire a good professional to design the trust and an excellent manager to manage the money, you will probably enjoy a nice return for the rest of your life.

It is true that many charities that have discovered this

fine arrangement insist on managing the money for you. But prudence on your part should tell you that your interests — the income — and the interests of the charity — the principal — are not the same. It's hard to predict how the charity will want the money invested. But you will want an aggressive strategy like the Donoghue Stock Market Strategy.

Also, managers can fit the cash flow from the trust to the needs of the donor. Depending on how the trust is designed, it is possible to slow or speed up the distribution of income from the trust. For example, if the donor is in his or her forties and does not need current income, the definition of income in the trust can exclude capital gains. Then, the money can be managed to emphasize capital gains to the exclusion of income-oriented investments. The trust can be structured to provide its income in the donor's later years.

To ensure that your interests are protected, you'll want to name most or all of the trustees and you'll want assurance that the investment manager will care for your interests.

Suppose you want your capital back?

What if you or your business later needs some of the assets you gave the charity? Think about it. You have a stream of income coming to you each year. Say you earn 10 percent a year in our example. That is $100,000 a year before taxes.

How much do you think that an astute banker would lend you if you had an annual cash flow of $100,000 a year? I will bet that if you had some life insurance to protect the bank if you died, you would be able to borrow back most of what you gave to the charity. So you are still in control of your investments and you can get most of the capital back if you need it.

You can replace the after-tax wealth you donated

How do you pay for the insurance? With the money you save on capital gains taxes and the deduction for the charitable contribution, you can buy both life insurance to protect the bank and life insurance to replace the after-tax money your heirs would have received when you died.

You save money a whole lot of ways. You are still in control of the asset if you appoint your accountant and/or lawyer the trustees. You are in control of how the money is managed if you tailor the trust's terms to your benefit. Finally, you have taken a portion of your estate sufficiently out of your control that it will be unavailable to your creditors; that may be beneficial if you are in a high-risk business.

The keys to success

The keys here are three: (1) You want influence over who manages the assets you donate; (2) you want control over how much you are paid each year from the trust; and (3) you want the tax savings to pay for insurance to replace the after-tax inheritance of your heirs. To provide all these benefits, an associate of W. E. Donoghue & Co., Inc., specializes in establishing Wealth Accumulation Trusts for private clients.

INVESTORS NEVER RETIRE

If you follow the strategies outlined in this chapter, you'll wind up with a nice collection of investments when you reach retirement age. But don't think investing stops then.

Too many people believe that because they've reached age sixty-five, they should cash out of their stock market mutual funds and put all their money in fixed-income investments. But in retirement, you should put special emphasis on managing your investments most effectively. In retirement, you have time to watch for "buy" and "sell" signals, and to look for special investment opportunities.

It does make sense to keep the money you intend to spend in the next twelve to eighteen months in a money market fund or other equally secure and accessible investment. You should also get out of volatile investments and increase your secure reserves if you are worried about possible health problems for you or your family. That way, if the stock market takes a short-term dip, the money you need in the short term will still be safe.

But your other investments should if anything be handled slightly more aggressively in retirement than when a full-time job occupied the bulk of your time. And your golden years can be truly golden.

12
LIFE INSURANCE TACTICS FOR TAX-FREE PROFIT

"**H**ow soon do you want to stop paying taxes on your investment earnings?" That's the pitch many astute investors have been hearing from a new breed of life insurance agents. Many investors have found the pitch too good to believe and have bought less worthwhile insurance products.

Don't be one of them. Unless the laws have changed dramatically by the time you read this, **single premium life insurance** is a truly great opportunity. Even though the government has tightened up on a few of the benefits of the policies, they're still among the most worthwhile ways to invest for the long term.

IT'S TIME TO ACT

Single premium insurance may be the last great way to save for your ultimate retirement kitty (over and above your IRA, Keogh, etc.). We mentioned it in chapter 6, but now it's time to examine all its glories (and complexities). Here's why it's so great:

▶ Its profits can be as reliable as a certificate of deposit's, *but* under present law no 1099 form at the end of the year will report your returns to the IRS unless you take them out of the policy, and as a result these returns are not taxable income at the federal or state levels and do not count as income for Social Security or Medicare purposes.
▶ It can produce tax-free returns like a municipal bond's, *but* you can avoid all market risk if you choose — and your investment will never decline in value.
▶ It protects you like a retirement annuity, *but* unlike a retirement annuity, it won't force you to take your distributions if you don't need them and you will never have to pay taxes on money you do not need to take.
▶ It offers secure, tax-sheltered gains like the ownership of your home. (Remember that if you are fifty-five or older before the day you sell your house, you can exclude up to $125,000 of the capital gains on that sale from taxes. This can be done only once in a lifetime.) You can borrow against your investment to obtain access to your profits as you do through home equity loans. But with this investment you'll either pay no interest at all when you borrow or else pay a tiny fraction of the rate you'd pay on a home equity loan.
▶ And it offers tax-free death benefits.

CONFUSING YOU TO DEATH?

Death *benefits*? I just saw a million readers frown. And I don't blame you. Yes, this investment program *is* (legally, anyway) a type of life insurance. And admittedly, single premium insurance does possess some of the drawbacks of most life insurance policies. Specifically:

1 It is so complex that you'll need the help of a financial services professional when you purchase it.
2 Once you sign up, you're married to it. After a few years,

you can start taking out most of your money. But you
must keep the program at least nominally in force for life
— or you will have to pay taxes on income you'd previ-
ously sheltered.
3 The government could change the rules and take away
more of the benefits.

But don't give up yet — at least if you've got $10,000 or
more and you'd like to shelter its income from taxes. Because
despite these drawbacks, nothing offers the advantages in tax-
sheltered investing today that you can get from single premium life insurance.

You say you don't need life insurance protection for your
family? Remember this: Single premium insurance can give
you more after-tax cash to spend after age 59½ than either
conventional investments or tax-free municipal bonds.

SAVING YOUR LIFE FROM TAXATION

As an investment, life insurance has always offered two enormous advantages:

▶ First, neither the U.S. government nor our state governments levy any taxes on the buildup in the cash value of
life insurance policies.
▶ Second, policy owners can borrow that cash value and
spend the money — and they never have to repay the
loans in their lifetimes. Thus the "borrowing" is like withdrawing money from a mutual fund account, except that
it is tax-free, or at least tax-deferred.

Policy owners therefore receive tax-free profits almost
like the owners of municipal bonds. The government allows
life insurance to serve as a tax shelter because it wants people
to provide for their long-term futures.

AN INVESTMENT, YES — BUT A GOOD INVESTMENT?

Are the returns of life insurance investing high enough to
make life insurance a good deal? Aye, there's the rub.

Twenty-five years ago, life insurance investing was a staid, conservative virtue that could just barely be justified by its tax benefits. Then interest rates rose sharply — and insurance yields rose slowly. Life insurance became a game for fools.

If you last looked at life insurance five or ten years ago, however, take another look today. Tax reform and new kinds of policies have recently made careful life insurance investing a super technique for smart people. It's time for a close examination of today's market.

SAVVY SHOPPERS FIND THE BEST OPPORTUNITIES

I believe that most people should:

▶ Buy good old-fashioned **term** insurance, which provides coverage inexpensively;
▶ Buy one of the two kinds of **single premium** life insurance, which work more like tax-deferred certificates of deposit or mutual fund investments than like life insurance policies; or
▶ Buy both term insurance and single premium insurance.

If you want to read only about "the good stuff" in the market, go ahead and skip a few pages to the section that explains **single premium whole life** ("Income Life"). Then read about **single premium variable life** ("Investment Life"). You'll discover some of the best tax-sheltering investment schemes around.

But before buying, read through this whole chapter. To deal with a professional financial person, you must understand all the major policies that exist. A salesperson may try to sell you something other than the policies recommended here. He or she *may* even have good reasons.

If possible, hire a fee-only financial planner (after carefully checking out his or her qualifications) to help with any big insurance purchase. If you pay an honest planner up front, there won't be any incentive to recommend a policy just because it pays a big commission. Even so, you can assure that a planner is treating you well only if you do enough homework to understand what is being said, and if you ask lots of intelligent questions.

Table 12.1 summarizes today's life insurance alternatives.

HOW MUCH LIFE PROTECTION DO YOU NEED?

Does your family need life insurance protection? You may answer "no," and still purchase a single premium life policy because of the magical way it can help your dollars compound tax-free. But knowing the "death benefit" you would like your insurance to provide (or knowing that you don't think you need any death benefit) still represents a key step in planning.

Most people with family responsibilities want to carry enough life insurance to make them confident that no dependent would become dramatically poorer if they passed away. At minimum, carry enough that your loved ones can survive without poverty.

Life insurance need not replace all the income you provide. Social Security will pay benefits to a family that has lost its sole support.

Suppose you are your family's sole support and you earn $42,000 a year, keeping $33,000 after taxes. Then suppose your local Social Security office tells you that your family would qualify for $8,000 a year, tax-free, if you passed on.

You figure that your family's consumption needs would decline by about $4,000 a year without you, since there is one less person to feed and clothe. So you'd like to carry enough life insurance to provide an income of $21,000 after taxes.

Your death would put your family in a lower tax bracket. So probably you want to produce an income of about $24,000 before taxes. Figuring a conservative 8 percent annual return, you'd need about $300,000 worth of insurance to provide that income every year without your family having to dip into the principal.

Now, where are you going to buy it?

TABLE 12.1 *Life insurance: types and uses*

Name	Amount of insurance protection provided	Investment value	Suitable for
Monthly (or quarterly) premium policies			
Term insurance	Considerable, at low cost for young people (price rises as customer grows older)	None	Anyone who needs inexpensive insurance protection, especially younger people with families
Standard whole life insurance	Substantially less than term insurance	Poor	No one
Universal life insurance	Varies	Mediocre	People who have trouble saving on their own
Single premium policies Buyers purchase the following policies paid up for a lifetime			
Single premium whole life	Little	Good	Anyone seeking a conservative, long-term, tax-deferred investment for $5,000 or more
Single premium variable life	Little	Excellent — money is invested in mutual funds and returns are based on the mutual funds' performance	Anyone seeking a flexible, long-term, tax-deferred investment

TERM INSURANCE: THE RIGHT CHOICE TO START

If you possess only a limited investment portfolio, you should probably buy the protection you need in **term** life insurance. You pay an insurance company a specified amount per year, and if you die the company pays a much larger amount to your family. Term insurance accumulates no cash value at all. It's pure protection. But because it has no investment value, its premiums are far lower for any given amount of protection than those of cash-value policies.

Term insurance is as simple as insurance gets.

You can sometimes buy good term insurance policies from savings banks or from companies that solicit credit-card holders by mail. Insurance agents who advertise prices in the newspaper may also be good sources.

The best way to buy term insurance is probably to get friends to recommend a couple of independent insurance agents, then ask two or more agents to search out the lowest-price term insurance from an insurance company which is rated A or A+ by A. M. Best & Co., the insurance company rating firm.

STANDARD WHOLE LIFE: PUT THE OLD WARHORSE OUT TO PASTURE

Usually, however, your neighborhood insurance brokers will be reluctant simply to write up the inexpensive term policy you need. Moreover, these agents may not even understand the single premium deals I'll discuss below. Instead, they'll try to sell you either an old-fashioned, monthly-payment **whole life** policy or a variant called **universal life**.

"Whole life" insurance was America's number one all-purpose way to provide for the future from the passage of the first income tax law until interest rates soared in the mid-1970s. The buyer of whole life pays the insurance company some cash every month, and not only receives insurance protection but also a buildup of cash value.

Once, this might not have been a bad deal. Of course, whole life always cost more than term insurance. With tax sheltering of the returns, however, a good whole life policy might build up cash value more rapidly than a program of simply buying term insurance and depositing the difference between the price of term and the price of whole life in the bank.

When interest rates soared, however, whole life insurance went sour. Whole life policies were essentially fixed interest rate investments yielding perhaps 6.5 percent. Only fools would buy them when they could obtain 15 percent and more by investing in money market mutual funds.

Today whole life returns have improved. You pay a fixed amount every month. A big chunk of your payment covers a hefty commission for the person who sells you the policy. Another part pays for the insurance protection. And another part goes to accumulate the policy's cash value. But you can't even tell exactly what fraction of your payments contributes to each.

Inflation can still destroy your investment. Moreover, you still abandon your financial future to the mediocrity of an insurance company's investment department. And it will take years before the tax advantages of a whole life policy compensate for the big commissions the salesperson gets.

Nowadays insurance companies know that consumers have been warned against whole life insurance. They often conceal the nature of the product by calling it something like "MasterLife Plus." Don't be fooled. If an agent tries to sell you a policy with fixed premiums and fixed benefits and can't tell you exactly what interest rate you will be receiving on your money, the policy is essentially old-fashioned whole life. Buyer beware.

UNIVERSAL LIFE: FOR THOSE WHO CAN'T SAVE

Universal life, a variant of whole life, can serve you a bit better than whole life because it is more understandable and flexible. With universal life, you and your insurance agent work out how your payments will be divided between insurance coverage and tax-advantaged savings.

The insurance company will even tell you just what interest rate you'll receive (though the rate may decline after an initial period of a year or so). Because insurance agents disclose interest rates, it is easier to compare policies, find a good deal, and be sure a policy suits your needs with universal life than with whole life.

Saving with universal life will never produce the returns of saving yourself and managing your money using the Donoghue strategies. If you can never remember to "pay yourself first" every month and therefore you require a form of enforced saving, universal life may be right for you. Most people, however, should buy term insurance and invest their savings themselves until they have built up a nest egg.

SINGLE PREMIUM WHOLE LIFE: "INCOME LIFE"

Life insurance makes perfect sense as an investment once you have accumulated a significant amount of money, however. There are two types of "single premium" policy. When whole life insurance is sold on a single premium basis, it offers excellent tax-free returns for conservative investors. And single premium variable life insurance, which I'll discuss at the end of this chapter, combines the tax shelter of life insurance with flexibility that will give you the returns of the Donoghue Stock Market Strategy.

I call **single premium whole life insurance** "Income Life." It can do everything a long-term fixed-income investment such as a long-term bond is supposed to do but never does:

▶ It can provide high, reasonably steady after-tax returns.
▶ It can protect your principal from ever declining in value.

As an unbelievable bonus, Income Life shelters your interest from taxes.

HOPE AT LAST

To buy single premium whole life (SPWL) insurance, you write one check, commonly for $10,000 or more. The insurance company will take a relatively small portion of your money for the agent's commission. It can keep the commission low because single premium insurance is not sold by high-pressure door-to-door insurance agents of the old school. No single premium policy is truly no-load. Insurance involves too much complexity to be sold the way no-load mutual funds are sold. But because the buyers typically know what they want, agents need not spend as much time selling single premium policies as they do selling whole life and universal life. So insurance companies need not include the same amount of commission in the price.

Another small portion of your check covers the cost of life insurance coverage, paid up for the rest of your time on earth. For example, if you purchased $30,000 in single premium whole life insurance at age fifty, you would immediately have paid-up insurance of approximately $60,000. You need never pay any more premiums.

But the cost of the insurance, too, consumes only a small portion of your payment. Moreover, because you invest for the long haul, the insurance company can invest your money in high-yielding long-term opportunities such as commercial mortgages. Therefore, it can pay the insurance agent's commission, reserve funds to cover the possibility that you may die sooner than it expects, and still have enough money to make a profit while crediting your account with interest on *the entire amount of your check* at tax-free rates that compete favorably with the fully taxable rates you would get from a bank on certificates of deposit.

The returns will still be mediocre compared to the returns you could achieve through the Donoghue Stock Market Strategy (which you can utilize if you choose single premium variable life, as I'll show below). But for an almost risk-free, fixed-income policy, the after-tax returns are terrific. A good single premium whole life insurance policy should pay rates that exceed those on tax-free municipal bonds (but fall below the rates on taxable investments such as high-yield "junk" bonds). If you compare them on an after-tax basis, of course, they will be larger than even the rates of "junk."

After an initial period (often seven to nine years), the insurance company will pay you the entire cash value of the policy if you wish. However, that would mean "surrendering" the policy, and you would owe income taxes on all the interest credited to your account plus a penalty tax if you're under age 59½. So instead, you take money out of the policy by "borrowing."

Typically you can "borrow" your interest without paying any fees at all (although you will owe income tax on the interest that you borrow). You can also borrow much of your original principal for a fee of 2 to 2.5 percent. Since you're borrowing your own money, the loans need never be paid back. If they're not repaid, loans simply reduce the death benefit when the insured person dies. (The term "death benefit" has to be the worst oxymoron ever. Death has no benefit.)

A good policy becomes a real gold mine when it's more than a few years old. A $30,000 policy in force for nine years at 8 percent interest, for instance, will have a cash value double the amount originally deposited. You won't have paid a penny in tax on the additional $30,000 accumulated. You can borrow some of that $30,000 and pay tax only on the money you take out. (If you borrow before age 59½, however, the government will impose a 10 percent "penalty tax" on the money you take.) On the other hand, if you leave your money in the policy and interest rates remain stable, it will produce another $60,000 in tax-free income over the next nine years.

Financial freedom

Here is a simple summary of the benefits of the single premium whole life program:

1 The insurance company credits interest on *all* your money *tax-free*.
2 *You never have to pay back the "loans" you take* until, of course, you die.
3 When you finally pass on your profits to your heirs, the death benefits are *free of all income tax*.
4 Unless you take your money out of the policy, returns from insurance policies do not count as income when

Social Security benefits and the new Medicare surtax are calculated. You still get the same benefits you would be entitled to without these returns.

Today, more than at any time in history, life insurance policies offer not only protection for your family but long-term wealth-building opportunities second to none.

Where's the catch?

Single premium whole life (Income Life) isn't perfect. The policies are complex. You lack total liquidity in the first years or when you're under 59½ years old. The policies' benefits may not outweigh their complexities unless you are in the 28 percent or higher tax bracket. Moreover, no one can guarantee that Congress won't change the law again to make single premium policies a less reliable tax shelter.

But almost all proposals would still allow companies to offer policies with wonderful investment benefits. Historically, moreover, the tax benefits of existing policies have usually been "grandfathered" under new tax legislation, so it seems unlikely that single premium policies purchased today would lose their advantages. But you can never tell.

Therefore, before you buy, watch the financial and political pages of your newspaper for a few weeks to be sure that no major threat to your tax benefits has advanced so far in Congress that the policy you are considering might lose its advantages. (Or write us for our free update before you buy: "Single Premium Update," 360 Woodland Street, Holliston, MA 01746.)

FINDING YOUR WAY

Throughout this book, I've tried to offer clear standards against which you can compare all financial opportunities. If a hotshot salesperson offers you a good-sounding deal, I've advised you to compare it to the results you could achieve for yourself following the Donoghue strategies.

A standard becomes especially important when you are evaluating single premium insurance. Dozens of companies offer plans with confusing features. No policy will offer every feature and guarantee you would like. Buying single premium insurance thus involves far more factors than investing in mutual funds, for instance.

To guide you, therefore, I want to take you on a leisurely walk through one single premium whole life policy. The policy is Pacific Fidelity's Life Link II.

This is not an endorsement of Pacific Fidelity. Our research has shown that Life Link II is one of the better policies available as this is written in mid-1988, but interest rates, guarantees, and other key factors change constantly. This policy is presented simply to illustrate my standards, which you can use as a shopping guide. Keep your eyes open.

A WALKING TOUR OF AN INCOME LIFE PLAN

Let's say you are a fifty-five-year-old male nonsmoker. You buy a Pacific Fidelity Life Link II single premium whole life policy by writing a check for, say, $30,000. What do you get for your money?

In mid-1988, you got paid-up life insurance with an immediate death benefit of $55,659. More important, your policy's cash value would immediately be credited with 8.5 percent a year interest on the entire $30,000, guaranteed for the policy's first two years. (You'd get 8.75 percent on policies over $40,000.)

These yields exceeded the before-tax yields on the best bank certificates of deposit, so on an after-tax basis these are very high yields. They exceeded the yields any tax-free municipal bond fund could offer. On the other hand, some other single premium whole life policies were paying as little as 7.3 percent at this time and guaranteeing the rate for only a year.

I suggest the following as the first two standards:

INCOME LIFE STANDARD NO. 1: COMPETITIVE YIELDS. *A single premium whole life policy should initially pay a net rate of return comparable to the pretax yields of long-term bank certificates* *of deposit* and exceeding the returns of all but the most aggressive (i.e., most risky) tax-free municipal bond mutual funds. (Be sure the interest rate you are quoted is "net" of all fees.)

INCOME LIFE STANDARD NO. 2: GUARANTEED COMPETITIVE YIELDS. *A single premium whole life policy should offer you the option of a guarantee* on its initial rate of return for at least two years. Three years is better. A one-year guarantee is too short. A five-year guarantee could hurt you if inflation and interest rates rise. (When inflation and interest rates rise, the insurance company's payment rate should rise, but your "locked-in" rate probably won't rise with it.)

What if I want my money back right away?

Life insurance is a long-term purchase, and you can't expect to make money if you demand your money back right away. But policies should be set up so you won't *lose* money, and so that you will get some return, if, for example, you have to cash in the policy after five years to pay unexpected doctors' bills.

The Pacific Fidelity policy has a one year "free look" period, in which you can ask for your money back with no surrender charge. After that, surrender charges apply for the next seven years. If you demand all your money back, you will pay 7 percent of your policy's value through the policy's third year, then 6 percent in its fourth year, 5 percent in its fifth year, 4 percent in its sixth year, 2 percent in its seventh year, and 1 percent in its eighth year.

The surrender charges for most other policies are comparable, but some policies' "free look" period is as short as ten days. Thus you could wind up getting back significantly less than you put in.

INCOME LIFE STANDARD NO. 3: 100 PERCENT MONEY-BACK GUARANTEE. *Be sure you can always get out at least as much as you invested* in the first place. Generally, this means insisting on policies with a one-year "free look" and an initial annual interest rate that at least equals the second-year surrender charge.

What happens after the initial two years?

After the initial guarantee period ends, insurance companies set a new rate "based on market conditions." All companies will lower the rate if interest rates in general have fallen. Most, but probably not all, will raise their rates if interest rates in general have risen.

All policies guarantee a minimum rate for the life of the policy. Pacific Fidelity guarantees a minimum of 5.5 percent. Others guarantee 6 percent or a rate indexed to the long-term yield of U.S. Treasury bonds. Some, on the other hand, guarantee only 4 percent.

An indexed minimum makes most sense. One policy from the North American Company for Life and Health Insurance guarantees whichever is higher, either 6 percent or the average yield on ten-year U.S. government Treasury notes. The only exception occurs if the Treasury note yield exceeds the policy's initial interest rate.

Indexed minimums remain fairly rare, however.

INCOME LIFE STANDARD NO. 4: A GUARANTEED MINIMUM YIELD. *Policies should guarantee a minimum rate of at least 5.5 percent.* A rate guarantee indexed to an easily verifiable statistic like long-term Treasury note yields is better.

What happens when I want my money?

When you want your money, you can simply call Pacific Fidelity and you will have a "loan" check within a week. There is no charge to borrow the interest your money has earned; you'll pay interest of 2 percent to borrow the principal you paid in. Avoid this before age 59½ to prevent penalty taxes. But after 59½, the liquidity of single premium whole life is a vital feature.

Two companies (General Services Life and American Life and Casualty) will issue checkbooks to policyholders so they can write their own loans. By taking a budgeted "loan" every month, you can get a regular cash flow from your Income Life investment.

In general, you should feel as free to borrow the interest your money has earned from these plans as you would to spend the income a bond investment produces. (The borrowing has no cost to you, other than income tax on the interest, and you don't have to repay it in your lifetime.)

If you want to spend the entire amount of your investment, on the other hand, it may be better to convert your policy into an annuity, as we'll discuss below. Avoid borrowing your principal, unless you plan to repay it within a few years. Interest at 2 percent a year (the fee Pacific Fidelity charges) doesn't sound like much, but it's too much to pay to borrow your own money.

INCOME LIFE STANDARD NO. 5: DON'T PUT YOUR EGGS IN A BASKET UNLESS YOU KNOW HOW TO GET THEM OUT. *You should understand exactly how you go about taking money out* of any policy and be satisfied that the approach will be appropriate for you.

What are my risks?

Never try to make a "one-decision" investment — to put your money away somewhere and just collect income. Any one-decision investment can turn against you — and most probably will.

On the other hand, if you plan to make only one investment decision in your life, then buying a carefully chosen single premium whole life policy is probably the least terrible "one decision" you can make. The value of your principal cannot go down; you benefit from tax sheltering, and the insurance company will *probably* keep its interest rate reasonably competitive.

Suppose the tax law changes? The Pacific Fidelity plan allows you to bail out of the policy without a surrender charge if that happens. Many policies offer this feature; insist on it if you are concerned about tax law changes. Even if a policy lacks this feature, however, you're unlikely to suffer greatly in tax law changes unless you buy shortly before they are voted in Congress and therefore do not benefit from "grandfathering."

Suppose the insurance company fails? That's unlikely, but not impossible. Even when insurance companies do fail, however, policyholders' losses are limited. State insurance regulations guarantee that insurance company assets are "reserved" and will be used to repay most if not all of the companies' obligations to policyholders.

To guard against the small chance of loss in an insurance company disaster, follow our advice to buy policies only from companies rated either A or A+ by A. M. Best & Co. (Whoever is selling you a policy should provide you with the insurance company's A. M. Best rating *in writing*.) If you put a large amount of money into single premium insurance, moreover, spread your investment among several insurance companies.

Still, the world contains no really good one-decision investments. In today's unpredictable world, policies must allow flexibility to insurance companies. (Insurance executives remember that a large firm named Baldwin United collapsed when interest rates fell after it had sold thousands of inflexible high-interest-rate policies. Policyholders didn't lose their money, but they wound up with lower-yielding annuities than they'd paid for.)

Unfortunately, rules that give companies flexibility can also allow them to do things that are not in the best interest of policyholders.

For example, Pacific Fidelity currently levies no net charge when you borrow out the interest your policy has earned. It charges only 2 percent a year when you borrow your principal. The company can change those borrowing rates, however. It can also impose a "mortality fee" — an additional charge for the insurance on your life on top of the charge that is hidden in the spread between the return it pays you and the earnings it receives by investing your money.

Policies contain provisions that allow you to bail out under certain circumstances. But no policy allows you to bail out in every circumstance where you might want to. The Pacific Fidelity plan allows you to bail out not only if the government changes the tax law, but also if the interest rate drops by 1 percent or more from the initial guarantee. That's a good deal. The biggest danger with single premium whole life policies is that insurance companies may fail to keep their rates competitive.

But Pacific Fidelity's bailout provisions won't protect you, for instance, if the company imposes an arbitrary mortality fee or raises the cost of borrowing out your money.

INCOME LIFE STANDARD NO. 6: BAILOUT FOR NONCOMPETITIVE YIELDS. *Unless a policy guarantees a minimum interest rate indexed to an easily verifiable statistic like U.S. Treasury note yields, the policy should allow you to bail out without a surrender charge* if the company reduces its interest rate by 1.5 percent or more.

A STANDARD FOR YOURSELF: KEEP YOUR EYES OPEN AT ALL TIMES. *Since no policy is guaranteed to remain competitive, reevaluate your policy every year or so.* Know how much your policy is currently worth and what interest rate it is currently paying. If the interest rate is significantly less than you could get elsewhere, consider either borrowing your interest out to invest elsewhere or switching to a different policy through a Form 1035 rollover. (See appendix 1.)

Choose your policy carefully. Keep an eye on your insurance company or have your investment advisor or financial planner do that for you. (See the discussion on financial planners below.) If you do, a single premium whole life policy will protect you better than any other long-term interest-paying investment.

SINGLE PREMIUM VARIABLE LIFE: "INVESTMENT LIFE"

In the end, single premium whole life has only one drawback that refuses to go away: The yields just won't make you *rich*. After taxes, they'll beat bank accounts, money market funds, and — usually — buy, hold, and pray long-term bonds or municipal bonds. But the returns probably won't match those of a carefully managed Donoghue Stock Market Strategy program that switches between stock mutual funds and money market funds — even on an after-tax basis.

Let's face it, 20 percent after taxes of 28 percent is still 14.4 percent, and that beats 10 percent tax-free.

One other insurance opportunity solves that little problem, however. I call it "Investment Life," and we previewed it in chapter 6.

Investment Life, whose proper name is **single premium variable life (SPVL)**, resembles single premium whole life. But instead of putting your money into an interest-bearing obligation of the insurance company, Investment Life companies invest your money in a family of mutual funds. Many of the best Investment Life policies are joint ventures between insurance companies such as Charter National and investment companies such as Scudder, Stevens and Clark. The value of your policy varies with the success or failure of your mutual funds and your success in trading those funds (hence the name "variable life").

You decide in which of these funds your money will be invested.

Thus in a bull stock market, you can invest your variable life account in growth stock mutual funds. When interest rates begin to rise, on the other hand, you can invest in a money fund to preserve your capital for the next bull market, which always shows up eventually.

Since the stock market has historically over the long run produced far higher returns than the mortgages and other unexciting investments in which insurance companies invest to pay interest to their whole life policyholders, you are likely to experience much better (though much less predictable) profit.

Investment Life seems to involve higher administrative fees than single premium whole life. In fact, it involves more fees than any other investment recommended in this whole book. But while the fees can be substantial, Investment Life offers a lot of investment flexibility. Other insurance products give the insurance company much more opportunity to hide its charges from you. With Investment Life, you see almost everything up front.

Typically, the life insurance company and the associated mutual fund company will between them collect 2.5 to 3 percent of your money each year for sales commissions, administration, mortality risk charge, fund advisory and management fees, etc. Investment Life also charges interest on all policy loans; your account will be charged about .75 percent per year whenever you "borrow" your own money. Surrendering the policy in its early years will produce fees comparable to those you'd pay if you surrendered a single premium whole life policy.

By comparison, the management fees of ordinary no-load stock mutual funds typically run .6 percent to 2 percent, and of course you can withdraw your cash without any fee at all. So you're paying about 1.5 percent of your capital each year for the advantages of single premium variable life: tax sheltering and a small amount of life insurance protection (comparable in amount to the protection you get from single premium whole life).

That can be a stupendous deal. If you invested on a fully taxable basis, averaged a 15 percent yearly return, and were in the 28 percent tax bracket, you'd pay more than 4 percent of your capital per year in taxes — far more than the additional cost of utilizing Investment Life. Even if you merely average a 7 percent return, you can come out ahead after taxes.

A STANDARD FOR TAX-DEFERRED INVESTING

Because you see everything up front and because there's so much to see, single premium variable life purchases seem even more complex and difficult to evaluate than single premium whole life.

So now let's take a slow walk through a typical single premium variable life policy. It will allow us to establish standards for purchase of this very attractive investment. The following standards for single premium variable life, in fact, are standards to which an active investor should compare all tax-deferred investments.

The policy we'll explore is Monarch Life Insurance Co.'s CaptnFlex, which uses mutual funds from Oppenheimer Management Corp. Again, this does not imply an endorsement; this was a pretty good policy in mid-1988, but fees, rules, and the management of the underlying mutual funds could have changed since then.

Choosing your investments

So suppose you write a $30,000 check to a broker or agent selling CaptnFlex. (You can invest any sum of $10,000 and up; $5,000 and up for children under age twenty.) Immediately, a fifty-year-old has life insurance with a $63,310 death benefit. (If you need more insurance protection than your single premium policy provides, buy an additional term insurance policy.)

You must immediately choose where you want your money invested. If your broker or agent has marketed CaptnFlex properly, you will have received a clear list of all your investment choices before you bought, and a clear statement of their past performance. In 1988 they included a money fund, a conservative long-term bond fund, a high-income (junk) bond fund, two stock market mutual funds, and a "multiple strategies portfolio." Demand a presentation of the funds' past performance that compares it to an index such as the Standard & Poor's 500 or the Wilshire 5000. Compare the money fund's performance to the Donoghue's Money Fund Averages.

CaptnFlex's multiple strategies portfolio showed the highest returns in the family in 1987, which means that the portfolio's managers recognized the dangers and pulled at least some of their assets out of stocks before the crash.

I recommend, however, that you invest primarily in stock and money funds and do your switching yourself, following the Donoghue Interest Rate Signal, at least until insurance-investment multiple strategies portfolios can show a four- to five-year record of success. The multiple strategies portfolio available through another Monarch plan, the Monarch/Merrill Lynch variable life policy Prime Plan V, was 85 percent invested in stocks at the time of the October 1987 market crash, and it lost 5.47 percent in value for the year — a poor performance.

INVESTMENT LIFE STANDARD NO. 1: MAKE SURE YOU HAVE AC-CURATE AND CURRENT PERFORMANCE DATA ON ALL THE FUNDS IN THE POLICY. *Marketing materials for an Investment Life program should clearly indicate each fund's past performance* and compare it to leading stock market averages. The choices should be diverse enough to allow you to follow the Donoghue strategies. Essentially, this means that at least one stock fund and a money fund should both show good track records over at least two years.

Warning: Do not invest in a policy that does not provide a convenient source for at least monthly disclosure of investment performance. Some single premium variable life policies do not offer convenient full disclosure.

The fees your account will pay

In most Investment Life programs, all of your money will be invested immediately. But that does not mean the product is no-load. The initial fees for CaptnFlex amount to 7 percent of your initial premium — a 4 percent sales load, 2.5 percent for state premium taxes, and .5 percent for administrative fees. Monarch will spread these amounts over years two through eleven, deducting approximately .7 percent per year to cover these costs. If you surrender your policy and demand all your money back before year eleven, the remainder of these fees will be deducted.

In addition, Monarch will deduct an annual "mortality and expense risk" charge of .6 percent of your principal and a "cost of insurance" that will depend on the age of the person insured. (For a fifty-year-old nonsmoking male, it will be about half a percent — .519 percent to be exact — of the value of the policy.) And Oppenheimer will receive advisory fees for managing your mutual funds.

Like most variable life mutual funds, Oppenheimer's CaptnFlex mutual funds currently charge lower management fees than the average mutual fund sold outside variable life policies. Currently, CaptnFlex fees average .3 to .5 percent of your principal. They could rise in the future.

INVESTMENT LIFE STANDARD NO. 2: THE 7 PERCENT SOLUTION.
The initial fees chargeable to your account should not exceed 7 percent of its value. Annual mortality, administrative, and miscellaneous fees should not exceed .75 percent of the policy's value. The "cost of insurance" should be comparable to the cost of a similar amount of term insurance. Mutual fund advisory fees should not exceed the management charges of comparable mutual funds purchased outside the policy (typically 1 percent or less).

Changing your investment strategy

Now suppose interest rates change direction. The Donoghue Signal says, "Sell." You can simply telephone Monarch and put all your money in a money fund. CaptnFlex allows unlimited free telephone switches. Other policies allow a limited number of switches; a few make nominal charges.

If you want to deposit more money in your policy later to obtain tax-free returns, you can do so with a check sent to your insurance agent or directly to Monarch. Additional deposits will pay the same fees and give you an increase in insurance protection comparable to that you received when you first invested.

INVESTMENT LIFE STANDARD NO. 3: A SWITCH IN TIME CAN SAVE YOUR _____ (FILL IN THE BLANK AT YOUR OWN RISK). *You should clearly understand how to switch investment strategies by telephone.*

INVESTMENT LIFE STANDARD NO. 4: ADDING MORE FUEL TO THE FIRE SHOULD BE EASY. *It should be easy for you to make additional deposits in your policy.*

When you want your money

When you want your money, you can simply telephone the insurance company for a loan. Monarch will even wire your money to your bank account, so you can use it the next day.

CaptnFlex and most other variable life companies charge a fee on all loans from a variable life account. CaptnFlex's fee is .75 percent of the loan amount during the first ten years of the policy and .60 percent of the loan amount after that. When you borrow, too, your money is removed from the investment portfolios, so it stops making money for you. A .6 to .75 percent fee may seem small, but it can be a significant consideration if for some reason (college tuition bills, illness) you want to borrow out most of the money in the policy,

especially during its first ten years. Moreover, as with Income
Life, you'll pay tax on your interest when you take money
out and a penalty tax if you take money out before age 59½.

Your original deposit, however, can be withdrawn tax-
free at the end of fifteen years as long as you maintain enough
cash value to keep the policy in force.

**INVESTMENT LIFE STANDARD NO. 5: KNOW THE RULES OF THE
ROAD BEFORE YOU DRIVE.** *Be sure you understand exactly how you can get your
money and what fees you will pay.*

An investment for life

Many of the cautions that apply to single premium whole life
also apply to Investment Life: Bear in mind that Congress
could change the law and cut into your tax benefits. Make
sure you understand *all* the fees that will be charged. Read
the contract carefully and be careful whom you buy from.
And deal only with insurance companies rated A or A+ by
A. M. Best.

But if you manage the money in an Investment Life policy
using the Donoghue Stock Market Strategy, the policy can
make you rich. Say you achieve 17.5 percent gross return on
your account. After deducting 2.5 percent or so in fees, your
account will grow at 15 percent a year. A $30,000 deposit will
turn into more than $120,000 after ten years; nearly $500,000
after twenty years.

Unless you're in a low tax bracket or you can't afford to
put money away for the long term, Investment Life is likely
to be a terrific deal. It's the only way I know in which you
can practice the Donoghue strategies in full force for whatever
purpose your heart desires. It lets you avoid taxes and retain
access to your money.

SINGLE PREMIUM LIFE OR AN ANNUITY?

Even with Congress's new restrictions, Income Life and Investment Life have important advantages over a product that
commissioned salespeople prefer to sell: annuities.

Annuities outsell single premium insurance policies by a margin of ten to one. The reason is the same as the reason that inferior investments outsell good investments at "full-service" brokerage houses: Salespeople sell what is easiest to explain.

Annuities are relatively simple. When you pay annuity premiums, the insurance company invests the cash and the returns are tax-deferred. Annuities also pay a higher rate of return than life insurance policies, because when you die the insurance company keeps most or all of your money.

When you retire, the annuity begins paying you a sum every month.

That's all there is to it — almost. See why investors sign up?

The annuity catch

When an annuity starts paying out, you *must* take your money every month — and pay taxes on it. The distribution can also cause you to pay a higher Medicare surtax. In an emergency, on the other hand, most annuities give you easy access to only a portion of your annuity's cash value.

A life insurance policy gives access to your money when *you* want it. If you don't need your money this month, it stays in the policy, earning income, and you pay no taxes.

In short, an annuity merely shelters your gain until you receive checks. A life insurance policy shelters your gain *until you surrender or "borrow" from your policy*. If you never surrender the policy, it shelters your gain *forever*. (As we have noted, death benefits are free of federal income tax to your heirs.)

The result is that a life insurance policy can sometimes produce *more* spendable cash after taxes than an annuity that costs the same amount — and also leave substantial benefits for your heirs.

If you are willing to borrow on your single premium whole or variable life insurance policy occasionally, rather than get the automatic checks from the annuity each month, you can save a lot of your money from being wasted on taxes.

The only time to buy an annuity

So why do people buy annuities? Well, the convenience of the check an annuity will send you every month is nice. If you're sure you want to spend most of your money before you die, the extra tax shelter benefits of a life insurance policy may not justify giving up the simplicity of an annuity.

An annuity also guarantees that regular payments will continue as long as you live. In the early years of retirement, the amount an annuity could guarantee you doesn't greatly exceed the amount you could comfortably take from a single premium insurance policy. But suppose you're in your seventies and you need an increase in cash flow. If you have some cash, a single premium annuity may be a good choice. Working with an insurance agent, you can also "roll over" a life insurance policy into an annuity at this point and guarantee that an income will continue for the rest of your life.

DO YOU NEED A FINANCIAL PLANNER?

If all this sounds a bit complex to you, you're not alone. That's why the profession of *fee-based financial planner* is growing throughout the United States. If you're in the 28 percent tax bracket and you have $60,000 or more to invest — or if you're contemplating the purchase of a product, such as a universal life insurance policy, that will involve substantial payments over a period of years — consider hiring a fee-based planner.

Some good financial planners have a hard time making a living even as high-pressure salespeople get rich off commissions. People resist paying large fees even when they know that the fees come to less than the commissions built into the cost of conventional insurance policies.

You should be smarter than that. If you're unsure what policy is best, yet you recognize that the right financial moves can mean tens or hundreds of thousands of dollars in the long run, don't turn your life over to a commissioned salesperson. Talk to a fee-based planner.

Ask your rich friends

But never seek a financial planner in the Yellow Pages. Too much is riding on your decision. Instead, look for a financial planner as you would seek a doctor or lawyer.

Ask smart, rich friends for recommendations. Ask other professionals, such as the lawyer who handles your will or the accountant who handles your taxes. Try to get names of at least two planners recommended by people you trust, and interview both.

Interviewing a planner

Your first question should be: "How do you get paid?" Ideally, you want a planner who charges you a fee — possibly a high fee — but who credits to your account any commission paid him or her by financial services companies.

Watch out for a planner who says he or she receives a "combination of a fee and commissions." Often this is just an ordinary commission-based salesperson who'll be glad to charge a fee to *you* on top of the commissions he or she receives.

Ask how much you should expect to spend. Then hold your breath. Most reliable financial planners will want you to pay them $1,500 or more, so they can take time to understand your entire financial situation.

Some fee-only planners may be willing to help you for $300 or so in a relatively simple transaction like the purchase of life insurance. But in general you should be suspicious of any fee of less than $600. A low fee suggests only that the planner either does not intend to spend much time with you or is getting rich with commissions on the side.

Next ask what financial services the planner typically recommends. If you hear mention of single premium insurance, no-load mutual funds, market timing services, and annuities, those are good signs.

Ask about educational qualifications. A degree in law, accounting, or business is helpful; an insurance background generally is not. The designation "Certified Financial Planner" is given by independent organizations genuinely concerned with professionalism, and indicates that a planner is at least knowledgeable and serious about his or her work.

Finally, ask about satisfied customers. Some consider their customers' names confidential. But if the planner won't give you the names of some customers, see if the person who recommended the planner can tell you.

Unless you're thoroughly convinced of a planner's professionalism by this time, ask your state securities commission and your local Better Business Bureau if they have received any complaints. Sometimes complaints are filed about excellent planners, and you may want to give a planner a chance to respond. But it's better to know about complaints *before* you pay any fees.

NEXT STOP, PROSPERITY

In investing, simple strategies work just as well as complex strategies. For example, investing in the stock market following the Donoghue Stock Market Strategy is likely to produce better returns in the long run than the most complex strategies on Wall Street.

Occasionally, however, something complicated can truly benefit you. That's the case with single premium insurance.

Using insurance well is probably the most demanding of all consumer financial maneuvers. But if you do it right, you'll make a big step toward assuring yourself a prosperous life.

13

THE DONOGHUE STRATEGIES — PUTTING IT ALL TOGETHER

Welcome to the Donoghue winners' circle. You are now ready to embark on an experience all too rare in this world: confident, successful saving and investing.

As you gain confidence, you will want to put your finances in order. Are you ready?

TRUST IS THE NAME OF THE GAME

The key to realizing your dreams is disciplined investing. With discipline, you can create a money machine. You must fully understand how that money machine functions, how it was developed, and how it works in real life, so you can trust its power and channel it to work for you.

Trust is the key word. You must learn the quirks and probabilities of success in each of the Donoghue strategies. You must learn to suffer calmly through an occasional false signal. You must accept occasional losses in the knowledge that you have dramatically increased the probability that you will succeed in the long run.

Remember, an understanding of the **probabilities** of success makes for a great long-term strategy. Never be tantalized by the tempting "possibilities" that salespeople use to sell the glamor of a recommendation.

YOU'VE COME A LONG WAY IN JUST A FEW HOURS

Chances are that when you started reading this book you had an investment portfolio that could only be described as "cats and dogs": a collection of bond mutual funds, insurance policies, money market fund accounts, a stock or two purchased through a full-commission broker, and perhaps an Individual Retirement Account at a bank, a company savings account, or a company stock purchase plan. You had no perceptible strategy. That's the way we all started out.

My fond desire is to see you clean up your financial house and bring all of your investments into a coordinated and assertive investment strategy. If this book has shifted you from low gear in bank CDs into high gear in mutual funds, I have done my job well.

Let's summarize what we know about our strategies and our investment choices. Then I'll give you a plan to put everything together to meet *all* your goals.

THE STOCK MARKET: THE BIGGEST OPPORTUNITY

Stock market mutual funds offer the greatest returns over the long term. Moreover, you can probably improve stock market returns dramatically while reducing risk by following the Donoghue Interest Rate Signal in the Donoghue Stock Market Strategy.

We have learned to:

1 **Stick to no-load funds.** They offer your best chance for profits. Occasionally, we'll consider a low-load fund (a fund with a sales charge of 3 percent or less) that has demonstrated superior performance.

2 **Invest in the best.** Choose stock market mutual fund investments from the Donoghue stock fund universe (appendixes 2 and 5).

3 **Stick with the top of the list.** Make choices from those recommended in this book, those that appear at the top of the lists in appendix 2, and those recommended by *Moneyletter*.

4 **When you can get good returns at lower risk, grab 'em.** Keep track of the Donoghue Interest Rate Signal, the 25-week exponential moving average of money fund interest rates. Never buy when it shows interest rates are rising. Always buy when it shows rates are falling. If you follow this strategy, it is probable that at least 40 percent of the time you will be sitting in a low-yielding but virtually riskless money market mutual fund. The probability is high that during that time a stock market investment will lose money.

5 **If you're lazy, find a lazy person's fund.** If you won't follow interest rate trends and trade your portfolio accordingly, choose a fund such as the lazy person's funds listed in chapter 6 — a fund that has a record of holding its value in down markets.

THE BOND MARKET

About the bond market, we have learned:

1 **The importance of timing.** *Never* invest in long-term bonds or bond mutual funds when interest rates are rising.

2 **Bonds will always be second-rate over time.** The best total returns on bond funds over the long term will seldom match the best total returns on stock funds. In our eight-year study, 46 of 46 stock funds beat the highest-yielding bond fund, when both were traded based on the Donoghue Interest Rate Signal. Careful studies have shown stocks regularly outperforming bonds all the way back to the 1920s.

3 Bond markets can decline a lot in a few weeks. Rapid bond market moves can cost you a lot of money, so pay close attention to protect your principal.
4 We can help. Following the Donoghue Interest Rate Signal can reduce risk and significantly improve your returns on bond funds over time.
5 Sometimes junk is good enough, even better. The highest-yielding bond funds — so-called "junk bond funds" — are often the best deals, although knowing when to sell is critical.

THE MONEY MARKET

In the money market, remember:

1 The importance of why. Money market investments can play the following roles:
a A parking lot between more aggressive investments to
● provide a safe haven in risky markets (i.e., rising-interest-rate markets);
● provide liquidity.
b An investment for the extremely cautious investor who is willing to accept low returns for minimal effort.
2 The importance of why not. Except when interest rates are rising, no long-term investor should keep the bulk of his long-term funds in the money markets. Even the most cautious investor should invest a significant fraction of his or her long-term money in the stock market when interest rates are falling.
3 The importance of where. The best money market investments are:
a Money market mutual funds. For short-term, liquid money, you just can't beat a real money market fund. Check appendix 3 in this book and Donoghue's Money Market Funds table in your newspaper for the highest-yielding money funds.
b Banks and thrifts. The banks and savings and loans that pay the highest rates on federally insured certificates of deposit and money market deposit accounts can give

good deals. But check their yields regularly to be sure they remain competitive. Compare the banks in your area to the highest-yielding banks and thrift institutions in the country, listed in a weekly table in *Barron's*.

c **Stockbrokers.** Brokers sell federally insured CDs offering excellent yields. You'll face easier paperwork than you would in dealing direct with the top-yielding institutions listed in *Barron's*, and you will deal with professionals rather than local bankers. Moreover, you can sell brokered CDs at a profit in a falling-interest-rate market.

d **Tax-free money funds.** If you are in a high tax bracket, consider a tax-free money fund. In high-tax states, compare the after-tax returns on double tax-free money funds to the yield on taxable money funds. Use the table in chapter 9. In New York City, look closely at triple tax-free money funds, which are exempt from state, local, and federal income taxes.

4 **The importance of when.** *All* investors should keep most of their money in extremely safe investments such as money market mutual funds when interest rates are rising. The Donoghue Average Maturity Signal is a good guide for appropriate times to invest in certificates of deposit. If the average maturity is under 40 days, keep your money in a top money fund until you see the average maturity show a rising trend over a period of four weeks or so. Invest in bank CDs only if the average maturity of money market mutual funds is over 40 days or is *rising*. Invest in CDs with maturity of more than six months only if the average maturity of money funds is over 45 days and is *either stable or rising*.

QUESTIONS TO ASK ABOUT YOURSELF

Remember these key questions about *you*:

▶ **Do I really want the higher returns that disciplined application of the Donoghue strategies will probably generate?** Let's face it. A lot of people simply do not want to take the trouble to earn more and take responsibility for their own investment results. You know people like that. I think we have all been like that at one time or another. (I changed when I learned how to increase the probability of investment success.)

▶ **Am I willing to discipline myself?** If you say yes, then you are making a time commitment of ten minutes a week — *every week*. It is your money that you are profiting from, so go for it.

▶ **Do I trust the Donoghue stock market or bond market strategies enough to risk my savings following them? Even if I lose money temporarily?** This is a very important question. If you have any doubt, go back and reread chapter 2 and sections dealing with other topics about which you are not yet convinced.

▶ **Do I really want to put all my money at risk in these new strategies?** You don't have to. You can, if you choose, leave part of your money in money market investments to reduce your risk.

AT THE REQUEST OF THE SEC, FULL DISCLOSURE . . .

The Securities and Exchange Commission requires that I warn you that past performance is no guarantee of future results. The Donoghue Signals, while based on earlier basic research, were developed after the crash of 1987, and the results in this book for specific mutual funds were backcasted. They do not represent actual returns on actual transactions.

However, I have to add that the only way to test improvements in investment strategies against actual market conditions is to backcast. I believe I have adequately described the inverse relationship between interest rates and the stock market and why it exists. This cause-and-effect relationship has worked well for the Donoghue Organization and has helped the readers of our publications to achieve superior returns for more than a decade.

THE BEST OF THE BEST STRATEGIES — FOR YOU

Your self-examination completed, you can now pull it all together. Make a list of all of your investments, including any passbook savings accounts, cash-value insurance policies, etc., you are holding as reserves. Total up their value.

Then review chapter 3 and make a complete list of your investment goals. This second list is the key. Break down your goals into three categories:

▶ Short-term (one to two years),
▶ Intermediate-term (three to five years), and
▶ Long-term (five to thirty years or more).

Short-term goals call for very conservative management

All investors will answer "yes" when you ask them if they are "conservative." By "conservative," they generally mean that the preservation of capital is their most important goal. They will not risk losing their money, either in the short run or in the long run.

Sophisticated assertive investors find, however, that making money involves losing small portions of their capital occasionally in order to earn large returns in the long run. They realize that, in the long run, the safest way to preserve their capital from the ravages of inflation, taxes, and emergency financial needs is to take the small short-term risks that will result in high long-term returns. Actually, they are just as conservative as the investor who refuses to take any risks at all — but only in the long run.

Real conservatism demands that you avoid all risk only on savings that are earmarked for very **short-term goals**. Typical short-term goals include a new car, a new TV or stereo, a wedding present for your son or daughter, or any other expenditure that you must make in a year or two.

If money invested for a short-term goal represents all the money you have or expect to have, you are not saving enough. Put another 5 percent of your after-tax pay into savings. It'll be painful for a while, but eventually you'll be glad you did it.

Use the Donoghue Average Maturity Signal to choose between money funds and CDs for this short-term money.

Aggressive readers may want to invest part of their short-term money in stocks when interest rates are declining. If you get caught in a downturn, you can always shift a little bit from your long-term money or even borrow to make up a shortfall. But *never* take significant risks with cash you need for short-term expenses if it's all you have.

Intermediate-term goals call for active, assertive management

If your investment goal is three to five years away, take some managed risks. This means investing in stock or bond market mutual funds with a well-thought-out strategy.

Typical **intermediate-term goals** are buying a larger home, buying a second home, paying for your teenagers' college education, accumulating cash to start a business, etc.

First, calculate whether you are saving enough to achieve your goal. If you achieve a 15 percent return on your money, will your present savings program give you enough when the bill comes due?

If it looks as though your money will be enough, then concentrate on investing following the Donoghue Stock Market Strategy to achieve that kind of return. If it will be more than enough, then you should still seek a 15 to 20 percent return, but rejoice — you can expect money left over. If 15 to 20 percent returns won't achieve your goal, start adding to your savings regularly, and build up your credit to get a loan when you are ready to realize your goal.

The stability of the CounterBalance system may also be suitable to intermediate-term goals (see chapter 6). But under the CounterBalance system you should not count on growth of greater than 12 percent a year.

Since you need the money at a specific time, the temptation is to "take care of it today and get it over with." Brokers and bankers love to sell zero-coupon bonds and bank CDs to people with intermediate-term goals. *Don't let 'em do it.* These investments produce mediocre returns in the best of times. If inflation runs higher than you expected, moreover, they'll leave you with insufficient cash even if you started with enough savings to have met your goal through wiser investments.

Remember these **dos and don'ts for active investors:**

The dos:

1 **Do** carefully select a few (three to five) of the top stock market mutual funds we have recommended. Use several, since not all funds will perform as well as their past track records. A portfolio of funds with excellent records will be likely to perform better than most other investments, however.

2 **Do** apply for the telephone exchange privilege, the automatic reinvestment of dividends, and the telephone redemption privilege for each mutual fund in case you need money in an emergency. Make sure that your name and tax ID number are identical on your fund account and your bank account, to eliminate snags in sending your money.

3 **Do** ask the fund family to tell you explicitly their policy on telephone switching. For example, the Twentieth Century family, which includes two of the top seven funds in both our eight-year and our four-year studies, prohibits switching out of a fund for 30 days after you've switched in. That is fine. Keeping your money in the wrong fund for a few extra days if you get whipsawed will have no long-term impact on your strategy. But you should know the rules.

4 **Do**, if you have enough money (more than $10,000) to invest in a separate investment pool, consider setting up a CounterBalance portfolio to add some additional stability to your investment program. Diversification among investment philosophies can be valuable.

The don'ts:

1 **Don't** invest in anything before looking at the trend of the Donoghue Interest Rate Signal. If it is saying, "Sell," or

if interest rates have started to rise to approach a "sell," hold on until it backs off. If it is in a clear "buy" mode, on the other hand, jump into stock market funds.

2 **Don't** try the easy way out and forget to keep up to date with the Donoghue Signals. That, my good friend, is gambling.

Long-term goals call for aggressive investing

The money you can segregate for **long-term goals** is usually targeted for the establishment of a second income, the college education of young children, and/or retirement. It also has the less specific but equally important goal of building up a good feeling of financial independence and a pool of wealth that gives you choices.

True riches are measured in the ability to make independent lifestyle choices. Wealth built carefully as the result of personal effort and wisdom gives a special feeling different from the impact of winning the lottery or inheriting some money.

Initially, I would start out by segregating your long-term money into three portfolios:

Portfolio A: new and doubtful long-term money. This portfolio houses money that you are not yet sure is really long-term money — money which may be needed for an emergency or to refund shorter-term portfolios if they fall short. Unexpected pregnancies, medical emergencies, or job changes can reshuffle your goals.

This money, then, must be liquid for emergencies. It has more patience than the shorter-term portfolios, yet it is not clearly committed to long-term goals.

It is best managed using the basic Donoghue Stock Market Strategy (see chapter 6). But it may be wise to add the 10 percent "stop-loss" rule in managing this money. If, at any time, any fund in your portfolio loses 10 percent from the fund's most recent high price, *sell*.

That will give you the confidence to invest aggressively with this money when the Donoghue Interest Rate Signal says, "Buy." It will also cost you in the long term, since it will sometimes cause you to sell prematurely and pay taxes on capital gains. But you are building confidence and preserving a fund that just might be needed for emergencies, and cutting losses is easier to swallow than too much volatility.

In addition, remember that this long-term money may be repositioned as shorter-term money if new short-term goals present themselves.

Portfolio B: your long-term taxable investment pool. This is the major portion of many investors' long-term money. It has the most freedom, and you pay the taxes to prove it.

This is where you show your patriotism. Taxes are a fee you pay for government services. But buy government services wisely. Many people seem to want to pay more tax than they need to. If you are on a long-term wealth-building program, buying a bond or a bond fund may not be good strategy, for example. The regular dividends they pay are all immediately taxable. That cuts heavily into your wealth-building power.

For this long-term pool, then, the wise investor will seek investments that produce the greatest after-tax returns and the greatest potential tax deferral.

The best investments for liquid, flexible wealth building are stock market mutual funds (much of whose income is capital gains, on which taxes may not be due right away) and the two kinds of money funds, taxable and tax-free.

Investing in stock market funds allows *you* to choose when you realize your profits. You owe taxes only on distributions from your fund until you sell at a profit. The tax-deferral effect of investing in stock funds is a critical part of their wealth-building effectiveness. Aggressive growth funds are often the best investments for long-term wealth building because they pay little in dividends and maximize capital growth. But deferring taxes is no reason to hang on when the Donoghue Interest Rate Signal says, "Sell." Paying tax on profits is better than watching them turn into losses.

Portfolio C: tax-deferred retirement savings. This money must, by law, be committed until you are at least 59½, or you will have to pay both ordinary income taxes and 10 percent of what you withdraw in excise tax penalty.

Once money is committed to a tax-deferred savings program, therefore, consider it your longest-term investment money — the most powerful investment money you have.

Manage this money aggressively. Consider a portfolio of several funds which have performed well over time using the Donoghue Stock Market Strategy. Since you can face complications with the Internal Revenue Service if you move your tax-deferred investments from one investment company to another, simply trade between two types of funds in a single family, for example:

▶ Fidelity Magellan and Fidelity Cash Reserves;
▶ Scudder Capital Growth and Scudder Capital Investment Trust;
▶ A portfolio of Twentieth Century Growth and Twentieth Century Select, both of which placed in the top five funds in our four-year study, and Twentieth Century Cash Reserve.

You will pay no taxes on this money until after you retire, so you can trade as often as you wish without fear of tax consequences. All profits are tax-deferred.

Portfolio D: the tax-preferred investments. You may need to tax-shelter the returns on more money than you can contribute to a self-directed retirement program. You may also want to tax-shelter investment income dedicated to another long-term goal, such as the education of young children.

Use single premium life insurance for these purposes. Choose one of the two delicious flavors:

▶ **Single premium whole life (SPWL),** or "Income Life," which is like investing in a tax-free fixed-income investment but without maturity risks and with returns as high as taxable investments.
▶ **Single premium variable life (SPVL),** or "Investment Life," which gives you an accumulation of profits not from interest paid by the insurance company but from the profit you can make from a portfolio of mutual fund investments.

WILL YOU AVOID THE NEXT CRASH?

Now we get down to the nitty and the gritty. With the terrifying experience of a stock market crash fresh in memory, many of us have given up believing in experts. I knew years ago that the tooth fairy was my mother and that investment gurus were a dime a dozen.

So you have every right to ask: What's the likelihood that even with all these portfolios, I could get caught in another 1987-style downturn?

The answer is: If you let a commissioned salesperson lead you like a sheep, it could happen very easily.

But if you pay attention and follow the Donoghue Strategies, you're quite safe.

Could another crash occur? It's possible.

Will another crash happen without the Donoghue Signals giving you a warning? Probably not. For as long as the world has had modern financial markets, great crashes have tended to occur only after increases in interest rates. This was as true in 1929 as it was in 1981 or 1987.

REMEMBER THE DONOGHUE WINNERS

Now let's look at the up side. If you really want to make big money — *and keep it* — simply learn to play the market following the Donoghue strategies.

The Donoghue winners are recommended mutual funds that allow you to play declining interest rates in the stock market, rising interest rates in the money market, and the entire cycle of bond market interest rates.

Most of all, the Donoghue strategies let you fulfill the long-delayed promise of the financial services revolution: They let *you* take control of your financial life and attain wealth and security achievable in no other way.

The life ahead of you is good. Go for it.

APPENDIXES

The following ten appendixes are designed to help you make the transition from uncoordinated investing to a disciplined, wise approach that can steadily make you richer.

Appendix 1 shows how you can free your money from mediocre investments you may own.

Appendixes 2–4 list specific mutual funds worthy of your consideration. The Donoghue Organization does not recommend all these funds at any given time; you can obtain current recommendations from a free current issue of *Donoghue's Moneyletter* (listed with other reliable investment publications in appendix 8). All the funds listed here, however, are well run, are large enough to offer a full array of mutual fund services, and offer telephone exchange privileges, so you can easily move your money to a money market mutual fund any day you choose.

Appendix 5 lists the mutual fund families to which these funds belong. Call the families for a prospectus and further instructions when you are ready to invest. Or call them simply to ask any questions you may have.

Appendixes 6 and 7 list some of the best single premium whole life and single premium variable life policies available as this is written. (See also chapter 12.) The free workbook will also have more up-to-date information in its Insurance Investing section. (To obtain a copy of the workbook, call 1-800-445-5900 or, in Massachusetts, 508-429-5930.)

Appendix 8 lists the newspapers currently carrying Donoghue's Money Market Funds table.

Appendix 9 discusses our three favorite asset management or cash management accounts, which represent opportunities to centralize much of your investing in one place.

Appendix 10 lists some of the best sources of further investment information.

Following the appendixes you'll find a glossary of important investment terms.

If you're confused about how to begin reorganizing your investment life, start by reading appendix 1 and taking its advice.

APPENDIX 1. HOW TO GET *OUT* OF THE WRONG STRATEGIES

The first big effort in successful investing is cleaning house — getting your assets out of the wrong types of investments and into the right ones, and dealing with the tax and emotional issues of selling. Freeing your money turns out to be less difficult than you might have thought.

Often readers never quite get started in wise investing because all their money is tied up in poor investments sold by commissioned salespeople. But the next few pages will point you toward the way out.

The first step: decide where you will keep your liberated cash

First, you need a place to escape *to*: a parking lot where you will receive an excellent return on your cash with nearly perfect safety, liquidity, and convenience. Then you won't have to wonder what to do with the money from investments that you are liquidating.

Many people use banks' money market accounts as their cash parking lots, but banks often pay much less interest than money market mutual funds. The three leading alternatives for your spare cash are:

▶ THE GOOD: For maximum convenience, simply park your cash in **the money market mutual fund of the no-load family that offers stock market mutual funds you find attractive**. Then you can accomplish a great deal of profitable investing with simple telephone calls to an 800 number.

▶ THE BETTER: For better yield, **choose one of the best-yielding money market mutual funds in the country from Donoghue's Money Market Funds table** in your local newspaper. Since some money market funds will let you write checks more or less as you could on an ordinary bank account, you can easily move your money anywhere you choose when you need it.

▶ THE BEST: A high-yielding money market fund attached to an **asset (or "cash") management account offered by a discount broker** will offer a yield competitive with the top-yielding money market funds in the country, together with maximum investment flexibility. The discount brokerage account will let you buy and sell a wide variety of investments by telephone. Charles Schwab's Schwab One account is particularly appropriate, because you can use it to buy and sell several hundred no-load and low-load mutual funds. (See appendix 9.)

Freeing yourself from a broker's yoke

If most of your money is tied up in investments purchased from a "full-service" broker, you have to consider several points before you can liberate it. Don't just sell all your investments through the broker and put the cash in a money fund account. Selling through a full-service broker can cost big dollars in commissions, and if any of your investments have risen in value, selling means you'll owe taxes on your profits.

If your account contains stocks or bonds (including tax-free municipal bonds), you can easily transfer them to an account at a discount brokerage house. Discount brokers are simply order takers; they will never try to sell you anything you don't want to buy or force you to sell anything you don't want to sell. They also charge commissions substantially less than you'd pay a full-service broker.

You can also transfer "closed-end" mutual funds to a discount brokerage account. These are funds that issue a fixed number of shares that must be bought and sold like stocks and bonds. Ordinary "open-end" mutual funds are usually better investments — if you ask to redeem your shares, the fund will simply sell enough assets to pay you an amount equivalent to your share of the fund's value. But many full-service brokers like to push closed-end funds on their clients. It's good to know that a discount broker can help you get rid of them, if you want.

Many discount brokers will take care of all details of transferring your account from your current broker if you just fill in a simple form or two. The process of transferring your assets may be time-consuming if your old broker doesn't cooperate efficiently, however, so you may prefer to have the old broker send all the stock certificates, all the bonds, and all the cash from your money fund directly to you. Then you can send the certificates directly to the discount broker and move the cash to your chosen parking lot. If there's any foot dragging by your old broker, you can personally call and complain.

Escaping isn't always this easy, however. Discount brokers generally can't help you get rid of ordinary "load" mutual funds, limited partnerships, tax shelters, unit trusts, or brokered CDs. You must either ask your old broker to sell them for you or leave them in your account at that broker.

If you own any of these investments, you should:

▶ Find out from the broker how much they are worth and how much commission the firm would charge to sell them;
▶ Learn how much you would pay in taxes if you sold — or, in the case of securities selling at less

than you paid, how much tax you would save if you took the loss. (Ask your tax preparer for help if you need it.)

▶ Make a separate decision to sell or continue holding each security in your brokerage account.

When you liquidate securities from a full-service broker, have the firm send you a check. Don't let the broker reinvest the money for you unless you are sure you trust him or her to advise you reliably in the future.

Rescuing an individual retirement account

Individual Retirement Accounts at banks and full-service brokerage houses can also be difficult to move.

Banks love to promote IRAs. But if you leave your IRA in a bank, you virtually guarantee that you will have far less at retirement than if you put your money in a no-load mutual fund family.

What do you do?

First, stop contributing to the bank IRA. Immediately set up an IRA at a no-load mutual fund family or a discount broker. You're allowed to maintain IRAs at two or more institutions, just so long as you never exceed the total annual contribution limits outlined in chapter 11.

Next, transfer the funds you've accumulated in the bank's or the full-service broker's IRA to the mutual fund family or discount broker. You can do this in two ways:

▶ You can fill out a simple form that most mutual fund families and discount brokers can provide, and the family or broker will carry out a "direct transfer of assets." This process is supposed to take two weeks to two months. A bank may charge you early withdrawal penalties for closing out any certificate of deposit. You can avoid that, however, by filling out a separate transfer-of-assets form for each CD, specifying that the transfer should be made to the money market fund of the fund family or discount broker when the CD matures.

▶ Because of the difficulties a direct transfer can produce — not just withdrawal penalties but also delays due to foot dragging and inefficiency — a second alternative may be better: a "sixty-day rollover." Simply ask the bank to give you the money in your account. (Or ask the broker to give you the cash and securities in your account.) Deposit it yourself within sixty days in your new IRA at the mutual fund family or discount brokerage. If you hold your money less than sixty days while moving your account from one institution to another, the IRS won't charge you for an early withdrawal. You'll owe no taxes whatsoever on the transaction. You can even spend any interest your money earns while it's between the two IRAs (though you'll have to pay tax on it).

Recovering your insurance money

Cash-value insurance policies are major assets to many people. But they are among the most difficult assets to put to good use. In your policy, you have accumulated tax-sheltered dollars. You can cash it in, but then you will owe taxes on every penny you have earned. Instead, try this approach:

First, ask your insurance company the current cash value of your policy and also its "maximum sustainable loan value." The maximum sustainable loan value is the total amount you can take out tax-free without restrictions. (In theory, you can usually borrow 90 percent of the value of an insurance policy tax-free. But generally you have to leave more than 10 percent of your money in the policy or else interest costs charged on your loan will reduce your balance below the 10 percent figure. If that happens, you'll owe a big tax bill.)

Also, ask the net interest rate that your money is earning in the policy. Remember that this interest rate is being earned tax-free. (If your insurance company won't tell you the current interest rate, you should definitely get your money out of that policy.)

Now, you have four choices:

▶ If the interest rate you're receiving is satisfactory and you are a risk-averse investor who likes such investments as long-term bonds and certificates of deposit, then you may want to leave your money in the policy.

▶ If you are in a low tax bracket, you may simply want to cash in the policy and invest the money on your own.

▶ If cashing in would create a painful tax burden and yet you want to manage your cash yourself, you can borrow the maximum sustainable loan value and manage the money yourself in such investments as no-load mutual funds.

▶ If you want to keep all the tax advantages of insurance but obtain better returns, you can do a "Form 1035 rollover" to move your money into a better-yielding policy, probably a single premium whole or variable life policy.

The Form 1035 rollover is the best step for most people whose policies have been in effect long enough to be exempt from surrender charges.

The insurance broker who sells you the better policy can simply fill in Form 1035 and ask you to sign it. That will transfer the cash value of your existing policy into your new policy.

Not all insurance brokers handle Form 1035 rollovers, but you can find one if you shop around.

APPENDIX 2. STOCK MARKET MUTUAL FUNDS — PERFORMANCE FOLLOWING THE DONOGHUE SIGNAL VS. "BUY AND HOLD"

All funds are no-load except that **low-load** funds (up to 4 percent load) are indicated with a +. Performance statistics have *not* been adjusted to take account of loads.

Funds' addresses, together with the names of other funds in the same families appear in appendix 5 under the name of the fund sponsors (also called the funds' "distributors"). Where the first word in the name of the fund distributor differs from the first word in the name of the fund, the name of the distributor appears after the fund name in parentheses in the table below.

EIGHT-YEAR TEST — JANUARY 1, 1980 THROUGH DECEMBER 31, 1987

Fund name	Phone number	Beta*	What $10,000 grew to trading using Donoghue Signal	Compound rate of return — trading	What $10,000 grew to "buy and hold"	Compound rate of return — "buy and hold"	Improvement in total returns Percent	Improvement in total returns Dollars	Rank—total returns Following Donoghue Signal	Rank—total returns Buy and hold
Fidelity Magellan +	800-544-6666	1.13	$104,460	34.08%	$74,284	28.49%	46.94%	$30,176	1	1
Hartwell Emerging Growth	800-645-6405	1.57	99,940	33.34%	25,560	12.45%	478.02%	74,380	2	31
20th Century Select	800-345-2021	1.11	81,022	29.89%	44,507	20.52%	105.82%	36,515	3	3
Stein Roe Capital Opportunity	800-338-2550	1.25	77,863	29.25%	26,254	12.82%	317.52%	51,609	4	28
Hartwell Growth Fund	800-645-6405	1.23	76,090	28.87%	35,610	17.21%	158.06%	40,480	5	11
20th Century Growth	800-345-2021	1.24	76,020	28.86%	36,720	17.66%	147.08%	39,300	6	9

EIGHT-YEAR TEST (continued)

Fund name	Phone number	Beta*	What $10,000 grew to trading using Donoghue Signal	Compound rate of return — trading	What $10,000 grew to "buy and hold"	Compound rate of return — "buy and hold"	Improvement in total returns Percent	Improvement in total returns Dollars	Rank-total returns Following Donoghue Signal	Rank-total returns Buy and hold
Axe Houghton Stock	800-431-1030	1.35	72,580	28.12%	18,990	8.35%	596.11%	53,590	7	46
Tudor Fund (Weiss, Peck)	800-223-3332	1.22	72,420	28.08%	37,410	17.93%	127.73%	35,010	8	8
Scudder Capital Growth	800-453-3305	1.07	63,979	26.11%	31,470	15.41%	151.42%	32,509	9	18
Columbia Growth	800-547-1037	0.99	63,650	26.03%	37,700	18.04%	93.68%	25,950	10	7
Janus Fund	800-525-3713	0.71	62,830	25.83%	39,030	18.56%	81.98%	23,800	11	5
Founders Special	800-525-2440	1.10	62,190	25.67%	27,314	13.38%	201.43%	34,876	12	27
Founders Growth	800-525-2440	1.00	60,570	25.25%	35,940	17.34%	94.95%	24,630	13	10
Evergreen Fund (Lieber)	800-235-0064	0.93	60,310	25.18%	33,280	16.22%	116.11%	27,030	14	13
T. Rowe Price New Horizons	800-638-5660	1.20	58,350	24.67%	24,160	11.66%	241.45%	34,190	15	34
Financial Dynamics	800-525-8085	1.33	57,600	24.47%	25,160	12.22%	213.98%	32,440	16	32
Manhattan Fund (Neuberger)	800-367-0770	1.09	57,060	24.32%	35,120	17.00%	87.34%	21,940	17	12
Financial Industrial Fund	800-525-8085	1.05	55,450	23.88%	31,460	15.40%	111.79%	23,990	18	19
Morgan Growth (Vanguard)	800-662-7447	1.06	54,420	23.59%	28,286	13.88%	142.92%	26,134	19	26
Value Line Special Situations	800-223-0818	1.30	53,910	23.44%	19,330	8.59%	370.63%	34,580	20	44
Explorer Fund (Vanguard)	800-662-7447	0.96	52,500	23.03%	23,910	11.51%	205.54%	28,590	21	35
Smith Barney Equity +	212-698-5353	0.89	51,940	22.87%	31,890	15.60%	91.59%	20,050	22	16
Scudder Development Fund	800-453-3305	1.17	51,930	22.86%	24,900	12.08%	181.41%	27,030	23	33
Value Line Fund	800-223-0818	1.11	51,050	22.60%	26,110	12.75%	154.81%	24,940	24	29
Guardian Mutual Fd (Neuberger)	800-367-0770	0.94	50,650	22.48%	29,960	14.70%	103.66%	20,690	25	23

Fund	Phone	Beta								
Fidelity Equity Income +	800-544-6666	0.73	50,330	22.39%	38,630	18.40%	40.87%	11,700	26	6
Acorn Fund (Harris)	312-621-0630	0.87	49,660	22.18%	30,200	14.82%	96.34%	19,460	27	22
Value Line Leveraged Growth	800-223-0818	1.13	49,240	22.05%	32,740	15.98%	72.56%	16,500	28	14
Founders Blue Chip	800-525-2440	0.97	48,750	21.90%	30,870	15.13%	85.67%	17,880	30	21
Vanguard World Fund — US Growth Portfolio	800-662-7447	n.a.	48,750	21.90%	41,690	19.54%	22.28%	7,060	29	4
Lexington Growth	800-526-0057	1.03	48,510	21.82%	19,170	8.47%	319.96%	29,340	31	45
Partners Fund (Neuberger)	800-367-0770	0.79	48,450	21.80%	47,230	21.42%	3.28%	1,220	32	2
Dreyfus Growth Opportunity	800-645-6561	0.88	47,670	21.56%	28,540	14.01%	103.18%	19,130	33	25
Financial Industrial Income	800-525-8085	0.81	47,210	21.41%	32,540	15.89%	65.08%	14,670	34	15
Selected Special Shares (Prescott, Ball)	800-553-5533	1.02	46,840	21.29%	22,270	10.53%	200.24%	24,570	35	42
Vanguard Index 500 Portfolio	800-662-7447	1.00	45,670	20.91%	31,080	15.23%	69.21%	14,590	36	20
Lexington Research	800-526-0057	0.93	45,490	20.85%	23,520	11.28%	162.50%	21,970	37	37
T. Rowe Price New Era Fund	800-638-5660	0.92	45,460	20.84%	29,090	14.28%	85.75%	16,370	38	24
Axe Houghton Fund B	800-431-1030	0.75	45,410	20.82%	22,970	10.95%	173.01%	22,440	39	40
Bull and Bear Capital Growth	800-847-4200	1.11	45,240	20.76%	21,280	9.90%	212.41%	23,960	40	43
Fidelity Contrafund	800-544-6666	1.09	42,840	19.94%	25,830	12.59%	107.45%	17,010	41	30
Babson Growth (Jones & Babson)	800-422-2766	1.02	42,780	19.92%	23,560	11.31%	141.74%	19,220	42	36
Safeco Equity	800-426-6730	1.04	41,740	19.56%	23,340	11.18%	137.93%	18,400	43	39
Franklin Income Fund +	800-342-5236	n.a.	38,760	18.45%	31,880	15.60%	31.44%	6,880	44	17
Dreyfus Third Century	800-645-6561	0.83	38,680	18.42%	22,350	10.58%	132.23%	16,330	45	41
Fidelity Trend Fund	800-544-6666	1.16	37,760	18.07%	23,360	11.19%	107.78%	14,400	46	38
averages, 46 funds			$56,174	23.69%	30,575	14.52%	124.41%	$25,609		

* **Beta** is a measure of the riskiness of a fund. The higher a fund's beta, the more its value is likely to rise and fall from month to month.
+ Low-load fund.
n.a. = not available

FOUR-YEAR TEST — JANUARY 1, 1984 THROUGH DECEMBER 31, 1987

Fund name	Phone number	Beta*	What $10,000 grew to trading using Donoghue Signal	Compound rate of return — trading	What $10,000 grew to "buy and hold"	Compound rate of return — "buy and hold"	Improvement in total returns Percent	Improvement in total returns Dollars	Rank—total returns Following Donoghue Signal	Rank—total returns Buy and hold
Hartwell Emerging Growth	800-645-6405	1.57	$24,123	24.63%	$10,088	0.22%	15948.86%	$14,035	1	47
Twentieth Century Growth	800-345-2021	1.24	23,601	23.95%	21,993	21.78%	13.41%	1,608	2	1
Fidelity Magellan +	800-544-6666	1.13	21,491	21.08%	18,181	16.12%	40.46%	3,310	3	2
Twentieth Century Select	800-345-2021	1.11	21,481	21.06%	15,744	12.02%	99.88%	5,737	4	14
Axe Houghton Stock	800-431-1030	1.35	21,349	20.88%	11,540	3.65%	636.95%	9,809	5	43
Value Line Fund	800-223-0818	1.11	21,132	20.57%	14,067	8.91%	173.72%	7,065	6	26
Value Line Leveraged Growth	800-223-0818	1.13	20,930	20.28%	15,133	10.91%	112.94%	5,797	7	17
SteinRoe Cap Opp	800-338-2550	1.25	20,853	20.17%	13,160	7.11%	243.45%	7,693	8	34
Scudder Cap Growth	800-453-3305	1.07	20,777	20.06%	14,982	10.63%	116.32%	5,795	9	18
Axe Houghton Fund B	800-431-1030	0.75	20,722	19.98%	13,590	7.97%	198.66%	7,132	10	28
Founders Growth	800-525-2440	1.00	20,695	19.94%	15,460	11.51%	95.88%	5,235	11	16
Financial Industrial Income	800-525-8085	0.81	20,602	19.81%	17,438	14.91%	42.54%	3,164	12	4
Founders Blue Chip	800-525-2440	0.97	20,442	19.57%	16,994	14.18%	49.30%	3,448	13	7
Vanguard Index 500 Portfolio	800-662-7447	1.00	20,379	19.48%	16,736	13.74%	54.08%	3,643	14	10
Vanguard World Fund US Growth Portfolio	800-662-7447	n.a.	20,290	19.35%	17,908	15.68%	30.12%	2,382	15	3
Hartwell Growth Fund	800-645-6405	1.23	20,163	19.16%	15,490	11.56%	85.12%	4,673	16	15
Lexington Research	800-526-0057	0.93	20,145	19.14%	14,616	9.95%	119.78%	5,529	17	22

T. Rowe Price New Era Fund	800-638-5660	0.92	20,058	19.01%	17,277	14.65%	38.22%	2,781	18	5
Lexington Growth Fund Inc.	800-526-0057	1.03	20,049	18.99%	14,621	9.96%	117.46%	5,428	19	21
Partners Fund (Neuberger)	800-367-0770	0.79	20,004	18.93%	17,172	14.47%	39.49%	2,832	20	6
Smith Barney Equity +	212-356-2600	0.89	19,989	18.90%	16,433	13.22%	55.28%	3,556	21	12
Safeco Equity Fund	800-426-6730	1.04	19,921	18.80%	14,469	9.68%	122.00%	5,452	22	24
Acorn Fund (Harris)	312-621-0630	0.87	19,895	18.76%	16,740	13.75%	46.81%	3,155	23	9
Evergreen Fund (Lieber)	800-235-0064	0.93	19,627	18.36%	14,872	10.43%	97.60%	4,755	24	20
Strong Total Return Fund +	800-368-3863	0.65	19,589	18.30%	16,892	14.00%	39.13%	2,697	25	8
Guardian Mutual Fd (Neuberger)	800-367-0770	0.94	19,475	18.13%	13,495	7.78%	171.10%	5,980	26	32
Morgan Growth (Vanguard)	800-662-7447	1.06	19,433	18.07%	13,536	7.86%	166.77%	5,897	27	30
Tudor Fund (Weiss, Peck)	800-223-3332	1.22	19,421	18.05%	13,581	7.95%	163.08%	5,840	28	29
SteinRoe Universe	800-338-2550	1.12	19,190	17.70%	11,705	4.01%	439.00%	7,485	29	41
Financial Dynamics	800-525-8085	1.33	18,976	17.37%	12,312	5.34%	288.24%	6,664	30	39
Financial Industrial Fund	800-525-8085	1.05	18,908	17.26%	13,834	8.45%	132.34%	5,074	31	27
Legg Mason Value Trust	800-822-5544	0.94	18,743	17.01%	13,500	7.79%	149.80%	5,243	32	31
Columbia Growth	800-547-1037	0.99	18,669	16.89%	14,932	10.54%	75.77%	3,737	33	19
Evergreen Total Return (Lieber)	800-235-0064	0.93	18,654	16.87%	16,121	12.68%	41.38%	2,533	34	13
Babson Growth (Jones & Babson)	800-422-2766	1.02	18,435	16.52%	14,186	9.14%	101.51%	4,249	35	25
Selected Special Shares (Prescott, Ball)	800-553-5533	1.02	18,120	16.02%	12,730	6.22%	197.44%	5,390	36	36
Fidelity Contrafund	800-544-6666	1.09	17,943	15.74%	11,786	4.19%	344.74%	6,157	37	40
Founders Special Fund	800-525-2440	1.11	17,729	15.39%	12,889	6.55%	167.53%	4,840	38	35
Dreyfus Third Century	800-645-6561	0.83	17,470	14.97%	13,444	7.68%	116.90%	4,026	39	33
Franklin Income Fund +	800-342-5236	n.a.	17,463	14.96%	16,590	13.49%	13.25%	873	40	11

FOUR-YEAR TEST (continued)

Fund name	Phone number	Beta*	What $10,000 grew to trading using Donoghue Signal	Compound rate of return — trading	What $10,000 grew to "buy and hold"	Compound rate of return — "buy and hold"	Improvement in total returns		Rank—total returns	
							Percent	Dollars	Following Donoghue Signal	Buy and hold
USAA Sunbelt Era	800-531-8000	1.21	17,208	14.53%	10,326	0.81%	2111.04%	6,882	41	46
Bull and Bear Cap Growth	800-847-4200	1.11	17,140	14.42%	11,682	3.96%	324.49%	5,458	42	42
Janus Fund	800-525-3713	0.71	16,805	13.86%	14,480	9.70%	51.90%	2,325	43	23
T. Rowe Price Growth and Income	800-638-5660	0.89	16,408	13.18%	12,550	5.84%	151.29%	3,858	44	38
Scudder Development Fund	800-453-3305	1.17	16,248	12.90%	11,280	3.06%	388.13%	4,968	45	44
Value Line Special Situations	800-223-0818	1.30	16,241	12.89%	8,124	-5.06%	n.m.	8,117	46	48
T. Rowe Price New Horizons	800-638-5660	1.20	16,003	12.47%	10,400	0.99%	1400.75%	5,603	47	45
Gateway Option Fund	800-354-6339	0.53	15,814	12.14%	12,607	5.96%	123.01%	3,207	48	37
averages, 48 funds			19,350	17.84%	14,326	9.08%	116.10%	5,023		

* **Beta** is a measure of the riskiness of a fund. The higher a fund's beta, the more its value is likely to rise and fall from month to month.
n.m. = not meaningful
n.a. = not available
+ Low-load fund.

230

APPENDIX 3. TOP-YIELDING MONEY MARKET MUTUAL FUNDS

The following lists show top-yielding money market mutual funds as of 1988. All these funds are no-load.

TAXABLE MONEY FUNDS

	12-month yield to August 1, 1988
Vanguard Money Market Reserves Prime 800-662-7447	7.14%
Flex-fund Money Market Fund 800-325-3539	7.06%
Strong Money Market 800-368-3863	7.00%
Value Line Cash Fund 800-223-0818	6.87%
Vanguard Money Market Reserves Federal 800-662-7447	6.84%
UMB Money Market Fund Prime (Jones & Babson) 800-422-2766	6.79%
Fidelity Cash Reserves 800-544-6666	6.78%
SAFECO Money Market Mutual Fund 800-426-6730	6.76%
USAA Money Market Fund 800-531-8000	6.72%
Merrill Lynch CMA Money Fund 609-282-2800	6.71%
Merrill Lynch Ready Assets Trust 609-282-2800	6.68%

MONEY FUNDS PRODUCING INCOME EXEMPT FROM U.S. TAX

	12-month yield to August 1, 1988
Calvert Tax-Free Reserves Money Market 800-368-2748	4.92%
Strong Tax-Free Money Market Fund 800-368-3863	4.89%
Franklin Tax-Exempt Money Market Fund 800-342-5236	4.83%
Vanguard Municipal Bond/Money Market 800-662-7447	4.82%
USAA Tax-Exempt Money Market Fund 800-531-8000	4.81%
T. Rowe Price Tax-Exempt Money Fund 800-638-5660	4.59%
Fidelity Tax-Exempt Money Market Trust 800-544-6666	4.56%
Babson Tax-Free Money Market Portfolio (Jones & Babson) 800-422-2766	4.53%
Merrill Lynch CMA Tax-Exempt 609-282-2800	4.53%
Lexington Tax Free Money Fund 800-526-0057	4.49%
The Tax-Free Money Fund, Inc. (Smith Barney) 212-698-5353	4.46%

MONEY FUNDS FREE OF STATE
AS WELL AS FEDERAL TAXATION
The following list is limited to funds that have been in existence long enough to have established a track record measured by the Donoghue Organization.

	12-month yield to August 1, 1988
California	
Vanguard California Tax-Exempt Money Market Fund 800-662-7447	4.80%
Franklin California Tax-Exempt Money Market Fund 800-632-2350	4.77%
General California Tax-Exempt Money Market Fund (Dreyfus) 800-242-8671	4.62%
Connecticut	
Reich & Tang Connecticut Daily Tax-Free 800-221-3079	4.08%
Massachusetts	
Fidelity Massachusetts Tax-Free Money Market Portfolio 800-544-6666	4.30%
New York	
General New York Tax-Exempt Money Market Fund 800-242-8671	4.25%
Reich & Tang Empire Tax-Free 800-221-3079	4.20%
Pennsylvania	
Fidelity Pennsylvania Tax-Free Money Market Portfolio 800-544-6666	4.48%
Michigan	
Reich & Tang Michigan Daily Tax-Free 800-221-3079	4.32%

APPENDIX 4. BOND MUTUAL FUNDS — PERFORMANCE FOLLOWING THE DONOGHUE SIGNAL VS. "BUY AND HOLD"

All funds are no-load except that low-load funds (up to 4 percent load) are indicated with a +. Performance statistics have *not* been adjusted to take account of loads. Tax-exempt funds are marked with x. Funds' addresses, together with the names of other funds in the same families, appear in appendix 5.

EIGHT-YEAR TEST — JANUARY 1, 1980 THROUGH DECEMBER 31, 1987

Fund name	Phone number	What $10,000 grew to trading using Donoghue Signal	Compound rate of return trading	What $10,000 grew to "buy and hold"	Compound rate of return "buy and hold"	Improvement in total returns		Rank — total returns	
						Percent	Dollar	Following Donoghue Signal	Buy and hold
Fidelity High Income	800-544-6666	$36,195	17.44%	$29,781	14.62%	32.43%	$6,414	1	1
Keystone Custodian Bond Series B-4 +	800-633-4900	31,730	15.53%	24,289	11.73%	52.08%	7,441	2	6
Dreyfus A Bond Plus	800-645-6561	30,869	15.13%	24,676	11.95%	42.20%	6,193	3	5
Merrill Lynch Corp. Bonds High Income Portfolio +	609-282-2800	30,687	15.05%	24,910	12.08%	38.74%	5,777	4	4
Fidelity Government Securities	800-544-6666	30,001	14.72%	23,244	11.12%	51.02%	6,757	5	8
Fidelity Intermediate Bond	800-544-6666	28,882	14.18%	26,674	13.05%	13.24%	2,208	6	2
Keystone Custodian Bond Series B-1 +	800-633-4900	28,186	13.83%	23,821	11.46%	31.58%	4,365	7	7
Vanguard Fixed Income — Investment Grade	800-662-7447	27,713	13.59%	25,035	12.15%	17.81%	2,678	8	3
Fidelity High Yield Municipals x	800-544-6666	26,161	12.77%	19,469	8.68%	70.67%	6,692	9	10
Franklin US Govt. Securities +	800-342-5236	26,010	12.69%	20,760	9.56%	48.79%	5,250	10	9
averages — 9 taxable funds only — 10 taxable and tax-free funds		$30,031	14.68%	$24,798	11.97%	26.12% 27.38%	5,231 5,377		

FOUR-YEAR TEST — JANUARY 1, 1984 THROUGH DECEMBER 31, 1987

Fund name	Phone number	What $10,000 grew to trading using Donoghue Signal	Compound rate of return trading	What $10,000 grew to "buy and hold"	Compound rate of return "buy and hold"	Improvement in total returns		Rank — total returns	
						Percent	Dollar	Following Donoghue Signal	Buy and hold
Fidelity High Income	800-544-6666	$19,335	17.92%	$18,054	15.92%	15.91%	$1,281	1	1
Fidelity Govt. Securities	800-544-6666	17,061	14.29%	15,190	11.02%	36.05%	1,871	2	9
Merrill Lynch Corporate Bonds High Income Portfolio +	609-282-2800	16,512	13.36%	15,650	11.85%	15.26%	862	3	5
Fidelity High Yield Municipals x	800-544-6666	16,496	13.33%	15,414	11.42%	19.99%	1,082	4	6
Fidelity Intermediate Bond	800-544-6666	16,450	13.25%	15,850	12.20%	10.26%	600	5	2
Keystone Custodian Bond Series B-4 +	800-633-4900	16,266	12.93%	13,424	7.64%	83.00%	2,842	6	13
Dreyfus A Bond Plus	800-645-6561	16,222	12.86%	15,361	11.33%	16.06%	861	7	8
USAA Tax Exempt High Yield x	800-531-8000	16,066	12.58%	15,180	11.00%	17.10%	886	8	10
Scudder Income Fund	800-453-3305	16,012	12.49%	15,805	12.12%	3.57%	207	9	3
Keystone Custodian Bond Series B-1 +	800-633-4900	15,666	11.88%	14,961	10.60%	14.21%	705	10	11
Value Line US Govt. Securities	800-223-0818	15,429	11.45%	15,745	12.02%	−5.50%	(316)	11	4
Franklin US Govt. Securities +	800-342-5236	15,311	11.24%	15,371	11.35%	−1.12%	(60)	12	7
USAA Tax Exempt Intermediate-Term x	800-531-8000	14,925	10.53%	14,462	9.66%	10.38%	463	13	12
USAA Tax Exempt Short-Term x	800-531-8000	13,756	8.30%	13,166	7.12%	18.64%	590	14	14
T. Rowe Price Tax-Free Short Intermed. x	800-638-5660	13,264	7.32%	13,040	6.86%	7.37%	224	15	15
averages — 10 taxable funds only		$17,033	13-11%	$16,059	11.55%	16.14%	$974		
— 15 taxable and tax-free funds						13.63%	$806		

APPENDIX 5. DONOGHUE'S FAVORITE MUTUAL FUND FAMILIES

Axe Securities Corporation
400 Benedict Avenue
Tarrytown, NY 10591
800-431-1030
914-631-8131
  Axe Houghton Fund B
  Axe Houghton Money Market Fund
  Axe Houghton Stock

Bull & Bear Service Center, Inc.
11 Hanover Square
New York, NY 10005
800-847-4200
212-363-1100
  Bull & Bear Capital Growth Fund
  Bull & Bear Gold Investors

Calvert Group
1700 Pennsylvania Avenue NW
Washington, DC 20006
800-368-2748
301-951-4820
  Calvert Tax-Free Reserves Money Market

Columbia Funds Management Co.
1301 SW 5th Avenue, P.O. Box 1350
Portland, OR 97207
800-547-1037
503-222-3600 (OR collect)
  Columbia Daily Income
  Columbia Growth Fund, Inc.

Dreyfus Service Corporation
666 Old Country Road
Garden City, NY 11530
800-645-6561
718-895-1396
  Dreyfus A Bonds Plus
  Dreyfus Growth Opportunity
  Dreyfus Third Century Fund
  General California Tax-Exempt
  General New York Tax-Exempt

† Low-load
No symbol: no-load fund

Evergreen Funds
550 Mamaroneck Ave.
Harrison, New York 10528
800-235-0064
914-698-5711
  Evergreen Fund
  Evergreen Money Market Trust
  Evergreen Total Return Fund
  Evergreen Value Timing Fund

Fidelity Distributors Corporation
82 Devonshire Street
Boston, MA 02109
800-544-6666
617-523-1919 (Mass., Alaska collect)
  Fidelity California T-F/M.M.P.
  Fidelity Capital Appreciation Fund
  Fidelity Cash Reserves
  Fidelity Contrafund
  Fidelity Europe Fund†
  Fidelity Freedom
  Fidelity Fund
  Fidelity Global Bond Fund
  Fidelity Gov't Securities Fund
  Fidelity High Income Fund
  Fidelity High Yield Munis
  Fidelity Intermediate Bond Fund
  Fidelity Magellan Fund†
  Fidelity Mass. T-F/M.M.P.
  Fidelity OTC Portfolio
  Fidelity Overseas†
  Fidelity Pacific Basin†
  Fidelity Pennsylvania T-F/M.M.P.
  Fidelity Select American Gold†
  Fidelity Select Precious Metals†
  Fidelity Tax-Exempt M.M. Tr.

Financial Programs, Inc.
P.O. Box 2040
Denver, CO 80201
800-525-8085
  Financial Daily Income Shares
  Financial Dynamics Fund
  Financial Industrial Income
  Financial Strategic Gold
  Financial Tax-Free Money Fund

† Low-load
No symbol: no-load fund

Founders Mutual Depositor Corp.
3033 E. First Avenue, Ste. 810
Denver, CO 80206
800-525-2440
800-874-6301 (Colo.)
  Founders Blue Chip
  Founders Growth Fund
  Founders Money Market Fund
  Founders Special Fund

Franklin Distributors, Inc.
777 Mariner's Island Blvd.
San Mateo, CA 94404
800-342-5236
  Franklin Gold Fund
  Franklin Money Fund
  Franklin Tax-Exempt M.M.F.
  Franklin U.S. Gov't Securities†

Gateway Investment Advisers, Inc.
P.O. Box 458167
Cincinnati, OH 45245
800-354-6339
513-248-2700
  Gateway Option Income Fund
  Money Market Portfolio Trust

Harris Associates L.P.
2 N. LaSalle Street
Chicago, IL 60602
312-621-0630 (collect)
  Acorn Fund

Hartwell Management Co., Inc.
515 Madison Avenue, 31st Fl.
New York, NY 10022
800-645-6405
  Hartwell Emerging Growth
  Hartwell Growth

Ivy Financial Services, Inc.
40 Industrial Park Road
Hingham, MA 02043
800-235-3322
617-749-1416
  Ivy International
  Ivy Growth
  Ivy Money Market

† Low-load
No symbol: no-load fund

Janus Capital Corporation
100 Fillmore Street, Ste. 300
Denver, CO 80206
800-525-3713
  Cash Equivalent M.M.
  Janus Fund
  Tax-Exempt M.M.

Jones & Babson, Inc.
2440 Pershing Road, G-15
Kansas City, MO 64108
800-422-2766
  Babson Growth Fund
  Babson Tax-Free M.M.P.
  UMB Money Market Fund Prime

Keystone Distributors, Inc.
99 High Street
Boston, MA 02110
800-633-4900
617-338-3400
  Keystone Custodian Series/B-1†
  Keystone Custodian Series/B-4†
  Keystone Tax-Free Fund†

Kleinwort Benson Investment Strategies
200 Park Avenue, Ste. 5610
New York, NY 10166
800-233-9164
212-687-2515
  Transatlantic Growth Fund, Inc.

Legg Mason Wood Walker, Inc.
P.O. Box 1476, 7 East Redwood Street
Baltimore, MD 21202
800-822-5544
800-638-1107 (Md.)
301-539-3400
  Legg Mason Cash Reserve Trust
  Legg Mason Value Trust

Lexington Management Corp.
P.O. Box 1515
Saddle Brook, NJ 07667
800-526-0057
800-526-0056
201-845-7300

† Low-load
No symbol: no-load fund

Lexington Goldfund
Lexington Growth Fund
Lexington Money Market Trust
Lexington Research Fund
Lexington Tax-Free M.F.

Merrill Lynch Funds Dist., Inc.
P.O. Box 9011
Princeton, NJ 08543
609-282-2800
CMA Money Fund
CMA Tax-Exempt
Merrill Lynch Corp. Bond: High Income†
Merrill Lynch Ready Assets Trust
Merrill Lynch Retmt Reserves M.F.
Summitt Cash Reserves Fund

Mutual Shares Corp/Qualified/Beacon Fund
26 Broadway
New York, NY 10004
800-858-3013
800-457-0211
800-553-3014
Mutual Shares Corporation

Neuberger & Berman Management, Inc.
342 Madison Avenue
New York, NY 10173
800-367-0770
800-237-1413
212-850-8300
Guardian Mutual Fund
Manhattan Fund
Neuberger & Berman Cash Reserves
Neuberger & Berman TF Money Fund
Partners Fund

Prescott Ball & Turben, Inc.
230 West Monroe Street
Chicago, IL 60606
800-553-5533
312-641-7862
Selected American Shares
Selected M.M.F., General Portfolio
Selected Special Shares

† Low-load
No symbol: no-load fund

Reich & Tang L.P.
100 Park Avenue, 28th Fl.
New York, NY 10017
800-221-3079
212-370-1240
  Reich & Tang/Connecticut Daily T-F
  Reich & Tang/Empire T-F
  Reich & Tang/Michigan Daily T-F
  Short Term Income Fund — M.M.

SAFECO Securities, Inc.
P.O. Box 34890
Seattle, WA 98124
800-426-6730
800-562-6810 (Wash.)
206-545-5530
  SAFECO Equity Fund
  SAFECO M.M.M.F.
  SAFECO TF Money Market Mutual

Scudder Fund Distributors, Inc.
175 Federal Street
Boston, MA 02110
800-453-3305
800-225-2470
  Scudder Capital Growth Fund
  Scudder Cash Investment Trust
  Scudder Development
  Scudder Global
  Scudder Income Fund
  Scudder International Fund
  Scudder TF Money Fund

Smith Barney, Harris Upham & Co., Inc.
1345 Avenue of the Americas
New York, NY 10105
212-698-5353
  Smith Barney Equity†
  The Tax-Free Money Fund, Inc.
  Vantage MMF — Vantage Cash Portfolio

Stein Roe & Farnham, Inc.
P.O. Box 1143
Chicago, IL 60690
800-338-2550
312-368-7826

† Low-load
No symbol: no-load fund

SteinRoe Capital Opportunities Fund
SteinRoe Cash Reserves
SteinRoe Tax-Exempt Money Fund
SteinRoe Universe Fund

Strong/Corneliuson Capital Mgmt., Inc.
815 East Mason Street, Ste. 1610
Milwaukee, WI 53202
800-368-3863
414-765-0934
Strong Money Market
Strong Tax-Free M.M.F.
Strong Total Return†

T. Rowe Price Investor Services, Inc.
100 East Pratt Street
Baltimore, MD 21202
800-638-5660
301-547-2308
T. Rowe Price Capital Appreciation
T. Rowe Price Equity Income
T. Rowe Price International Bond Fund
T. Rowe Price International Stock Fund
T. Rowe Price New Era
T. Rowe Price New Horizons
T. Rowe Price Prime Reserve
T. Rowe Price T-E M.F.
T. Rowe Price Tax-Free Short-Intermediate

Tucker Anthony Mgmt./Freedom Dist. Corp.
One Beacon Street, 3rd Floor
Boston, MA 02108
800-225-6258
800-392-6037 (Mass.)
617-523-3170
Freedom Global Fund†
Freedom Global Income Plus†
Freedom Money Market Fund
Tucker Anthony TE M.M.

Twentieth Century Investors, Inc.
P.O. Box 419200
Kansas City, MO 64112
800-345-2021
816-531-5575
Twentieth Century Cash Reserve
Twentieth Century Growth
Twentieth Century Select
Twentieth Century Ultra

† Low-load
No symbol: no-load fund

USAA Investment Mgmt. Co.
USAA Building
San Antonio, TX 78288
800-531-8000
512-498-8000
USAA Gold Fund
USAA Money Market Fund
USAA Tax-Exempt Fund High Yield
USAA Tax-Exempt Fund Intermed. Term
USAA Tax-Exempt Fund Short Term
USAA Tax-Exempt M.M.F.

United Services Funds, Inc.
P.O. Box 29467
San Antonio, TX 78229
800-873-8637
United Services Gold
United Services New Prospector†
United Services Treasury Securities

Value Line Securities, Inc.
711 Third Avenue
New York, NY 10017
800-223-0818
Value Line Cash Fund
Value Line Fund
Value Line Leveraged Growth Investors
Value Line Special Situations
Value Line TE Fund — M.M.P.
Value Line U.S. Gov't Securities

Vanguard Group, Inc.
P.O. Box 2600
Valley Forge, PA 19496
800-662-7447
800-662-2739
Vanguard 500 Portfolio
Vanguard M.M.R. Federal
Vanguard M.M.R. Prime
Vanguard Morgan Growth
Vanguard Muni. Bond/M.M.
Vanguard Special Gold
Vanguard World Fund International
Vanguard World Fund U.S. Growth

† Low-load
No symbol: no-load fund

Weiss, Peck & Greer
One New York Plaza
New York, NY 10004
800-223-3332
212-908-9582
  Tudor Fund
  Short-Term Income Fund
  W.P.G. Tax-Free Money Market

† Low-load
No symbol: no-load fund

APPENDIX 6. SAMPLE SINGLE PREMIUM WHOLE LIFE POLICIES

These policies can be called "Income Life": Their cash value increases tax-free, at interest rates competitive with those of taxable certificates of deposit. You can "borrow" the interest, and the loan need not be repaid during your lifetime. (See chapter 12.) In sum, single premium whole life policies not only provide a small amount of life insurance, paid up for life; they also offer the income opportunities that many conservative investors seek elsewhere and cannot find.

The policies listed below represent some of the best available in mid-1988. Note, however, that policy provisions change constantly, and these may not be the best available when you go shopping. Moreover, not every policy listed here meets all the standards for single premium whole life policies offered in chapter 12. Use the listings here along with the standards in chapter 12 as guidelines to indicate what you can expect — and what you can insist on. For late developments, write to "Single Premium Update," 360 Woodland Street, Holliston, MA 01746.

Company, policy name	Interest rate in initial period (as of mid-1988)	Guarantee period	Minimum rate after guarantee period	Surrender charges	Can you bail out free if interest rate is cut after guarantee period?	Can you bail out free if tax laws change?	Free look period	Special features
Midland Mutual Horizon	7.8%	1 year	Indexed to 5-year Treasury securities	8% in year 1, 7% year 2, then 6%, 5%, 4%, 3%, 2%, 1% charge from 9th year.	No. Indexed guarantee protects you.	No	10 days	Company cannot add charges for "cost of insurance."
Pacific Fidelity Life Link II	8.5% on first $40,000; 8.75% over $40,000	2 years	5.5%	Depends on age & gender of insured; generally 4% year 2; 3% in years 3 and 4; 2% in years 5 and 6; 1% in years 7 and 8. No charge from 9th year.	Yes, if decline is 1% or more.	Yes	1 year	
Lincoln Benefit Life (AllState affiliate) Valedictorian	8.5% 8.25% 8.1%	1 year 3 years 5 years	6%	8% first 2 years; 7% in year 3, then 6%, 5%, 4%, 3%, 2%, 1%. No charge from 10th year.	Yes, if decline is more than 1.25%.	No	10 days	You can bail out free if company ever adds a "mortality charge" or increases the borrowing interest rate.
Kemper Living Life	8.05%	1 year	4%	7% for first 7 years. No charge from 8th year.	No.	No	20 days	
Jackson National Single Premium Whole Life	8.5%	1 year	6%	9% for first year, decreasing 1% a year. No charge from 10th year.	No.	No	1 year	

American Investors SPWL V	8.25%	1 year	5.5%	8% first year, 7% second & third year, 6% fourth year, then declining 1.5% per year. No charge from 8th year.	Yes, if rate is 1.5% less than current 91-day Treasury bill.	Can exchange policy for an annuity	10 days	You can "write your own loans" with a checkbook provided.
American Life & Casualty Passport	8.15% 7.15%	1 year 3 years	4%	9% first 3 years, then 8%, 7%, 6%, 5%, 4%, and 2% in each of following years. No charge from 10th year.	No.	No	20 days	
Life of Virginia Single Premium Life	7.75%	1 year	6%	7% first 3 years, then declining at 1% per year. No charge from 10th year.	Yes. Can bail out free if rate drops below initial rate during any years when surrender charge would apply.	Yes	Always get at least the premium back	
Metropolitan Life SPL	7.25% 7.5%	1 year 3 years	6% or 1.75% below month's average 5-year Treasury note rate	6% first two years, then declining 1% per year. No charge from 8th year.	No, but indexed minimum provides some protection.	No	Always get at least the premium back	

Company, policy name	Interest rate in initial period (as of mid-1988)	Guarantee period	Minimum rate after guarantee period	Surrender charges	Can you bail out free if interest rate is cut after guarantee period?	Can you bail out free if tax laws change?	Free look period	Special features
North American Kaleidoscope	8%	1 year	6% or average 10-year U.S. Treasury note yield	7% first 3 years, then 6% in 4th year, 5% in 5th year, 3% in 6th year, and 2% in 7th year. No charge from 8th year.	Indexed minimum provides good protection.	No	20 days	
	7.75%	2 years						
	7.25%	3 or 5 years						
General Services Life Single Premium Plus	9.1% for first month; total of 7.6% guaranteed for first year.	Hybrid contract. —Company will pay you all it earns on your money minus 1.5%	4%	6 months' interest, years 1 through 10.	"Pass-through" provision provides good protection.	Yes	1 year	Checkbook for instant access to policy's cash value. Zero cost borrowing on both interest and principal.

Source: Independent Advantage Financial, 10960 Wilshire Blvd., Suite 2320, Los Angeles, CA, 90024-3883

APPENDIX 7. SAMPLE SINGLE PREMIUM VARIABLE LIFE POLICIES

These policies, which I call "Investment Life," combine the tax benefits of life insurance and the growth power of mutual funds. You choose which of several portfolios you want your money invested in. They have many of the benefits of the single premium whole life policies listed in appendix 6 (such as tax-free borrowing of the cash value of your policy), but will produce greater long-term returns if the portfolio you choose increases in value.

The listings here show policy provisions in effect in the second half of 1988. Use them together with the standards in chapter 12 as guidelines to what you can expect — and what you can insist on. Note in the listings that the total of all fees, expenses, and interest costs of the policies that acknowledge charging a "load" — Monarch's and Guardian's — may be *less* than the total fees, expenses, and interest costs of policies that seem to be "no-load." Selling single premium insurance is a complicated job, and somehow the people who do it must be paid.

As with single premium whole life, new tax laws could change the legal status of these policies. For late developments, write to "Single Premium Update," 360 Woodland Street, Holliston, MA 01746.

	Charter National Life InVest	Prudential Discovery Life Plus	National Home Pacer Choice	Monarch Resources Prime Plan V	Monarch Resources CaptnFlex	Guardian Value Plus
Investment manager:	Scudder, Stevens & Clark	Prudential	Fidelity Investments	Merrill Lynch	Oppenheimer	Guardian and Value Line
Investment accounts available	· Money market · Managed bond · Managed equity · Managed diversified · Managed international · Natural resource/gold · Zero coupons	· Money market · Bond · Common stock · Aggressively managed · Conservatively managed · Real estate · Fixed · Zero coupons	· Money market · High income · Equity income · Growth · Overseas · Zero coupons	· Money reserve · Intermediate govt. bond · Long-term corp. bond · High-yield · Capital stock · Growth stock · Multiple strategy · Global · Natural resource · Zero coupons	· Money market · Growth fund · Capital appreciation · Multiple strategy · Bond · High-income bond · Zero coupons	· Money market · Centurion fund (capital growth) · Stock · Bond · Govt. securities · Zero coupons
Telephone switches annually	3 free	4 free (except fixed and real estate)	12 free	5 free	Unlimited	Every 30 days
Reports to policy owners	Semiannually and with each switch	Semiannually and with each switch	Quarterly	Quarterly	Quarterly	Quarterly
Additional deposits allowed after initial purchase?	Yes	No	Yes	Yes	Yes	No
Minimum deposit	$10,000	$10,000	$5,000	$10,000	$10,000	$5,000
Life insurance benefits — male, age 55, $50,000 deposit	$126,337	$143,377	$108,500	$91,927	$98,887	$92,125
Annual fees and expenses	Approximately 2.5% of the policy value	Approximately 2.25% of the policy value	Approximately 3% of the policy value	Approximately 2.5% of the policy value	Approx. 2.75% of the policy value	Approx. 2.5% of the policy value

Net cost of borrowing						
· Interest	0.25%	0.5% on 10% of deposit	0%	0.75% (all loans, years 1–10) 0.60% (all loans thereafter)	Same as Prime Plan V	0.75% on principal and interest
· Principal	1.25%	2% on loans over that amount	2%			
Surrender charge						
· Policy years:	1|2|3|4|5|6|7|8|9 8|7|6|5|4|3|2|1|0	1|2|3|4|5|6|7 9|8|7|6|5|4|0	1|2|3|4|5|6|7|8|9 8|8|7|6|5|4|3|2|0	Unrecovered load (load is 7% of initial premium, charged against account at 0.7% per year in years 2–11)	Unrecovered load (load is 7% of initial premium, charged against account at .7% per year in years 2–11)	Unrecovered load (load is 7.5% of initial premium, charged against account at .75% per year in years 2–11)
· % of policy value:						

APPENDIX 8. NEWSPAPERS CARRYING DONOGHUE'S MONEY FUND TABLES

TAXABLE AND TAX-FREE FUND TABLES

Los Angeles Daily News
Los Angeles, CA

Los Angeles Times
Los Angeles, CA

The Orange County Register
Santa Ana, CA

The Sacramento Union
Sacramento, CA

The San Diego Union
San Diego, CA

Colorado Springs Gazette Telegraph
Colorado Springs, CO

The Denver Post
Denver, CO

Hollywood Sun-Tattler
Hollywood, FL

The Ledger
Lakeland, FL

The Orlando Sentinel
Orlando, FL

The Boston Globe
Boston, MA

Morning & Sunday Sun
Baltimore, MD

Barron's
New York, NY

The Plain Dealer
Cleveland, OH

The Oregonian
Portland, OR

Philadelphia Daily News
Philadelphia, PA

The Journal-Bulletin
Providence, RI

The Houston Chronicle
Houston, TX

San Antonio Light
San Antonio, TX

TAXABLE FUND TABLE ONLY

Arkansas Democrat
Little Rock, AR

The Arizona Daily Star
Tucson, AZ

The Fresno Bee
Fresno, CA

Monterey Peninsula Herald
Monterey, CA

Oakland Tribune
Oakland, CA

The San Francisco Chronicle
San Francisco, CA

Examiner
San Francisco, CA

Mercury
San Jose, CA

The Stamford Advocate
Stamford, CT

Ottaway News Service
Washington, DC

The Washington Post
Washington, DC

News & Sun Sentinel
Fort Lauderdale, FL

Gainesville Sun
Gainesville, FL

The Miami News
Miami, FL

Palm Beach Post
West Palm Beach, FL

Tallahassee Democrat
Tallahassee, FL

The Tampa Tribune
Tampa, FL

The Columbus Ledger & Enquirer
Columbus, GA

The Honolulu Advertiser
Honolulu, HI

The Idaho Statesman
Boise, ID

Chicago Tribune
Chicago, IL

The Journal Star
Peoria, IL

The Indianapolis News
Indianapolis, IN

The Evening Gazette
Worcester, MA

Morning Herald
Hagerstown, MD

The Detroit News
Detroit, MI

The Manchester Union Leader
Manchester, NH

The Asbury Park Press
Neptune, NJ

Albuquerque Journal
Albuquerque, NM

Las Vegas Review-Journal
Las Vegas, NV

Times-Union
Albany, NY

The Buffalo News
Buffalo, NY

New York Times
New York, NY

Watertown Daily Times
Watertown, NY

The Columbus Dispatch
Columbus, OH

Dayton Journal Herald and News
Dayton, OH

Pittsburgh Post-Gazette
Pittsburgh, PA

Observer-Reporter
Washington, PA

The Wilkes-Barre Times Leader
Wilkes-Barre, PA

The Greenville News
Greenville, SC

The Dallas Morning News
Dallas, TX

The Milwaukee Journal
Milwaukee, WI

APPENDIX 9. RECOMMENDED ASSET MANAGEMENT ACCOUNTS

Invented by Merrill Lynch in 1977, asset (or cash) management accounts have become a popular way for investors to consolidate cash and securities into one liquid, manageable brokerage account. But as with all financial services, there are a variety of asset management accounts on the market.

The standard features of most include a choice of money market mutual funds for the cash portion of the account, the ability to margin (borrow against) securities, check writing, a nationally known credit or debit card, monthly statements, and year-end transaction summaries. Different financial services firms offer variations of these features; it's up to you to compare and choose the account that best suits *your* needs.

	Minimum initial investment	Minimum balance required	Annual account fee	Check-writing privileges	Debit card	Number of money funds available	Automatic sweep into money fund?	Cash/margin securities?	Additional features
Fidelity USA	$25,000	$5,000	$3/month	Yes	Gold Mastercard ($24/year) or Premier Visa ($24/year)	3	Yes	Yes	· 24-hour toll-free service line for quotes and trading · Access to Fidelity's 75 mutual funds · Subscription to *Standard & Poor's Investment Market Letter*
Merrill Lynch CMA	$20,000	None	$65/year	Yes	Visa or Premier Visa ($25/year)	3	Yes	Yes	· Insured Bank Money Market Deposit Accts. · Subscription to Merrill Lynch *Marketletter*
Schwab One	$5,000	None	None	Yes	Visa	2	Yes	Yes	· 24-hour toll-free service line · Access to Schwab Mutual Fund Marketplace

Charles Schwab's Schwab One Account
The account for investors willing to pay for convenient no-load investing
The Schwab asset management account is set off from its Fidelity and Merrill Lynch peers by its low $5,000 initial minimum and lack of annual account maintenance fees. It also allows investors access to the Schwab Mutual Fund Marketplace, where they can trade among 250 no- and low-load mutual funds. This, of course, in addition to Schwab's discount brokerage services.

The Schwab One is the best account for individuals with small stock, bond, and mutual fund portfolios who do their own research and want to consolidate their investments.

Merrill Lynch CMA
The best asset management account for full-service brokerage clients
In addition to the standard asset management account fare, Merrill Lynch's CMA offers the option of storing reserves in federally insured bank money market deposit accounts (MMDAs). CMA holders also receive a subscription to the *Merrill Lynch Marketletter* for investment advice and economic outlook. If you are a semiactive stock and bond trader and you want (or need) the luxury of a personal account executive to do research and watch over things for you, the CMA is a good deal at $65 per year. However, it may not be worth it if you have a small or relatively inactive account — remember, you're paying full-cost commissions for trades.

Fidelity USA Account
The best asset management account for low-load investors
For a minimum initial investment of $25,000 and a minimum balance of $5,000, Fidelity's Ultra Service Account (USA) allows holders access to a twenty-four-hour toll-free service line through which they can inquire about their accounts, receive quotes, and trade in Fidelity's seventy-five mutual funds and discount brokerage. Account owners also receive the *Standard & Poor's Investment Market Letter*. If you hold Fidelity mutual funds and also have stocks, bonds, CDs, etc., the USA may be just the thing to create a more easily managed account.

APPENDIX 10. SOURCES OF INVESTMENT INFORMATION

Donoghue's Moneyletter
Box 6640
Holliston, MA 01746
800-445-5900 (in Mass., 508-429-5930)

A twice-monthly newsletter on no-load stock market and money market mutual funds for do-it-yourself individual investors. The newsletter describes and recommends no-load mutual fund investment strategies that maximize after-tax returns. The basic strategies followed during the past five years have outperformed the vast majority of all mutual funds in existence while minimizing risk. *Moneyletter* has been named "Best Financial Advisory Newsletter" by the Newsletter Association. Sample issue available.

Price $99 per year (24 issues)

Donoghue's Money Fund Report
Box 6640
Holliston, MA 01746
800-343-5413 (in Mass., 508-429-5930)

An authoritative weekly newsletter providing statistics on comparable yields and portfolio holdings in the $400 billion money market mutual funds industry. It includes commentary, trend analysis, and a statistical summary of each fund's sales, redemptions, net charge, and yields. *Money Fund Report* is circulated primarily to financial institutions.

Price $695 per year (52 issues)

Quarterly Report on Money Fund Expense Ratios
Box 6640
Holliston, MA 01746
800-343-5413 (in Mass., 508-429-5930)

Lists annualized expense ratios (the ratio of total expenses to net assets of the fund), as well as average quarterly expense ratios for 448 money market mutual funds.

Price $325 per year (4 issues)

Donoghue's Mutual Funds Almanac
Box 6640
Holliston, MA 01746
800-445-5900 (in Mass., 508-429-5930)

Now in its nineteenth edition, this 216-page volume is a complete, accurate, and convenient source that will enable you to evaluate over 1,800 mutual funds. Includes addresses, toll-free numbers, investment objectives, fund services, fees, five- and ten-year performances, expense ratios, and more.

Price $23 (annual)

Best's Insurance Reports (Life-Health)
A. M. Best Company
Oldwick, NJ 08858
201/439-2200

An annual compendium of comprehensive statistical reports on the financial position, history, and operating results of insurance companies operating in both the United States and Canada. Best's rating system evaluates various factors affecting the overall performance of insurance companies.

Available in most public libraries.

Price $390 (annual)

Hulbert Financial Digest
643 South Carolina Avenue, S.E.
Washington, DC 20003
800-443-0100, ext. 459 (in D.C., 202-546-2164)

Monthly newsletter that evaluates performance of over one hundred financial newsletters.

Price $135 per year (12 issues)
    (5-month trial subscription $37.50)

Johnson's Charts
246 Homewood Avenue
Buffalo, NY 14217
716-876-4669

Annual performance charts of 503 funds arranged by investment category. Quarterly reports list over 1,300 funds.

Available at most public libraries.

Price $295 (1 annual edition plus 4 quarterly reports)

Mutual Fund Sourcebook
Morningstar, Inc.
53 West Jackson Boulevard
Chicago, IL 60604
800-876-5005 (in Ill., 312-427-1985)

A quarterly survey of mutual funds. Comprehensive coverage of over 700 mutual funds, including risk-adjusted ratings, fund portfolios, investment criteria, performance data, and fund operations information.

Available at most public libraries.

Price $175 per year (4 issues), $55 per issue

Mutual Fund Values
Morningstar, Inc.
53 West Jackson Boulevard
Chicago, IL 60604
800-876-5005 (in Ill., 312-427-1985)

Complete mutual fund advisory service, including twice-monthly publication which reviews fund performance and portfolio holdings.

Primarily for financial planners, but publication available in some public libraries.

Wiesenberger Investment Companies Service
A Division of Warren, Gorham & Lamont
One Penn Plaza
New York, NY 10119
800-922-0066 (in N.Y., 212-971-5599)

Complete service includes hard-cover annual directory of funds, a monthly current performance and dividend record, a monthly mutual fund investment report, a quarterly review of management results and an annual mutual fund data panorama.

Directory available in most public libraries.

Price $375 per year

GLOSSARY OF FINANCIAL TERMS

accrued interest: The interest due on a bond or other fixed-income security that must be paid by the buyer of the security to the seller.

annuity: A contract where the buyer (annuitant) pays a sum of money to receive regular payments for life or a fixed period of time.

asked price: The net asset value per share plus sales charge, if any. The asked price of a stock refers to the price at which the seller is willing to sell.

asset: Any item of value. Several classifications include: tangible asset — an item that can readily be assigned a dollar value (hard assets, such as gold and silver, fall into this category); current asset — an item that can be turned into cash in a year or less; fixed asset — an item used for business, such as machinery; intangible asset — an item that cannot be readily assigned a dollar value, like the goodwill of a business.

automatic reinvestment: A plan that allows shareholders to receive dividend distributions in the form of new shares instead of cash.

automatic withdrawal: See check-a-month plan.

average maturity: The dollar-weighted average time between today and when the investments in a portfolio mature (are paid off at maturity). Donoghue's money fund average maturity (the Donoghue Average Maturity Signal, see chapter 2) is an example. It is the arithmetic average of the individual average maturities of the

money funds that report to *Donoghue's Money Fund Report.*
The reason it is not dollar-weighted is that one of the largest
funds, Merrill Lynch Ready Assets Trust, performs in an atypical
manner due to its valuation methodology; it would skew the
statistics and make them less valuable if a dollar-weighted average maturity were used.

back-end load: The fee paid when withdrawing money from a fund.
See load.

balance sheet: A financial statement showing the dollar amounts of
a company's or person's assets, liabilities, and owner's equity.

balanced fund: A mutual fund which has an investment policy of
"balancing" its portfolio, generally by including bonds, preferred
stocks, and common stocks.

bankers' acceptances (BAs): Short-term, non-interest-bearing notes
sold at a discount and redeemed at maturity for full face value.
Primarily used to finance foreign trade. BAs represent future
claims on U.S. banks that provide lines of credit to U.S. im-
porters. A BA is collateralized by the goods to be sold and is
guaranteed by the importer's U.S. bank.

basis point: Term used to describe amount of change in yield. One
hundred basis points equal 1 percent. An increase from 8 percent
to 10 percent would be a change of 200 basis points.

bear market: A sustained period of falling stock prices usually
preceding or accompanied by a period of poor economic performance known as a recession. The opposite of a bull market.

beta: Term used to describe the price volatility of securities. Standard & Poor's 500 Index is assigned a beta of one; anything with
a beta above one is considered to be more volatile than the Index;
anything below one has less volatility than the S&P Index.

bid price: The price at which someone will buy a security. For a
mutual fund, the price at which the fund's shares are bought back
by the fund, usually the current net asset value per share.

blue chip: The common stock of a major corporation with a long,
relatively stable record of earnings and dividend payments.

bond: A security representing debt; a loan from the bondholder to
the corporation. The bondholder usually receives semiannual
interest payments, with principal being refunded at maturity.

bond fund: See fixed-income fund.

broker: A person in the business of effecting securities transactions
for others, for a commission. There are two types of brokers:

full-service brokers, who give advice, and discount brokers, who do not give advice (the investor must do his own research).

bull market: A stock market that is characterized by rising prices over a long period of time. The time span is not precise, but it represents a period of investor optimism, lower interest rates, and economic growth. The opposite of a bear market.

capital appreciation: An increase in value, such as in real estate, stock, or bond prices.

capital gain: A long-term capital gain is a profit from the sale of a capital asset, such as a security, that has been held for over six months. A short-term capital gain is the profit from selling a capital asset in less than six months. Both are subject to federal income tax at ordinary income rates. Congress and the IRS, however, have kept this important distinction for future tax legislation.

capital loss: A loss from the sale of a capital asset. Up to $3,000 may be deducted from taxable income in one year, and if the loss is greater than the amount allowed for one year, it may be carried forward to future years until it is used up.

cash flow: The cash flow from an investment is the total of dividends, interest payments, realized profits, and any return of principal you receive. If you choose to reinvest your dividends and capital gains as suggested throughout this book, the checks sent to you under a check-a-month automatic withdrawal plan (like the one suggested in Stock Strategy #3 on page 90) are, in effect, although not for tax purposes, the cash flow from your investment.

certificate: The actual piece of paper which certifies ownership of stock in a corporation. Mutual funds normally do not issue certificates but rather issue confirmations of transactions and monthly statements.

certificate of deposit (CD): Generally, a short-term debt instrument certificate issued by commercial banks or savings and loan associations. (Euro CDs are issued by foreign branches of U.S. banks; Yankee CDs are issued by U.S. branches of foreign banks.)

check-a-month plan: An arrangement many open-end investment companies have which enables investors to receive fixed payments, usually monthly or quarterly. The actual payout is determined by the investor.

closed-end investment company: A company that issues a fixed number of shares that usually must be traded in the securities market. Closed-end investment company shares are usually bought and sold through brokers.

collectible: A physical object that has value by virtue of its rarity or intrinsic or artistic value.

commercial paper (CP): Unsecured promissory notes of corporations and various financial institutions, with maturities of up to 270 days. Used as a money market instrument.

commission: The fee paid to a broker for buying or selling securities as an agent.

common stock: Securities that represent ownership in a corporation.

compound interest: Interest computed on the interest as well as the principal.

consumer price index (CPI): Index that analyzes the change in prices for consumer goods and services over time.

contingent deferred sales load (CDSL): The fee paid by the shareholder when fund shares are sold. The fee usually is reduced each year the shares are owned.

convertible securities: A bond, debenture, or preferred stock that gives its owner the right to exchange that security for common stock or another type of security issued by the same company.

correction: Used in conjunction with a bull market. It is a sustained period of stock price declines in the midst of long-term rising stock prices. A correction is usually followed by another period of rising stock prices. A major correction refers to a decline of 10 percent or more in the widely accepted stock market indexes.

coupon: A promise to pay interest when due, coupons are usually attached to a bond. In the past, people actually clipped coupons and deposited them for collection. Currently, nearly all bonds are registered and "clipping coupons" is a colorful but outdated memory. Checks are simply sent to the registered owner of the bond.

custodian: The organization which holds in custody and safekeeping the securities and other assets of a mutual fund or individual.

dealer: A person or firm who regularly buys and sells securities for others from his or her own account of securities. In contrast, a broker acts as an agent for others. Frequently, broker and dealer functions are synonymous.

debenture: A bond secured by the general credit of the corporation, and usually not secured by any collateral.

debt instrument: Any instrument that signifies a loan between a borrower and a lender.

declaration of dividends: Announcement by issuer of bonds or equities of their decision to make a payment to their shareholders. Some companies do this on a regular basis, while others may declare a dividend only when company earnings have reached a certain predetermined level. Many money funds declare dividends daily but pay monthly.

deep discount bond: A type of bond that is selling at a market price far below its par (face) value. The face value of a bond is usually $1,000.

default: Failure to pay principal and/or interest when due.

depreciation: The decline in value of a security, CD, or mutual fund due to market risk; for example, when interest rates rise, bond market values or prices depreciate or fall. Accountants usually use the following definition: The estimated decline in the value of property due to use, deterioration, or obsolescence over a period of time.

discretionary accounts: An account in which an investment advisor or broker has the full right to buy and sell securities without consultation or authorization of the investor.

discount: The amount by which a preferred stock, bond, or other security may sell below its face value.

distribution fee: Under the 12b–1 plan, a fund or fund family that does not have its own sales force is allowed to take a percentage of the assets as a fee to pay independent brokers for selling its fund(s).

distributions: Dividends paid from net investment income and payments made from realized capital gains of a mutual fund.

distributor: The principal underwriter — either a person or a company — that purchases open-end investment company shares directly from the issuer for resale to others.

diversification: The policy of spreading investments among a number of different securities to reduce the risk inherent in investing. Diversification may be among different types of securities, different companies, different industries, or different geographical locations.

diversified investment company: To be so classified, the Investment Company Act requires that 75 percent of a fund's assets be allocated so that not more than 5 percent of its total assets are invested in one company. In addition, it can hold no more than 10 percent of the outstanding voting securities of another company.

dividend: A payment declared by a corporation's board of directors and made to shareholders, usually on a quarterly basis.

dollar cost averaging: Method of investing equal amounts of money at regular intervals regardless of whether the market is moving upward or downward. The theory is that the investor's average cost will be lower than if he or she invested larger amounts irregularly over the same amount of time.

Dow Jones Averages: Stock market indexes issued by Dow Jones & Company to indicate changes in industrial, transportation, financial, and composite groups of stocks.

equity: Represents stock ownership of a company.

equity fund: A mutual fund that invests primarily in stocks.

equity-income fund: A mutual fund whose primary objective is income. Its portfolio typically consists of high-yielding common stocks, preferred and convertible issues, and bonds.

Eurodollars: U.S. dollars deposited in foreign branches of U.S. banks or foreign banks located outside the United States.

exchange privilege: The right to take all or some of the shares of one fund and put them into another fund within the same family of funds. This is considered a sale and new purchase for tax purposes. (Same as a switching privilege.)

ex-dividend date: The date on which stock is sold without dividend. Under the five-day delivery plan, buyers of the stock on the fourth business day preceding the stockholder of record date will not receive the declared dividend. Most stock exchanges operate on the five-day plan.

expense ratio: Annual expenses paid by a fund (including management fees, custodial fees, transfer agency fees, legal fees, investment advisory fees, and distribution or "12b–1" fees) divided by the average shares outstanding for the period. The expense ratio does not include loads or commissions paid for the investor's purchasing, reinvesting, or selling the fund's shares.

face value: The value that appears on the face of a bond, usually $1,000. This is the amount the issuing company will pay at maturity, but it does not necessarily indicate market price.

family of funds: A group of mutual funds managed by the same investment company. One company may manage several different funds, each with different objectives such as growth, income, or tax-exempt funds.

FDIC (Federal Deposit Insurance Corporation): The federal agency which insures deposits up to $100,000 per person at member banks. FDIC also makes loans to buy assets from member banks to facilitate mergers or help prevent bank failures.

fiduciary: An individual or corporation who is entrusted with certain assets for a specified purpose. Also known as trustee, executor, guardian.

fixed annuity: An annuity contract that provides for fixed payments at regular intervals.

fixed-income fund: A mutual fund whose portfolio consists primarily of fixed-income securities or bonds. The fund's objective is normally income rather than capital appreciation.

401(k): A qualified employee benefit plan where employee contributions are made on a pretax basis. Both employer and employee contributions compound tax-free until withdrawn.

front-end load: A sales charge for buying into a mutual fund. The sales charge typically can run as high as 4.0 to 8.5 percent and legally can be 9.0 percent or more.

FSLIC (Federal Savings and Loan Insurance Corporation): The federal agency established to insure funds on deposit (up to $100,000) at member savings and loans.

fully invested: One hundred percent invested position. All money is considered to be earning dividends, capital gains, interest, or a mixture of any of these, in contrast to only a portion of the invested money having earning capabilities.

fund assets: The total market value of the assets invested by a fund.

fund representative: A federally licensed (registered representative) individual qualified to give investors information about, and sell, a fund.

GNMA (Government National Mortgage Association): U.S. government agency whose primary function is to buy mortgages or mortgage purchase commitments and to resell them at market prices to other investors. It also designs and issues new mortgage-backed securities. Called "Ginnie Mae."

government securities: A general term that refers to any instruments of debt issued by the U.S. government or its agencies or instrumentalities.

gross income: Income before any deductions or expenses are deducted (subtracted).

growth fund: A mutual fund that has growth of capital as its primary objective, to be obtained principally through investments in common stocks with growth potential. This type of fund will primarily generate capital gains rather than pay dividends.

growth/income fund: A mutual fund whose objective is to provide both income and long-term growth.

high-yield bonds: See junk bonds.

holding company: A company that owns the majority of stock or securities of, as well as manages, one or more other companies.

illiquid: An asset that is difficult to quickly convert into cash.

immediate annuity: An annuity contract that starts making payments to the annuitant almost immediately — within one year of the contract's purchase.

income fund: See equity-income fund.

Income Life: William Donoghue's informal name for single premium whole life insurance.

index: A mathematically derived number used as an indicator of trends in the market. For example, Dow Jones Industrials Average, Standard & Poor's 500, or Donoghue's Money Fund Average.

inflation: The economic condition of rising prices for goods and services. It is characterized by an increasing volume of currency in circulation and a decline in the buying power of cash.

institutions-only mutual funds: Mutual funds that allow only institutional clients, bank trust departments, corporations, stock brokers, depository institutions, or pension funds to buy shares. Some funds which claim to be institutions-only will allow individuals to invest if they can meet the (usually high) minimum initial investment or invest through an institution.

interest: Periodic payments made to a lender of money by the borrower for use of the money borrowed.

investment company: Generic term including mutual funds, unit investment trusts, and other types of companies that sell their shares to the public and invest the proceeds according to stated investment objectives.

Investment Life: William Donoghue's informal name for single premium variable life insurance.

investment objective: The specific goal, such as long-term capital growth or current income, which the investor or mutual fund pursues.

IRA (Individual Retirement Account): A retirement plan that can be started by anyone who earns employment income. Investment earnings on IRA money is tax-deferred, usually until retirement at age 59½ or older. The tax deductibility of annual IRA contributions is limited to taxpayers who meet income guidelines defined in the Tax Reform Act of 1986.

IRA rollover: The removal of IRA money from one investment and placement of this money into another investment. A rollover involves the individual receiving the money and reinvesting it. Rollovers must be completed within 60 days and are allowed only once every twelve months.

IRA transfer: Movement of IRA funds from one trustee to another. The IRA investor does not receive the money; it goes directly to another trustee. For example, a common transfer is from a bank money market deposit account to a no-load mutual fund family. Both banks and mutual fund families are permitted to be IRA trustees.

junk bonds: High-yielding, non–investment quality, lower-rated bonds.

Keogh plan: A tax-qualified retirement program for self-employed individuals and their employees.

leverage: The use of borrowed money with invested funds to increase returns. The effect is to magnify profits or losses and increase the amount of risk.

liability: Any debt owed by a company or an individual. Usually classified as a current liability (due in one year or less) or a long-term liability (due in over one year).

liquid: May be easily converted into cash or exchanged for other assets.

liquidate: To convert an asset into cash.

load: A portion of the offering price that goes toward selling costs such as sales commissions and distribution. A front-end load is the fee charged when buying into a fund. A back-end load or redemption fee is the fee charged when getting out of a fund. Low loads like those for some Fidelity Investments funds such as Fidelity Magellan are paid directly to the mutual fund family rather than to a salesperson, since they are sold directly in the same way no-load funds are sold.

long-term investment: For tax purposes, an investment held for over six months.

management company: A company that manages the day-to-day operations of a mutual fund or investment company.

management fee: The amount paid to the administrator and/or management company (who may also serve as an investment advisor) for services rendered to the fund and included in the expense ratio.

margin account: A brokerage account that allows an investor to buy or sell securities on credit. An investor can purchase additional securities against the value of cash and securities in the account.

margin, buying on: Buying securities on credit from a broker.

market order: An order to buy or sell a stated amount of a security at the best possible price as soon as it can be accomplished.

market price: The last reported price at which a security has been sold.

market rate: A general term used to describe the current interest rate on a given instrument.

maturity: The scheduled date for repayment of the principal amount of a debt instrument.

money market fund: Mutual fund which invests in short-term, relatively riskless money market instruments such as bank certificates of deposit, bankers' acceptances, commercial paper, and short-term government securities.

money market instruments: Short-term debt instruments such as Treasury bills, repurchase agreements, bankers' acceptances, certificates of deposit, and commercial paper.

moving average: A mathematical method for determining trends in the stock market or stock market indicators. A moving average is calculated by adding a series of values for a certain time period and dividing the total by the number of values added. For the next figure, the earliest value is dropped and the current one is added.

municipal bond fund: An open-end company or unit investment trust which invests in diversified holdings of federal tax-exempt securities issued by state, city, and local governments.

municipal securities: Debt obligations issued by states, counties, cities, towns, school districts, or other municipal agencies. The interest paid on these securities is generally exempt from federal income taxes and state and local taxes in the state of issuance.

mutual fund: An open-end or closed-end investment company which pools the money of its shareholders into one professionally managed account; investments are made in a wide variety of securities.

net asset value per share: The total market value of an investment company's shares — securities, cash, and any accrued earnings — minus its liabilities, divided by the number of shares outstanding. The price per share of a no-load mutual fund is the net asset value per share. A load fund adds a sales commission for purchases, reinvestment of dividends, and/or redemptions.

net income: Income less expenses and deductions.

no-load mutual fund: A fund which does not charge a sales charge for investment, reinvestment of dividends, and/or redemptions.

odd lot: The usual amount when buying shares of stock is 100 shares (a "round lot"). When you buy fewer than 100 shares it is called an odd lot; commissions vary with the number of shares bought.

offering price: The lowest price at which shares are offered for sale. (Also called asked price.)

open-end investment company: An investment company that continuously sells and redeems shares, e.g., a mutual fund.

option: The right to buy (call option) or sell (put option) a fixed quantity of a security, at a stated price, within a specific amount of time.

option income fund: A mutual fund which sells options on the shares in its portfolio to increase its income.

ordinary income: Income taxed at the maximum rate schedule, such as employment income or income from a business.

over-the-counter: The nationwide network of brokers/dealers who buy and sell securities that, for the most part, are not listed on an exchange.

par value: See face value.

payroll deduction plan: An agreement between an employee and employer whereby the employer is authorized to deduct a stated amount from the employee's paycheck and invest it, usually in a specified mutual fund.

penny stock: Any stock that is very low-priced and often speculative.

periodic payment plan: An arrangement which allows an investor to purchase mutual fund shares periodically, usually with provisions for the reinvestment of income dividends and the acceptance of capital gains distributions in additional shares.

portfolio: The total investment holdings owned by an investment company or an individual.

preferred stock: A class of stock that has prior claim on dividends before common stock shares. In the event of corporate liquidation, preferred stockholders have a prior claim on assets over common shareholders.

premium: The amount by which a bond, closed-end mutual fund, unit investment trust, preferred stock, or other security sells above its face value or, in the case of a closed-end mutual fund, above its net asset value per share.

profit: The amount earned when the selling price is higher than the cost.

prospectus: The legal written document that describes a mutual fund, or any security, and offers it for sale. In the case of a fund, the prospectus contains information required by the Securities and Exchange Commission on investment objectives and policies, services, investment restrictions, officers and directors, procedure to buy and sell shares, fees, and financial statements.

proxy: The written transfer of voting rights to someone who will then vote according to the wishes of the shareholder. Usually done if the shareholder cannot be present at the stockholders' meeting.

qualified retirement plan: A private retirement plan that meets the rules and regulations of the Internal Revenue Service. Contributions to a qualified retirement plan are, in most cases, tax deductible, and earnings on such contributions are always tax-sheltered until retirement. Most company pension plans are qualified retirement plans.

Examples of qualified retirement plans are pension plans, IRAs, Keoghs, 401(k) plans, and 403(b) plans.

record date: The date by which mutual fund (or other security) holders must be registered as share owners in order to receive a forthcoming distribution such as dividends or capital gains.

redeem: To buy back shares from the present owner. See redemption price.

redemption fee: See back-end load; load.

redemption price: The amount per share a mutual fund shareholder receives when he or she cashes in shares (also known as "liquidating price" or "bid price"). The value of the shares depends on the market value of the company's portfolio securities at the time.

reinvestment privilege: A service provided by most mutual funds for the automatic purchase of additional shares with the shareholder's dividends and capital gains distributions.

repurchase agreement (repo): A financial transaction in which one party "purchases" securities for cash and a second party simultaneously agrees to "buy" them back in the future at specified terms.

return on investment: Percent gain including reinvestment of capital gains and dividends, if any.

risk: The chance or possibility of loss associated with a particular investment.

rollover: A term normally associated with IRAs and similar qualified retirement plans, it simply means substituting one legal trustee for another and transferring the assets to the new trustee. The IRS permits you to do this once every twelve months if you take possession of the assets for less than sixty days in the interim. (See appendix 1 for details.)

round lot: The accepted standard number of shares (100) used to trade stocks. It is also the number of shares to which prevailing broker commission rates apply.

sales charge: The amount charged in connection with public distribution of fund shares. It is added to the net asset value per share in computing the offering price and is paid to the dealer and underwriter.

SEC (Securities and Exchange Commission): An independent agency of the U.S. government which administers the various federal securities laws for the protection of the shareholder.

SEP (Simplified Employee Pension): A qualified employee retirement plan where the employer makes contributions to the employees' IRAs.

series funds: A broad range of funds offered by a fund family. Each fund has its own investment philosophy, whereby it invests in only certain industries or companies.

short-term investment: An investment of less than one year. For tax purposes, short-term is now considered less than six months.

signature guarantee: A required signature by a fiduciary representative (banker or broker) to verify the identity of the shareholder.

SIPC (Securities Investor Protection Corporation): A corporation backed by federal guarantees that provides protection for customers' cash and securities that are on deposit with an SIPC member firm, should the firm fail. Unlike FDIC or FSLIC insurance, SIPC insurance insures your right to the assets rather than insuring their value. It is designed to protect your assets left with a broker against the brokerage's creditors in the event of its bankruptcy. Protection is limited and is usually supplemented by additional private insurance purchased at the expense of the brokers.

single premium variable life (SPVL) (Investment Life): Similar to single premium whole life except that the premium is invested not in a separate account similar to a bank CD but in accounts similar to mutual funds. Some policies offer several choices of mutual fund–like investments, as do mutual fund families.

single premium whole life (SPWL) (Income Life): Under current law, the single premium is fully invested in a CD-like investment, the buildup of cash value is tax-free, and death benefits are exempt from federal income taxes. Annuities are an acceptable savings alternative for many investors.

specialized mutual fund: A fund that focuses on a particular segment of the market and has a philosophy or stipulation the fund must follow or meet when investing.

speculative: Considered to have a high degree of risk.

stock dividend: A dividend paid in securities rather than cash.

stock split: An increase in the number of shares outstanding through the issuance of new shares to existing shareholders. Often designed to lower the cost of a share, making it more attractive. In the case of a 2-for-1 split, shareholders receive one additional share for each one held. In effect, it is like a 100 percent stock dividend from the investor's point of view and does not affect a shareholder's proportional interest in the company.

switch: See exchange privilege.

tax avoidance: Legal actions that may be taken to reduce, defer, or eliminate tax liabilities.

tax-deferred: Income on which a tax is levied only when it is distributed.

tax-exempt fund (tax-free fund): A mutual fund whose portfolio consists of securities (usually municipal bonds or money market obligations) exempt from federal income tax.

tax-exempt securities: Usually refers to municipal bonds and other obligations that are exempt from federal taxes. Some municipal bonds, known as triple exempt bonds, are also exempt from state and local taxes, depending on the state laws where the bond was issued and where the buyer of the bond resides.

tax shelter: An investment used for deferring, eliminating, or reducing income taxes.

technical analysis: The study of internal movements of the stock market such as patterns of price movements, in an effort to forecast the future direction of the stock market.

total return: A performance calculation which includes the fund's percentage change in net asset value plus the value of capital gains and dividends distributed and presumed reinvested over a given time period.

Treasury bill (T-bill): Short-term debt issued by the U.S. government at a discount from its face value. Maturities are three months, six months, and one year. Minimum order is $10,000 with subsequent multiples of $5,000.

Treasury bond: Debt obligation issued by the U.S. government with a maturity ranging from ten to thirty years and with $1,000 as the lowest denomination.

Treasury note: Debt obligation issued by the U.S. government with a maturity between one year and ten years. Lowest denomination issued is $1,000.

trustee: The individual or institution that maintains administrative control over another's assets: a commercial bank, savings and loan association, mutual savings bank, trust company, or stockbroker.

Truth-in-Lending Law: A federal law stating that a lender must specify the terms and conditions of a loan to the borrower.

turnover ratio: The extent to which a fund's portfolio securities are replaced in a one-year period.

12b-1 plan: A plan created by the SEC that allows a fund to use shareholder money to pay marketing and distribution expenses.

unit investment trust (UIT): A type of mutual fund that buys a fixed number of debt or fixed-income obligations and sells them to investors in units. The portfolio is not actively managed and is liquidated after a specified amount of time.

variable annuity: An insurance annuity contract under which the dollar payments received are not fixed but fluctuate with the market. Most frequently, investors will have a choice of stock, money, or bond funds.

variable life insurance: In contrast to straight life insurance policies, variable life lets you direct some or all of the cash value into the financial markets, most commonly through mutual funds.

wash sale: For tax purposes, a wash sale occurs if securities (or options to buy them) are purchased within thirty days before or after the sale of substantially the same securities. The loss on the sale of the original securities may not be taken for tax purposes in such cases.

whole life insurance: Often called traditional life. Purchasers pay a fixed annual premium for a fixed death benefit and a cash value which grows at an interest rate determined by the insurer.

wire transfer: Use of a bank to send money to a fund or vice versa.

withdrawal plan: A mutual fund plan that allows a specified amount of money to be withdrawn at specified intervals.

yield: Income earned from investments, usually expressed as a percentage of market price.

yield curve: The relationship between interest rates (or the current yield of the security) to the maturity of a security. May be used to forecast the future direction of interest rates.

zero-coupon bond: A bond sold at a deep discount on which no periodic interest payments are made prior to maturity. Payment of principal at maturity provides an effective yield on the amount for which it was purchased. These are the most highly volatile fixed income securities in existence. A small rise in interest rates can cause a dramatic decline in market value of such a bond. They are clearly not recommended for the safety-conscious investor under any circumstances.

INDEX

Acorn Fund, 87
Active investors, 45–46
Aggressive strategies for long-term
   goals, 96, 212–214
Alternative minimum tax and mu-
   nicipal bonds, 112
Annualized yields for Treasury
   bills, 143
Annuities, 197–199
   from Income Life, 188
   from Investment Life, 102
Asset management accounts, 77,
   142, 220, 256–258
Auctions for Treasury bills, 143
Average maturity
   for bonds, 106–109
   See also Donoghue Average Ma-
   turity Signal
Axe Houghton Stock Fund, perfor-
   mance of, 30, 81

Bailouts from life insurance, 188–
   190
Bankers' acceptances, 51
Banks
   IRAs at, 222–223
   for money market deposit accounts, 131, 133–136, 151,
   206–207, 219
   and Treasury bills, 143
Bent, Bruce, 52–53
Best & Co., A. M., 179, 189, 197
Boesky, Ivan, scandal of, and mutual fund prices, 22
Bond market, 205–206
   average maturity of, 106–107
   buy, hold, and pray strategy for,
   119–120
   for income, 105

   and interest rates, 11–13
   risk with, 21, 106–111, 115–116
   transferring out of, 220
Bond market mutual funds, 57,
   113–116
   performance of, 234–235
   in RIGS strategy, 94–95
Borrowing. *See* Loans
Brokered CDs, 138–141
   disposing of, 221–222
Businesses, effect of interest rates
   on, 11–12
Buy, hold, and pray investment
   strategy, 85–89
   for bonds, 119–120
Buy signals, 74
Buying with lazy person's investment strategy, 86–88

CaptnFlex single premium variable
   life insurance policy, 193–197
Cash Equivalent Fund (Kemper),
   151
Cash flow. *See* Income investment
   strategy
Cash Management Account (Merrill Lynch), 65, 142, 257–258
Cash management accounts, 77,
   141–142, 220, 256–258
CDs (certificates of deposit), 51
   and average maturity signal, 17
   compared to brokered CDs, 138–
   141
   compared to money market deposit accounts, 17
   long-term, 136, 153–154
   and money market accounts,
   134–135
   penalties with, 222–223

ABOUT THE AUTHOR

William E. Donoghue, "America's Do-It-Yourself Investment Guru," is publisher of *Donoghue's Moneyletter* and author of the books on mutual fund investing, *William E. Donoghue's Complete Money Market Guide* and *William E. Donoghue's No-Load Mutual Fund Guide*, both major national bestsellers. His nationally syndicated personal finance column and money fund yield tables are read by more than seven million readers. He is a Certified Public Accountant, holds an M.B.A. in finance from Temple University, and is President of W. E. Donoghue and Company, Inc., a registered investment adviser.